Blitzkrieg!

Bryan Perrett was educated at Liverpool College. He served in the Royal Tank Regiment and was awarded the Territorial Decoration. A professional and bestselling military historian for many years, he was Defense Correspondent at the Liverpool Echo.

BRYAN PERRETT

BLITZKRIEG!

CANELOHISTORY

First published in the United Kingdom in 1983 by Robert Hale Limited

This edition published in the United Kingdom in 2022 by

Canelo
Unit 9, 5th Floor
Cargo Works, 1–2 Hatfields
London, SE1 9PG
United Kingdom

A CIP catalogue record for this book is available from the British Library.

Print ISBN 978 1 80436 070 5
Ebook ISBN 978 1 80436 069 9

Look for more great books at www.canelo.co

Printed and bound in Great Britain by Clays Ltd, Elcograf S.p.A.

1

The supreme excellence is not to win a hundred victories in a hundred battles. The supreme excellence is to defeat the armies of your enemies without ever having to fight them.

Sun Tzu, *The Art of War*, 500 B.C.

Foreword

by General Sir John Hackett

It is widely thought, in the impatient and often indolent Western culture of our time, that to find an acceptable name for something is to explain it. To tie a label on anything is too often held to be an adequate substitute for (or even identical with) its analysis. The use of the term *Blitzkrieg* – lightning war – offers a case in point. The word is universally employed to indicate a specific, highly effective mode of offensive action on the land battlefield. Precisely what that mode is remains somewhat obscure. Since the name given to it is far from precise this is scarcely surprising. The frequency of the term's application to what has happened in twentieth-century warfare suggests the importance of discovering what we are really talking about. The real purpose of the historical analysis presented in this book is to do precisely that.

Lightning strikes swiftly, in unexpected places and with enormous violence. Even when the probability of a lightning strike is known to be high, its target cannot be predicted with confidence and the blow, when it falls, comes with complete and often devastating surprise. But it is a single instantaneous event. Reflection on the nature of the operations to which the term *Blitzkrieg* is applied suggests that for that reason it is an inaccurate description of them. For although these operations may be conducted with speed, violence and initial surprise, it is not through instantaneous, but in sustained action that they succeed. The duration of the operation may be relatively short (though some of those to which the term is applied have been protracted) but it is in the unremitting maintenance of pressure during the whole of it that success lies. This is not at all the single, flashing, violent sword-stroke that the name implies.

The strategic essence of *Blitz* warfare is the indirect approach. Probably the most authoritative and comprehensive examination of the indirect approach in war is contained in Liddell Hart's book under that title.[1] He examines twelve wars, which decisively affected the course of European history from ancient times onwards, starting with what can probably be described as the first "Great War" in European history, that between the Greeks and Persians in the fifth century BC. He goes on to consider the eighteen major wars that followed, up to 1914 – counting the Napoleonic Wars as one. In these thirty conflicts there were more than 280 campaigns. In only six of these campaigns, Liddell Hart points out "did a decisive result follow a plan of direct strategic approach to the main army of the enemy". "With the exception of Alexander," Liddell Hart claims, "the most consistently successful commanders when faced by an enemy in a position that was strong naturally or materially, have hardly ever tackled it in a direct way. And when, under pressure of circumstances, they have risked a direct attack, the result has commonly been to blot their record with a failure." His enquiry leads him to two final conclusions. "The first is that, in face of the overwhelming evidence of history, no general is justified in launching his troops to a direct attack upon an enemy firmly in position. The second, that instead of seeking to upset the enemy's equilibrium by one's attack, it must be upset before a real attack is, or can be successfully launched." In *Blitzkrieg*, as we have come to know it, that is to say, in the application of the principles of the indirect approach through what have been found to be the most appropriate tactical methods, the destruction of the enemy's equilibrium, both physically and psychologically, forms the essential basis of success. The attack itself, launched swiftly, violently, with maximum surprise and sustained with great speed and destructive force, is built upon it.

Tactically the *Blitz* method demands the swift exploitation of successes achieved in deep penetration between, or round, main centres of resistance, which are left for later reduction by follow-up forces. This is just the reverse of the practice to which so much of the appalling slaughter on the Western Front in World War I was due – the committing in the attack of the strongest forces against the enemy's strongest defensive positions. The basic principle of *Blitzkrieg* is to seek out for attack the points where the enemy is weakest and least expecting to be attacked; then, having broken in to secure a foothold, to pour in whatever can be found to develop, out of the break-in, a break-through. Liddell Hart, in analysing the theory after World War I, used to apply the descriptive term "expanding torrent" to indicate the nature of the follow-through.

There was not really anything odd or esoteric and certainly nothing new in all this. A brilliantly successful practitioner of the indirect approach in the Western Desert in World War II, General Dick O'Connor, denied that he was applying any theory at all. What he did, he said, was dictated only by common sense.

The full development of the method in the land battle, however long its history, had to await the introduction of appropriate means, providing greater troop mobility, higher speeds and more effective mobile fire power. The wide application of the internal combustion engine in World War I, and the appearance in battle of the tank and the aeroplane, opened the door to *Blitzkrieg* as we have come to know it. The term may be imprecise, but it is now generally accepted and it is probably sensible to continue to use it.

The First World War already offered examples of the method, pregnant with warning of what could happen as weapons and equipment developed further. General Oskar von Hutier's action for the crossing of the River Dvina and the capture of Riga in September 1917 was a classic case. A more than usually competent Russian general, Klembovsky, commanding the 12th Army, expected to be attacked in his defence of the river line but was confident that the attack would fall first upon his own bridge-head, into which he had consequently put his best troops. Hutier, commanding the German 8th, played it the other way round, ignoring the bridgehead and crossing the Dvina elsewhere. He then by-passed the stronger positions and, having thrown the whole structure of the defence out of balance, swept on to the swift capture of Riga, the second port in Russia. In October of that year the same method was used by von Below's 14th Army in Italy to cause the complete collapse of the Italian 2nd Army at Caporetto on the Isonzo, driving the Italians back seventy miles to the River Piave. If Below had had cavalry, or better still armoured cars, the rout would probably have been such as to drive Italy out of the war.

The tank had already made its appearance. In November 1917 it was used on the Western Front to break the Hindenburg Line at Cambrai and open a way for British cavalry to drive through to the German rear. The follow-up was too slow and a great opportunity went unused. The German counter-offensive that followed was a stunning success: all ground that had been lost to the tanks was by 7 December recovered. Few people understood why. It was not widely appreciated, or even known, that the Germans had now added aircraft to the equation. The outline pattern of what we know as *Blitzkrieg* was complete.

The author points out, as a matter of interest, that in the Caporetto campaign two men who were in the Second World War to show a high mastery of the method were on opposite sides. They were O'Connor and Rommel, both light infantrymen. This prompts me to reflect that the swiftness with which early tactical success is exploited and the flexibility of command structures that makes such exploitation possible are two keys to the successful application of the method. In Vienna in 1946, after a war in which I had experienced Rommel's use of it at first hand, and after diligent search, I found a copy of Rommel's own book *Infanterie Greift an*[2] based on his experiences as a junior officer in the *Infanterieregiment Konig Wilhelm I. (6. Wurttemberger)*, in which he started the war as commander of No. 7 Coy. It should be remembered that the companies in a German infantry regiment were numbered consecutively all the way through, the battalion (a major's command) being more of an administrative than a tactical headquarters.

The use of the German regimental structure to swing companies about in reinforcing success is here most graphically explored and illustrated. Rommel himself as a captain sometimes found himself in command of four, six or even eight companies of infantry, when the hole that his own had punched in the enemy position had made an opening into which they could be thrust. On one occasion, in Rumania in August 1917, the *Abteilung* under Rommel's command grew to 16.5 companies, bigger than the normal regiment.[3] This is an outstanding example of what Liddell Hart calls the "expanding torrent". Rommel's book is perhaps of no more than minor historical interest now, but I have never seen a translation of it into English and find it hard to understand why.

The First World War ended without the full exploitation of the capability of armour for deep penetration, though some remarkable episodes such as the action of Carter's armoured cars in the 17th Battalion of the Royal Tank Corps and the truly astonishing run of Lieut. Arnold's single Whippet tank *Musical Box* hinted at what lay ahead. World War II, on the other hand, after a rehearsal in the Spanish Civil War, opened at the very outset with a full-scale and totally successful German *Blitz* campaign in Poland.

Though the country that first brought tanks onto the battle-field (this one) had in the inter-war years largely neglected them, the Germans had not, and had also been developing the other elements essential to modern *Blitz* warfare – air striking power, ground troop mobility and intense and fast-moving fire support. The history of the land battle in World War II is in large part the history of *Blitzkrieg* itself and the author of this book does a great service in looking at it in this way. It is fascinating to follow the accelerating development, under the pressure of war, of suitable tools for the job. It is illuminating to observe, from the failures of the method, its weaknesses when applied by those who did not fully understand it – when, for example, the political leaders would step in and override the advice of the professionals. Hitler offers a prime example here. Amateurs could be found among regular soldiers in professional armies, however, as the history of the fighting in North Africa shows. True *Blitzkrieg* is only for bold and highly skilled professionals, and for youngish professionals at that.

It is inevitable in a book reflecting on one aspect of war that there will be occasional lack of balance and over-statement, and perhaps even some dubious conclusions. In exploring antidotes to *Blitzkriegs* for example, I find the emphasis placed on the United States Tank Destroyer Force a little unconvincing. There will be readers, however, I am sure, who will never have heard of the American TDF and a little overemphasis in correcting a weakness is sometimes no bad thing. The debate as to how effective the United States Tank Destroyer Force actually was, or could have been, is worth opening up, especially at a time when it is still far from certain whether the dominant element in the attack on armour should be ATGW or the high-velocity gun. There is probably little doubt that the best tank-destroying weapon of the war was the Jagd Panther, with its 88-mm gun, introduced in 1944. The anti-tank defence was now too good: the tank's total domination of the battlefield was at an end. From now on what had been becoming more and more apparent for some years was accepted as blindingly obvious – only the most highly integrated co-operation of all arms together could offer any confident hope of success on the modern battlefield.

Particularly rewarding chapters in this book are those that explore German success and failure on the Russian Front. The failure of "Barbarossa" – due in large measure to Hitler's interference, which according to Halder was "throwing everything into disorder" – destroyed the German confidence, hitherto complete, in lightning victories. In the indirect attack that destroyed the 6th German Army of von Paulus, pinned in Stalingrad by the Fuhrer's decree, Zhukov gave the Russians their first *Blitzkrieg* victory – untidy but genuine. The writing for the Germans was now clearly on the wall.

This penetrating and highly informed book is worth reading and reflecting upon, and not only by military readers. It throws a clear light, often from a novel angle, on what is probably the single most important development in land fighting of the century, a development that continues to dominate it today and is likely to do so for a long time to come.

Chapter 1: The Return of Mobility

At 0730 the long bombardment ceased abruptly. All along the German line officers' whistles shrilled as men came tumbling up from the deep dug-outs, belts stuffed with stick grenades and dragging heavy boxes of machine-gun ammunition. In places the intense shellfire had obliterated the parapets and fire steps of the trenches, so that the men were forced to form a rough firing-line in the craters beyond. The machine-guns were dragged out of their protective shelters and hurriedly emplaced.

There were a few seconds in which men realised that they had emerged from sinking semi-darkness into a beautiful midsummer day. The sun was climbing into a peerless blue sky; larks sang and pipits twittered above the scarlet carpet of poppies that stretched away to the British position. And then the image of beauty faded with the realisation that from that position was rising a menacing phalanx of steel helmets, punctuated by the rippling glitter of fixed bayonets.

"The first line appeared to continue without end to right and left," wrote a German officer of the 180th Infantry Regiment. "It was quickly followed by a second line, then a third and fourth. They came on at an easy pace as if expecting to find nothing alive in our front trenches.

"'Get ready!' was passed along on our front from crater to crater, and heads appeared over the crater edges as final positions were taken up for the best view.

"A few moments later, when the leading British line was within a hundred yards, the rattle of machine-gun and rifle broke out along the whole line of shell holes. Some fired kneeling so

I

as to get a better target over the broken ground, while others, in the excitement of the moment, stood up regardless of their own safety, to fire into the crowd of men in front of them. Red rockets sped up into the blue sky as a signal to the artillery, and immediately a mass of shells from the German batteries in rear tore through the air and burst among the advancing lines. Whole sections seemed to fall, and the rear formations, moving in close order, quickly scattered. The advance rapidly crumpled under this hail of shells and bullets. All along the line men could be seen throwing up their arms and collapsing, never to move again. Badly wounded rolled about in their agony, and others, less severely injured, crawled to the nearest shell hole for shelter.

"The British soldier, however, has no lack of courage, and is not easily turned from his purpose. The extended lines, though badly shaken and with many gaps, now came on all the faster. Instead of a leisurely walk they covered the ground in short rushes at the double. Within a few minutes the leading troops had advanced to within a stone's throw of our front trench, and while some of us continued to fire at point-blank range, others threw hand grenades among them. The British bombers answered back, while their infantry rushed forward with fixed bayonets. The noise of battle became indescribable. The shouting of orders and the shrill cheers as the British charged forward could be heard above the violent and intense fusillade of machine guns and rifles and bursting bombs, and above the deep thunderings of the artillery and shell explosions. With all this were mingled the moans and groans of the wounded, the cries for help and the last screams of death. Again and again the extended lines of British infantry broke against the German defence like waves against a cliff, only to be beaten back."[4]

Here and there the British effected a penetration, which was quickly overrun by German counter-attack. Everywhere men pressed forward through the few gaps in the uncut wire, to find themselves the specific targets of machine-gunners. Soon the gaps were choked with heaps of dead and dying, but still they came on, to fall in their turn, while others died hanging in the wire itself, trying to force their way through.

And then suddenly it was over as the attack finally sank into the ground. Glutted with slaughter, and with their admiration tinged with pity for the men who had sought death so willingly and found it so easily, Germans left their trenches to give what help they could. As one of their officers put it, it had been "an amazing spectacle of unexampled gallantry, courage and bulldog determination on both sides".

The date was 1st July 1916, the first day of the Battle of the Somme, the bloodiest day in the entire history of the British Army. In a little over an hour 57,470 casualties had been sustained, of whom some 20,000 lay dead in an area several hundred yards wide and eighteen miles long. When the battle ended in November each side had suffered well over 600,000 casualties without any decisive result being obtained. It has been said that the magnificent German Army was never quite the same afterwards, but the same can be said of the British, who never quite trusted their leaders again.

Most of the battalions that took part in the 1st July attack belonged to Kitchener's New Army. Many of them were called Pals' battalions, since they were composed of volunteers from the same town, neighbourhood or business who had joined so that they could fight together. For many small communities the losses suffered were indeed the death of a generation.

As they had marched up to the line, the Pals had been promised that the artillery preparation would be so thorough that the German wire would be universally cut and the defenders of the front-line trenches completely eliminated. This was not so and the sharp grief at the deaths of so many kinsmen and friends was neither forgotten nor forgiven.

If a man survived the Somme there were worse experiences to follow. The 1917 Flanders offensive, sometimes called Third Ypres or Passchendaele, was fought in such torrential rain and mud that tanks sank up to their roofs, pack animals to their bellies, and men disappeared altogether if they strayed from the slimy duckboard tracks at night. Soldiers advanced at a snail's pace, their boots encased in balls of clinging mud, and if they were wounded they stood as much chance of drowning as of bleeding to death.

One can but wonder at the fortitude of men who experienced this, saw their fellows dismembered or driven insane, and yet still fought on, week after week, month after month; wonder too that they can look back with warmth on those days, recalling with pleasure the close comradeship and the shared experience. They belonged to a mentally tough and completely self-reliant generation, and they will tell you, with some justice, that "men aren't like that any more".

In human terms, the Western Front was one of Mankind's greatest catastrophes, and for this the generals are usually blamed, a little unfairly. Naturally, armies that expanded as rapidly as those of 1914 contained a proportion of senior officers who were too elderly or who were unable to respond to the demands of modern warfare, but in due course these men were replaced. The majority of generals loathed trench warfare and sought only to end it. For many, the appalling casualties remained an intolerable burden on their consciences for the rest of their days. Nor should it be forgotten that the generals received their own orders from politicians, the despised "frocks", war at the highest level being simply a matter of politics.

The generals were not fools, and recognised that most simple of military truths so concisely expressed by Guderian, that "only movement brings victory". They were, however, faced with a problem unique in military history, namely that barbed wire, machine-guns and quick-firing artillery gave the defence power out of all proportion to that possessed by the attack. They felt that if only they could break through the enemy's defended zone and exploit beyond with mobile troops, which meant cavalry, a war of movement would be restored, which would eventually result in a decisive victory.

All energies were therefore directed to securing the all-important breach. Millions of tons of shells were fired and hundreds of thousands of lives were sacrificed to this end, but the enemy's front remained unbroken, and the reason for this was simply that it was easier for the defenders to rush reinforcements into a threatened sector over unspoiled ground than it was for the attackers to bring up their supports, artillery and cavalry over the shell-torn battlefield with its festoons of barbed wire and deep trenches. In such a situation, with both sides employing the horse as a prime mover, it was inevitable that the defence was always going to be one move ahead.

By the spring of 1917 it was clear that neither the soldiers nor the civilian populations of the major combatants were going to tolerate this method of waging war forever. In March, Russian soldiers sided with rioters to sweep away their medieval monarchy and its corrupt train of incompetent officials; the combination of battlefield slaughter and starvation in the cities was more than the most absolute states could bear. In May, the French Army was convulsed by a series of mutinies following the disastrous failure of an offensive planned by its over-optimistic Commander in Chief, General Robert Nivelle, who had rashly hinted that at last he had found a formula that would break the trench deadlock; it did not, and the carnage was the last straw for regiments that had already been bled white at Verdun. At sea, the effects of unrestricted U-boat warfare were beginning to bite deep into British food supplies, while the Royal Navy's blockade was slowly forcing the German population onto a starvation diet.

The writing was on the wall for generals and politicians alike to read. A solution must be found, a solution that was rapid and total in its efficiency and which did not cost a river of blood to achieve; the alternative was revolution. It was fortunate that human ingenuity provided at that moment not one, but two, solutions which would make the 1918 battles very different from those of the previous years.

In 1968, I visited a small shop in one of the few areas of pre-war Berlin still standing. The shop was owned by a kindly man named Werner Scholtz, who manufactured *Zinnfiguren*, these beautifully engraved military miniatures known as "flats" for which Germany is famous.

In 1916, Scholtz was serving on the Somme front as an infantryman, and he witnessed the first British tank attack. When the alarm whistles blew, he had taken his place on the fire-step and stared out across No Man's Land. A number of unfamiliar rhomboidal shapes had left the British lines and were moving very slowly towards the German trenches, nosing their way in and out of the shell craters and trailing clouds of exhaust smoke. Machine-gunners and riflemen opened up, only to see their rounds flying off the hard boiler-plate in a shower of sparks.

Rockets roared up out of the trench, calling for emergency defensive fire from the German artillery. But the gunners were not used to ranging on moving targets, and the tanks came on through their barrage unscathed as the shell splinters rattled off their sides. They were moving at about one mile per hour, but their movement was continuous, and this in itself filled the waiting infantrymen with a dreadful sense of their menace.

The tanks' own machine-guns and 6-pounders began to fire as the monsters clawed their way inexorably through the dense outer belt of barbed wire. Panic spread like an electric current, passing from man to man along the trench. As the churning tracks reared overhead the bravest men clambered above ground to launch suicidal counterattacks, hurling grenades onto the tanks' roofs or shooting and stabbing at any vision slit within reach. They were shot down or crushed while others threw up their hands in terrified surrender or bolted down the communication trenches towards the second line.

The action took place on the Flers sector on 15th September and resulted in the capture of Flers village.[5] At first German reaction was one of horror at the new weapon's potential, and prisoners described the use of tanks as "bloody butchery"; Werner Scholtz and his comrades referred to them as the Devil's Coaches. In fact, they killed comparatively few, and their main effect was to induce terror and destroy the will to fight, so providing some of the primary ingredients for what was to become known as *Blitzkrieg*.

The tank was the British and French solution to the problem of trench deadlock, and it had been under development since 1915.[6] The French, who were several months behind the British, at first favoured a simple armoured box containing a 75-mm gun and several machine-guns, mounted on a short commercial tractor chassis. The arrangement was a clumsy one, with overhangs fore and aft, so that while the vehicles performed reasonably well on all but the worst going, their ability to cross trenches was poor.

The British had taken the ability to cross trenches as the prime requirement of their design. The best mechanical shape for such a task is that of a huge wheel, but a wheel requires a great deal of power and has a heavy ground pressure. The British designers therefore compressed the wheel into a rhombus, a stroke of genius that combined the benefits of the wheel's obstacle crossing capacity with an acceptable ground pressure.

The rhombus was of course the basic tank hull, around the outside of which passed the tracks. The vehicle was powered by a 105-h.p. Daimler sleeve-valve engine mounted internally along the centre line. Most of the tank's armament was carried in sponsons slung on either side of the hull, the Male version being equipped with two 6-pounder guns and four Lewis or Hotchkiss machine-guns, and the Female with six machine-guns. Of the eight-man crew, no fewer than four were required to steer and change gears on the Tanks Mark I-IV, but the Mark V, powered by the more sophisticated 150-h.p. Ricardo engine, could be driven by one man. No one has yet succeeded in producing a fighting vehicle to equal the cross-country performance of those early tanks, but they had very limited mechanical reliability, and after doing seventy miles required a complete overhaul.

Another limiting factor was the physical endurance of the tank crews themselves. Inside, the concentrated heat of the engine produced a working temperature similar to that of a sauna; the noise level was appalling, a compound of roaring engine and the thunder of tracks passing along the top run of the hull – so bad, in fact, that drivers had no way of knowing whether the guns were in action unless they looked round; the unsprung track rollers produced a hard ride as the vehicle faithfully followed every short pitch and roll of the ground; the air was heavily polluted by a combination of hot oil and exhaust fumes, thickened by the drifting smoke of expended cordite, and often overlaid with the sharp stink of bile as men's stomachs rejected the total experience. Add to this the strains of combat and it is small wonder that returning crews, after several hours in this environment, deafened, exhausted and semi-asphyxiated, simply collapsed beside their vehicles and remained incapable of further effort for long periods.

It has often been said that the initial employment of tanks in small numbers on the Somme was a tactical blunder, and that it would have been better to wait until several hundred machines became available and then deliver a concentrated blow with the new weapon, so preserving the element of surprise. There is much to be said for this argument, but there is another side to the coin as well.

Once the Germans had recovered from their initial shock, they set about evaluating a number of tanks that had fallen into their hands. They found that not only were they mechanically unreliable, they were vulnerable to direct gunfire as well. In the opinion of many German officers the tank was a freak terror weapon of limited efficiency and with a strictly local potential. Special anti-tank ammunition, known as the K round, was developed for use by the infantry, and guns brought into the front line for use in the direct fire role. Of greater importance was the German decision *not* to divert resources to manufacturing their own tanks, a decision that seemed entirely justified by the sight of British vehicles wallowing their way into bottomless mud-holes during the 1917 Flanders offensive. But the German evaluation contained a number of blind spots. It was wrong to assume that the British would not improve the mechanical efficiency of their tanks; wrong to assume that armour thickness would not be increased, so reducing the K round to impotence almost as soon as it was issued; and, above all, wrong to assume that tanks would *always* be employed across the least suitable going.

The Tank Corps, as the Heavy Branch Machine Gun Corps became, had as its commander thirty-six-year-old Brigadier-General Hugh Elies, a Royal Engineer officer who had advised Haig during the tank's development stage. Elies' Chief of Staff (GSO 1) was Lieutenant-Colonel J.F.C. Fuller, an intellectual soldier who had originally served with the Oxfordshire and Buckinghamshire Light Infantry, and who would later become a distinguished military historian.

Fuller possessed an insight that amounted to genius. Although at first he was somewhat less than lukewarm to the tank idea, his conversion was total. Like many such men, he had little patience with those who failed to grasp what he considered to be an essential truth, treating them with caustic scorn. The cavalry he considered to be completely useless, the artillery an over-subscribed fraternity whose principal contribution was to smash up the ground that his tanks would have to cross. During the Passchendaele fighting he had a board erected outside Tank Corps HQ, saying,

> DON'T BE PESSIMISTIC! THIS IS THE LAST
> GREAT ARTILLERY BATTLE!

Elies made him take it down; it was too close to the truth not to make enemies.

Both Elies and Fuller worked unceasingly for the chance to show what their Corps could achieve fighting *en masse* and on good going. Haig, more often remembered for his premature comment that the tank was "a pretty mechanical toy" than for the later support he gave to the Corps, granted their request after some prompting from General Sir Julian Byng, whose Third Army sector contained the most promising ground for the attack, consisting of rolling chalk downland as yet little cut up by shellfire.

The object of the offensive was to seize the enemy's communications centre of Cambrai. The tanks would breach the formidable Hindenburg Line in conjunction with Third Army's infantry, and the Cavalry Corps would exploit beyond. Artillery preparation was limited to a short hurricane bombardment at H-Hour.

The tank Corps had available a total 376 Mark IV gun tanks, plus a further thirty-two fitted with grapnels for clearing wire from the cavalry's path, eighteen supply tanks and a handful of communication and bridging vehicles. The Hindenburg trenches were dug both wide and deep, and were considered to be tank-proof by the Germans. To counter this, many tanks carried huge bundles of brushwood, known as fascines, on their roofs, which could be released into the trenches, so forming a bridge.

The attack was to commence on the morning of 20th November 1917, and the evening before Elies sat down to scribble his now famous Special Order No. 6.

> 1. Tomorrow the Tank Corps will have the chance for which it has been waiting for many months – to operate on good going in the van of battle.
>
> 2. All that hard work and ingenuity can achieve has been done in the way of preparation.
>
> 3. It remains for unit commanders and for tank crews to complete the work by judgement and pluck in the battle itself.
>
> 4. In the light of past experiences I leave the good name of the Corps with great confidence in their hands.
>
> 5. I propose leading the attack of the centre division.
>
> Hugh Elies,
> B.G.
> Commanding Tank Corps.
> 19th Nov. 1917
> Distribution to Tank Commanders.

Elies led out his men in the tank *Hilda* of H Battalion, proudly flying his Corps' brown, red and green standard. He had chosen the colours deliberately as a demonstration that the tanks could and would smash through the mud and blood of trench deadlock and advance into the green fields beyond.

That morning, the Tank Corps affirmed another essential element of *Blitzkrieg* – overwhelming concentration of force at the point of impact. The Germans could offer little effective resistance and fled, routed and panic-stricken, leaving a huge six-mile gap yawning in their laboriously constructed defence system.

For a brief period, the cavalry had the chance to break out into open country. They did not take it, since their Corps Commander had installed himself in a headquarters several miles in the rear, and kept his subordinates on a tight rein. By the time he was fully conversant with what was taking place and authorised a general advance, the enemy had rushed in reinforcements to seal the gap, and the moment had passed; in addition, the horses had been on the move or standing to all day, and badly needed watering. Here again was a lesson that would be absorbed into subsequent *Blitzkrieg* techniques – that the commander of an exploitation force must travel with the leading troops if he is to make the most of the opportunities he is offered.

But for the moment that did not seem to matter; what really mattered was that at last a way had been found to break the German defences at a comparatively trivial cost in lives. For the only time during the Great War the church bells of Britain rang in joyous celebration of a great victory.

During the next few days, battle casualties and mechanical attrition progressively reduced the numbers of tanks available for action. The tempo of the battle slowed and the front seemed to reach a state of stabilisation again. The tanks were gradually withdrawn and despatched by rail to their base.

Then, on 30th November, the unbelievable happened. The Germans counter-attacked with a speed and drive that had never been experienced before on the Western Front. Whole units were isolated and cut off, while others went down fighting to stem the tide. The few tanks that had not been shipped away, often battlefield recoveries, were formed at commendable speed into provisional units, which succeeded in eroding the weight of the German effort, but by 7th December much of the ground taken during the great tank attack had been recaptured, and a little more besides. The Battle of Cambrai had ended with honours exactly even, and for the British this was as humiliating as it was inexplicable.

Reports were called for, containing an explanation for the disaster. Neither Haig nor Byng, nor the corps and divisional commanders, could offer any militarily intelligible explanations. To the eternal disgrace of their authors, those reports that were submitted sank to unplumbed depths of moral cowardice in that blame was laid squarely on the shoulders of the regimental junior officers and even NCOs, who, it was said, had failed to exercise proper leadership. These were the very men who had died resisting the German attack, and to whom military discipline denied any right of reply if they survived.

Obviously, the general public was not going to accept this outrageous suggestion without making a great deal of trouble for the Government and the military Establishment. Some sort of quasi-plausible excuse was cobbled together, based on the lack of reserves, which, it was said, had been absorbed by the Flanders sector or which were in transit to the Italian Front; but it did not explain why the German infantry had managed to break through the defences so quickly. The plain fact was that nobody really knew.

One officer, Captain G. Dugdale, diagnosed one of the symptoms when he wrote his own record of the battle.[7] He wrote that "The German aeroplanes were very active, flying over our lines in large numbers, very low. They were shooting with machine guns at the troops on the ground, and I am quite sure this did more to demoralise our men than anything else." Here was something that would be instantly recognisable to the *Blitzkrieg* generation – the use of air power in conjunction with the ground attack to eliminate centres of resistance and induce fear.

This was part of the answer, but only part. The Germans had in fact perfected their own method of breaking the trench deadlock, and the Cambrai counter-stroke was only a foretaste of what was to come.

The story began three months earlier in the most unlikely of settings, on the Baltic coast at Riga. Here the Russian Twelfth Army under General Klembovsky held a bridgehead along the west bank of the River Dvina. Their opponents were General von Hutier's Eighth Army, which had the task of eliminating the bridgehead and capturing Riga as a prelude to an advance on Petrograd.

Klembovsky knew he was to be attacked, but imagined that von Hutier would first eliminate the bridgehead before crossing the river. He therefore retained his more reliable troops in the bridgehead itself and detailed divisions of doubtful quality to hold the river line.

However, von Hutier's strategy was the exact opposite. His plan was to force a crossing of the river and then swing north towards the coast, so placing the defenders of Riga inside a trap. In so doing, he was employing the strategic principle of *Blitzkrieg* known as the Indirect Approach, a recognition that an enemy position could be made untenable as a result of successful operations elsewhere rather than by direct assault.

Apart from the overall strategy of the Riga operation, its tactical execution is of great interest as well. The first German attempts to use poison gas had been clumsy, involving the release of chlorine from cylinders in the front line when a favourable wind was blowing, but of course any change in wind direction tended to make this a very two-edged weapon. Since the early experiments chlorine had been replaced by phosgene, otherwise known as mustard gas, which required only one part to four million of air to be effective. It was, therefore, possible to incorporate a small cylinder of the gas into the filling of a conventional high explosive artillery shell, thus ensuring its accurate delivery. The beauty of the device, if that is quite the right word, was that the recipients were unaware that they were being gassed until it was too late. The results were extremely unpleasant, consisting of painful blistering and violent attacks of vomiting, with a consequent reduction in both the capacity and the will to fight. The new shell had not been used in offensive operations before, and von Hutier's artillery was to treat the Russians to a very stiff dose.

The German infantry, too, would be employing new tactics. Once across the Dvina, the assault troops would rely on speed and infiltration to work their way through the enemy's successive defence lines, while waves of ground attack aircraft raked the trenches with machine-gun fire.

They went in on 1st September, following a five-hour bombardment, a mere disturbance by Western Front standards, but enough to drench the Russian positions with gas, shake their occupants with high explosive and blind them with smoke. When the German infantry swarmed across the river, their rapid advance *past* sectors that were still holding out completely unnerved the remainder of the defenders, who began streaming away to the east in panic. Within hours the front had been broken.

The very speed with which success was attained prevented von Hutier from reaping the full fruits of his victory. He had prepared a strict timetable, which had been overtaken by events, and it took him some time to accelerate the northern thrust that was meant to be decisive. In that time, Klembovsky, reacting with a promptness foreign to the majority of Russian general officers, re-appraised the situation and withdrew the remainder of his army through Riga and along the coast road to Pskov.

Casualties in terms of killed and wounded had been negligible for both sides, although 9,000 Russians had been taken prisoner. The Kaiser, delighted at von Hutier's almost bloodless capture of Russia's second most important port, paid him the compliment of a personal visit.

On 24th October the same tactics were employed again, this time against the Italian Second Army on the Caporetto sector of the Isonzo front, by General von Below's Fourteenth Austro-German Army. The Italian Commander in Chief, General Luigi Cadorna, had suspected that this sector had been chosen as a target for a major offensive, and had given instructions for a defence in depth to be prepared; his instructions were ignored, with catastrophic consequences.

The German bombardment, erupting among the surprised Italians, disrupted all communications with the rear, so that formation headquarters were left floundering in a fog of war as dense as that which enveloped their choking front-line troops. And then came the assault infantry, sinister grey ghosts flitting in groups through the zone of gas and on towards the artillery and administrative areas, followed by more substantial formations, which eliminated any centres of resistance that had been by-passed. Regiments shredded away from the front, while those on either flank, bereft of instructions from the paralysed command system, were forced to conform to the movement. Soon the whole of Second Army was straggling towards the rear, thus compelling the withdrawal of Third Army on its right as well.

Cadorna hoped to check the flood along the line of the Tagliamente, but the pursuit was as rapid as it was ruthless. Crossings were forced before the Italians could reorganise their shattered forces, Second Army HQ being reduced to the common lot of fugitives, incapable of organising a coherent front from the drifting wrack of its troops. Not until 7th November did the Italians turn and fight again, manning a hastily dug defence line, which followed the southern bank of the River Piave.

In less than three weeks they had sustained a staggering 300,000 casualties, lost 2,500 guns, and been propelled back more than seventy miles from their original front line. It was a blow that almost knocked Italy out of the war, and which caused the urgent despatch of sorely needed British and French divisions from the Western Front to stiffen the defence.[8]

The conduct of war is subject to certain inescapable rules, one of which is that the power of the attack diminishes in proportion to the distance it has covered. The operation of this rule had given the Italian Army the time it needed to form a new front; von Below had available neither armoured cars nor cavalry with which to exploit the sudden collapse, and the pursuit had been carried out by infantry who had reached the limit of their endurance.

Riga, Caporetto and the Cambrai counter-stroke all pointed to the way in which the German Army planned to fight its 1918 battles, but the evidence was too fragmented by distance for the Western Allies to draw any firm conclusions. Riga had been fought against troops already war-weary and demoralised by revolution; the Italians were not considered to have a first-class army, and anyway, mountain warfare was different; and of course, Cambrai remained an enigma.

Meanwhile, the Germans were refining their techniques, forming their *Stosstruppen* into special battalions that would form the spearhead of their respective divisions. The Storm Troopers were chosen from among young, fit men of proven initiative and represented the cream of the army. They moved in groups, their favourite weapons being the grenade, of which each man carried at least one bag, the light machine-gun and the man-pack flamethrower. They came on at a run, rifles slung, taking advantage of all available ground cover, and if they encountered opposition they worked their way round it, jumping trenches without pausing to fight for them. Their object was to get into the enemy's artillery zone, overrunning batteries and pressing on towards brigade and divisional headquarters with little respite. Continual movement was the essence of their tactics. On occasion, an attack might make ground so quickly that it was in danger of running into its own supporting artillery fire, and a system of rocket signals was evolved to inform the gunners when to lift onto the next target.

Behind the Storm Troops would come the Battle Groups, specially trained to reduce strong-points that had been left unsubdued, followed by the mass of the infantry divisions, which would eliminate the last pockets of resistance and secure the captured ground. The whole system resembled a gigantic snake in that once the tail had caught up, the head would shoot off again.

Overhead flew the *Schlachtstaffeln* (Battle Flights), more specialists who concentrated on ground strafing enemy troops in the immediate path of the Storm Troopers. Generally, the *Schlachtstaffeln*, consisting of up to six Hannoverana or Halberstadt machines, attacked from a height of about 200 feet, sometimes dropping bundles of grenades to supplement the fire of their guns.

Both the Royal Flying Corps and the German Imperial Air Service had begun ground strafing in mid-1917. The RFC did not, however, believe it necessary to form special units for the work, which was considered to be an extension of normal squadron duties, and employed a variety of machines of which the best remembered is the famous Sopwith Camel. The British produced the better results by flying at ground level, there being several recorded instances of German soldiers being knocked flat by the wheels of British aircraft. The moral effect was considerable, provoking bitter complaint from the Storm Troops that the *Schlachtstaffeln* were not doing their job properly. An enjoyable diversion for the British pilots was the pursuit of motor-cycle despatch riders and staff cars – not quite the trivial occupation it sounds, since the undelivered message and the general prevented from exercise command can both contribute to the failure of an operation already plagued by difficulties. The French formed a large organisation for heavy local ground support, the *Division Aerienne*, which could be moved about the front as required.

In previous offensives along the Western Front it had been the practice of the higher command to commit its reserves against the strongest resistance encountered. The strategy of infiltration differed radically in that only *successful* penetrations were reinforced; in this way the merest trickle through a broken defence could become a flood and ultimately a torrent. Whereas offensives had until now burst like a wave against the rock of defence, the new system could be likened to an in-coming tide, probing insidiously into the channels between sandbanks, flowing round them yet still maintaining its advance against the shore, while behind came the great mass of water under which the sandbanks would ultimately vanish.

As 1917 drew to a close it appeared that of the two alternative forms of attack, only the German method produced lasting results. For General Erich von Ludendorff, effective commander of the German armies in the west, it seemed as though the New Year was to be one of great promise.

Russia had at last staggered out of the war and was preoccupied with her own internal struggles, while it would be some months before American troops could reach the battlefields in any significant numbers. In the period before the American presence could make itself felt, the troops released from the Eastern Front could be used to deal the tired British and French armies a series of knock-out blows.

In Ludendorff's eyes, Great Britain had become the dominant partner in the Alliance, not merely at sea, but also on land. He reasoned that if the French were beaten into surrender, the British would continue to fight; that the reverse did not apply; therefore, the next major offensive must be designed to inflict a severe defeat on the British and physically separate them from their Allies.

The offensive, codenamed *Michael*, would begin with a massive attack on the Arras – Cambrai – St Quentin sector. The strategic objective would be the communications centre of Amiens, and a mere twenty miles beyond lay an even more glittering prize, the Somme estuary and the sea. If only the sea could be reached, the Western Front would be ripped apart and the British armies confined to a coastal enclave; from that point onwards, the British would be fighting for survival and not for victory. It was an attractive strategy, and one which, some twenty-two years later, would form the basis of a plan presented to the Fuhrer by Field Marshal von Manstein.

On the forty-mile stretch of front no less than sixty-seven divisions of the German Seventeenth, Second and Eighteenth Armies had been concentrated against a total of thirty-three belonging to Gough's Fifth and Byng's Third Armies. In addition, Ludendorff's team would include a number of very important names, including those of von Hutier, hero of Riga, and von Below, the victor of Caporetto.

Also present was a Colonel Bruchmuller, who had fired the crucial opening bombardment at Riga. Bruchmuller was a brilliant artilleryman who commanded a "travelling circus" of medium and heavy guns, which moved up and down the line throughout Ludendorff's 1918 series of offensives. He insisted that all batteries under his command should register their targets by mathematical survey rather than by the more usual ranging shell-fire, thus achieving total surprise when they did open up. During its career, the Bruchmuller Circus consistently achieved such spectacular results that the colonel became known throughout the army as Durchbruch Muller (Break-Through Muller).

In great secrecy the German artillery was focused against Gough and Byng, so that 4,010 field guns opposed only 1,710, and 2,588 medium and heavy pieces were ranged against the 976 available to the British.

In the meantime, events on the other side of the wire were also tending to further the success of the German plans. Not only had more of the front been taken over from the French, a new system of defence was being developed as well. This contained three elements: a Forward Zone, consisting of a series of strong-points that were in effect little more than fortified outposts; a Battle Zone trench system manned by about one third of the defenders, some two to three miles behind the Forward Zone; and a Rear Zone trench system, housing the reserves, some four to eight miles beyond the Battle Zone.

Every aspect of the system played right into Ludendorff's hands. The Forward Zone provided the Storm Troops with the very opportunities they sought to infiltrate: the Battle Zone was within range of the German artillery yet lacked dug-outs in which the troops could shelter during bombardment;[9] and in places the Rear Zone had not even been dug, its location being marked by a line of spit-locked turf. The system was, in short, a recipe for complete disaster, revealing how little the British understood of the new German artillery and infantry tactics, compounded by the fact that each nine-battalion division was badly below strength, battalions containing an average of 500 effectives in contrast to the 1,000 with which they had gone to war.

Deserters had warned of the impending offensive, but none of the defenders had the slightest inkling of just what was in store for them.

At 0440 on 21st March almost 7,000 guns rocked the atmosphere with the opening salvo of the most concentrated bombardment in the history of the war. It is said that when the 2,500 British guns opened up in reply there was no appreciable difference in the noise level, since the air was too disturbed by continuous shock waves to conduct more than an impression of sound.

From 0440 until 0640 Bruchmuller's men fired a mixture of gas and high explosive shells into the British gun batteries, command posts, communication centres and bivouac areas, punctuated at 0530 by a ten-minute switch directly onto the Forward Zone. At 0640 there was a thirty-minute pause to rest the sweating gun crews, during which batteries fired check rounds only.

At 0710 the guns thundered out again, hammering the British trench systems while the heaviest pieces engaged targets in the rear. By 0940 the whole area had been combed and swept several times, and what was not smashed by high explosive was drenched in gas and shrouded in drifting smoke. At 0900 the fire rose to a crescendo, its pattern changing ominously to a barrage that obliterated what remained of the Forward Zone, then lifted 300 metres, halted for three minutes, lifted 200 metres, halted for four minutes, and lifted again, maintaining a steady progress into the Battle Zone.

0940 was the Storm Troopers' H-Hour. Their rapid advance across No Man's Land was cloaked by a natural mist and they met little resistance in the shattered Forward Zone. They pressed on into the Battle Zone, their green signal rockets soaring to request an acceleration of the creeping barrage, and were seen working their way through gaps in the main trench line. Behind came the Battle Groups, isolating and subduing small pockets of stubborn defenders, and in their wake followed the main weight of the attack. Only the *Schlachtstaffeln* were absent, grounded by the mist, but as this cleared, they began to arrive over the battlefield about midday, their activities covered by a swarm of fighters.

One characteristic of the British soldier is his stubborn immobility in defence. With their telephone links to the rear cut by shellfire, battalions fought their battles with little direction from their higher formation. Some, the luckier ones, were able to withdraw, doggedly covering the retreat of the artillery; others, more quickly surrounded, fought on to the death and were never heard from again. These, and little group of cooks, clerks, batmen, signallers and drivers, rushed into the line at a minute's notice, all took toll of their attackers, but the fact remained that by nightfall a forty-mile gap had been punched in the line and Fifth Army was on the point of disintegration.

The week that followed was one of deep trauma for the British both in France and at home. The Flesquiers salient, last remnant of the great tank attack at Cambrai, was swallowed up in the first day's advance; four days later all the ground that had been bought so bloodily during the Somme battle was once more in German hands. British and French divisions, hurrying to plug the gap, found themselves caught up in the general retreat.

The crisis was of such proportion that on 26th March the Allies appointed a Supreme Commander, Marshal Ferdinand Foch, to coordinate counter-measures. Everyone appreciated the strategic significance of Amiens and divisions from both the British and French sectors were despatched quickly into the danger area. By 5th April the line had been stabilised at Villers-Bretonneux, a mere ten miles east of Amiens, partly because of these counter-measures and partly because the German offensive was running down in obedience to the laws of the attack.

The Storm Troops, having advanced up to forty miles in a week in the van of a hard-fought battle, were exhausted and had suffered a fiercer rate of attrition than had been allowed for. Their casualties been caused by the stubborn defence, by the RFC's universal ground-strafing, and by encounters with tanks fighting in the counter-attack role.

These last encounters are of interest, for while it is true to say that tanks can take ground but not hold it, they can buy time, which in war is the most priceless commodity of all. On a number of occasions tanks caught Storm Troop and Battle Group units in the open and dispersed them with some slaughter, effectively blunting divisional spearheads and so delaying the advance of the main body until a reorganisation could be affected.

There was another influence at work too, a factor that could not have been foreseen by either side. God tends to remain aloof from Man's foolishness, but the devil does not and the battlefield is his playground. On 28th March German air reconnaissance reported that the country between Albert and Amiens was clear of Allied troops, but for no intelligible reason the advance did not proceed beyond the town of Albert itself. A staff officer was sent forward by car to investigate. On arrival he found a state of complete bedlam. Drunken men, some wearing top hats and other looted clothing, were staggering about the streets, helping themselves to whatever they fancied, quite beyond the control of their officers. By the time the advance was resumed, Amiens was no longer attainable.

Elsewhere along the front similar scenes were taking place whenever an Allied supply depot was captured. Weary Storm Troopers, suddenly presented with stocks of drink, real tobacco, real coffee and items of food that the British maritime blockade had long since made a memory in Germany, found themselves unable to resist the temptation to gorge themselves with unaccustomed luxuries; even such mundane things as boot polish and notepaper had not been seen in the trenches for many months, and now they were to be had for the taking.

The advance was resumed as soon as order had been restored, but the Storm Troops' keen psychological edge had been dulled and the *elan* of the early days was lacking. The daily advance rate became slower and slower until it was clear that the *Michael* offensive was over.

Disregarding the demoralising effects of the Allied supply depots, it must be admitted that Ludendorff had it within his power to capture Amiens. That he did not do so stemmed from a decision taken as early as 23rd March. Instead of maintaining the westward march of his three armies, he dispersed their effort, insisting that Seventeenth and Eighteenth Armies should turn respectively north-west and southwest, while in the centre Second Army alone continued along its original axis.

This can be justified only in part as the conventional strategy of building protective shoulders for the huge salient that was forming, but it also denied a basic military tenet and fundamental principle of *Blitzkrieg*, namely Maintenance of the Objective; in other words, having set Amiens as his primary strategic objective, the *majority* of his effort should have been directed at capturing the city in accordance with the aims of his original plan.

His decision, in conjunction with the various other factors already mentioned above, did not merely cost him a meticulously planned and gallantly executed infantry *Blitzkrieg* victory; ultimately it cost Germany the war.

The following month, Ludendorff would attack again, this time in Flanders, recovering all the ground lost during the 1917 British offensive, and in May the French were forced back more than thirty miles on the Chemin des Dames sector, but neither operation possessed the same strategic menace as had the great drive on Amiens.

Not that Amiens had been forgotten. On 24th April the Germans mounted a surprise attack on Villers-Bretonneux, heralded as usual by an intense bombardment with gas and high explosive. This time, however, it was not the Storm Troops who emerged from the morning mist but tanks of a totally unfamiliar design.

The tanks' break-through at Cambrai had at last convinced the Germans that they must, after all, form their own Panzer Corps. Experiments had been going on in a dilatory sort of way since October 1916, conducted by the secret Allgemaine Kriegsdepartment 7 Abteilung Verkehrswesen (General War Department 7, Traffic Section), known as A7V for short, which also gave its name to the finished product, of which only a handful had been built by the spring of 1918.

In form the A7V followed the French concept of an armoured box on a tracked chassis. Its armament consisted of one 57-mm Russian Sokol gun in the front plate, two machine-guns on each side and two at the rear. Although possessing a sprung suspension the vehicle was a poor cross-country performer and had a high centre of gravity. Inside no less than eighteen men were stuffed in supreme discomfort into a space measuring twenty-four feet by ten feet, which also housed two 100-h.p. Daimler engines.

In conjunction with five captured Mark IVs, four A7Vs had been used in penny packets on the first day of the *Michael* offensive. Their use had gone unrecorded by the British, since those who had seen the tanks had either been killed or captured. Thereafter, the tanks' low mechanical endurance had prevented them from keeping up with the advance.

At Villers-Bretonneux the Germans led their attack with a total of twelve A7Vs. The effect of the tanks on the British infantry was precisely the same as it had been on the German. A three-mile gap appeared in the line, through which the Storm Troops poured into the shattered town.

However, a little way to the south-west lay the Bois de l'Abbe, and lying up in the wood were two Female and one Male Mark IVs of No 1 Section A Company 1st Battalion Tank Corps, commanded by Captain J.C. Brown. The crews were still suffering from the effects of gas but those who had not been totally incapacitated manned their vehicles and proceeded towards the still unbroken Cachy switch-line. Throughout the subsequent action Brown controlled his tanks on foot, running across open ground between them to direct their movement.[10]

No sooner had No 1 Section emerged from the wood than they were warned by the infantry of the presence of German armour. The following extracts are taken from an account of the engagement written by Lieutenant Frank Mitchell, commanding the Male tank.

"I informed the crew, and a great thrill ran through us all. Opening a loophole, I looked out. There, some 300 yards away, a round, squat-looking monster was advancing; behind it came waves of infantry, and farther away to the left and right crawled two more of these armed tortoises."

Mitchell's right-hand gunner at once engaged the German vehicle with his 6-pounder. He worked under the greatest difficulty, being all but blinded by gas, and was forced to load for himself while the Male pitched in and out of shell holes, his usual loader being one of those left behind in the wood. Meanwhile the A7V, *Elfriede* of 3rd Panzer Abteilung, was firing at the other tanks in the section with its 57-mm gun. The two Females, being armed only with machine-guns, were powerless to reply and were quickly forced to retire with holes blown in their armour plate. Simultaneously the A7V's machine gunners were engaging Mitchell's vehicle, sending the crew diving to the floor as a continuous shower of sparks and splinters flew off the inside of the hull. Mitchell decided to halt so as to give his gunner a better chance.

"The pause was justified; a well-aimed shot hit the enemy's conning tower, bringing him to a standstill. Another round and yet another white puff at the front of the tank denoted a second hit! Peering with swollen eyes through his narrow slit, the gunner shouted words of triumph that were drowned by the roar of the engine. Then once more he aimed with great deliberation and hit for the third time. Through a loophole I saw the tank heel over to one side; then a door opened and out ran the crew. We had knocked the monster out! Quickly I signalled to the machine gunner and he poured volley after volley into the retreating figures."

Elfriede's driver, probably concussed by the thunder-clap explosion of the first 6-pounder round against what Mitchell calls, with some justice, the conning tower, had lost direction and run his tank slantwise onto a steep slope. The second and third hits seem to have caused little damage, but the ground had given way beneath the A7V, which slowly toppled onto its side into a sand pit.

Well pleased with the result of the action, Mitchell set off in a slow-motion pursuit of the two remaining German tanks, which had begun to retire towards their own lines. Unfortunately, a direct hit from an artillery shell brought an end to the chase and Mitchell and his crew were forced to evacuate their vehicle and shelter in the nearest infantry trench.

The state of play was now as follows. On the British side, Mitchell's Male had been immobilised and Brown's two Females had retired with battle damage; to balance this one German tank had been knocked out and two more had voluntarily withdrawn, leaving the Storm Troops vulnerable to counter-attack if more British tanks appeared.

That this actually occurred was rather the result of personal initiative than of any grand design. An RFC pilot, flying over the area of the tank battle, had observed the stalled German infantry preparing to advance again towards the switch-line and had dropped a message to that effect into the harbour area of a 3rd Battalion Tank Company three miles west of Cachy.

The tank company consisted of seven Whippets[11] commanded by Captain T.R. Price, who at once set his vehicles in motion. As he approached the battle area Price deployed his tanks into line abreast and advanced at top speed over good going. The Germans, amounting to two battalions, were taken completely by surprise while forming up in a hollow and were massacred as the Whippets tore into them, machine-guns blazing. At the end of their run the tanks wheeled round and combed the area again, the crews later being sickened by the discovery that their tracks were "covered in blood and human remains". Both German battalions were utterly dispersed with the loss of 400 men killed. British casualties amounted to three killed and two wounded. Three Whippets were slightly damaged by shellfire. A fourth, which against Price's orders had shown itself on a skyline, was knocked out – at the time it was thought by artillery, although it was later found to have fallen victim to a solitary A7V that remained in the area.

So ended the first tank battle in history. The Germans abandoned their attempt to take Cachy and during the night an Australian attack threw them out of Villers-Bretonneux.

In the meantime, Fuller had been analysing the lessons of the previous six months. Cambrai had shown that tanks could break trench lines and infuse fear, but it also confirmed that on the Western Front cavalry could not be relied upon to exploit the breach. In future it would have to be the tanks themselves that carried out the exploitation. Of the vehicles available only the Whippet offered the slightest chance of achieving this aim, but its limited speed was not corrected in its planned replacements the Mediums B and C. However, Tank Corps thinking was already running along the lines of a much faster vehicle that had not yet reached the production stage although the principles of its design were well advanced. This was the Medium D, which travelled on articulated "snake" tracks, suspended from cables and which was powered by a 240-h.p. aero engine. An experimental version had already reached a speed in excess of 20 m.p.h., and it was hoped that the vehicles would begin to reach the battlefield in quantity during 1919.

The Storm Troops' infiltration tactics also appealed to Fuller, particularly the paralysis caused by their striking at the lower formation headquarters in the early stages of the battle. Obviously, the effect of the paralysis increased in proportion to the importance of the headquarters, but again the Storm Troops' rate of advance on foot and their limited physical endurance prevented them from snapping up any of the really large prizes, the Corps and Army Headquarters, which remained obstinately beyond their grasp. If Medium Ds were substituted for men on foot those very headquarters could be eliminated within a matter of hours.

Fuller committed his thoughts to paper and on 24th May submitted them in the form of a battle plan. His main point was that the enemy's command structure should be eliminated *before* the main attack on his front was launched. During the first phase he envisaged a Disorganising Force, consisting of Medium Ds with air cover, effecting a penetration and driving deep into the enemy's rear to destroy senior headquarters, which he felt could be reached in about two hours. Meanwhile, bombers and ground attack aircraft would add to the confusion by strafing road and rail centres, and supply dumps.

As soon as the command system had been eliminated, a Breaking Force of heavy tanks, infantry and artillery would shatter the enemy's front. The confusion and panic already caused by the Disorganising Force would ensure that resistance would not be protracted.

Once the front had been broken a Pursuing Force of fast tanks, lorry-borne infantry and cavalry would harry the routed army ruthlessly. Fuller saw the pursuit being maintained for 150 miles, following which the enemy's will to fight would have been broken.

The plan was accepted by Foch as the basis for operations to be carried out the following year, and was for this reason referred to as Plan 1919.[12] For decades to come it would be the keystone of the *Blitzkrieg* philosophy.

Following the easing of German pressure against Amiens, it was decided to mount a minor attack against the ridge at Hamel, to the north of Villers-Bretonneux. This would be useful in gauging German morale and also provide an opportunity of testing the newly arrived Mark V in action.

The attack was made by ten battalions of the Australian Corps with four American companies under command, and was supported by five companies of tanks on a three-and-a-half-mile frontage. It went in at 0310 on 4th July, the date being chosen in honour of the Americans, following a rolling barrage fired at H-Hour by 600 guns. Within an hour all objectives had been secured at a trivial cost of only 775 Australian casualties and 134 American. 1,500 prisoners were taken and 171 machine-guns captured. It was a brilliant little success, which Fuller considered did more to establish the reputation of the Tank Corps than Cambrai.

On 18th July the French launched a heavy armoured counterattack against the flank of the Marne salient. Unheralded by any form of bombardment 211 Schneider and St Chamond tanks, followed by 135 of the new two-man Renault FTs, burst out of their woodland cover and smashed through the German front. By the end of the day the French had advanced four miles and taken 25,000 prisoners.

There was now reason to believe that German morale was falling in spite of the substantial gains made in the spring. The overall numerical superiority with which Ludendorff had begun his offensives had now disappeared with the arrival of more and more American divisions, and the scales were beginning to tilt irrevocably against Germany. The elite Storm Troops, the cream of the Army, had been decimated time and again, and were no longer the proud force they had been in March; and inevitably the rest of the Army, having already surrendered its best to the *Stosstruppen*, was of inferior quality. Worst of all, these men had been promised that their efforts would result in the longed-for peace. They had not, and they began to lose hope as the Allies gained strength and went inexorably over to the counter-attack. These and other troubles that beset the German Army were willingly recounted by deserters to Allied intelligence officers.

Encouraged by such signs and by the results of the recent Allied tank attacks, Haig suggested to Foch that the entire British Tank Corps should be assembled secretly east of Amiens with a view to striking a concerted blow, which would not only clear the enemy away from the city but also recover several strategic railway lines that had been submerged by the German advance. Foch readily agreed and detailed planning was commenced at once by General Rawlinson's Fourth Army Staff.

The right flank of the operation would be covered by XXXI Corps of the French First Army; the main thrust would be delivered by the Canadian Corps, supported by the 1st, 4th, 5th and 14th Tank Battalions, and by the Australian Corps, which had been allotted the 2nd, 8th, 13th and 15th Tank Battalions, plus the 17th Battalion, which was equipped with Austin armoured cars;

north of the Somme the left flank was covered by the British III Corps with 10th Tank Battalion in support. Ready to exploit the breach was the Cavalry Corps, with which would be working the 3rd and 6th Battalions, each with 48 Whippets.[13]

The nine heavy battalions were equipped with Mark Vs and two, the 1st and 15th, had the larger Mark V Stars, which in addition to their normal duties were to carry two infantry machine-gun teams per vehicle onto the objective. In addition to the 324 heavy tanks and ninety-six Whippets, forty-two vehicles were held in mechanical reserve and 120 used as supply carriers, while twenty-two gun carriers would follow in the wake of the attack. In total the 604 fighting vehicles represented the largest concentration of armour ever achieved in the Great War.[14]

The Royal Air Force, which had come into being on 1st April following the amalgamation of the RFC and the Royal Naval Air Service, had already achieved a total superiority over the battle zone, effectively preventing German intruders from examining the preparations for the attack. As the tanks came forward in their hundreds to move into their hides after dark the sound of tracks and engines was drowned by low-flying bombers droning up and down the line. For the attack itself a large number of squadrons had been detailed for ground support and some of these had the specific task of dealing with enemy artillery batteries that lay in the tanks' path.

On the German side of the thirteen-mile front were two armies, von der Marwitz's Second with ten divisions in the line and four in reserve, and von Hutier's Eighteenth with eleven in the line and four in reserve, all well below strength. Of these only a handful were still considered to be battle-worthy, while the morale of the remainder was low. Army staffs tended to dismiss recurrent tank alerts as being symptomatic of general nervousness.

At 0400 on 8th August the tanks began to move forward towards the start line, their noise still masked by aircraft engines. At 0420 they passed through the infantry to go into the lead while simultaneously 3,500 guns opened fire, one third dropping a rolling barrage ahead of the attack, the remainder firing into the German battery positions.

Dense mist shrouded the advancing vehicles. In some areas direction was lost, but for the defenders, already shaken by the opening barrage, the sound of the invisible tanks moving slowly towards their position was, if anything, even more frightening than being able to see them. All along the line, SOS flares shot skywards, but it was too late.

The bulky shapes loomed out of the mist, crushed their way through the wire and towered over the parapets. Where resistance was met it was swept away in a blast of 6-pounder case shot and machine-gun fire. Some men took to their heels, but the majority surrendered and the attack rolled on.

Morale in the artillery was higher than in the infantry and the German gunners tended to stick to their weapons until the last minute, accounting for no less than 109 tanks, a quarter of those engaged. But it was not enough to halt the flood of armour, which by mid-morning had broken through the trench system.

The cavalry divisions began to pass through, but failed to make the most of their opportunity, preferring to wait for specific instructions from their Corps HQ, which had not yet caught up with the advance. A supply column was captured during a charge near Harbonnieres, but the horsemen's principal contribution to the battle was in rounding up the thousands of enemy who had been left behind by the assault wave. Long before dusk they were retiring from the field to attend to their mounts, taking with them the Whippet battalions, to the fury of Elies and Fuller.

The Tank Corps Staff had argued strenuously that horses and armour just did not mix, and their views had been justified. When there was no opposition the horsemen had cantered ahead, leaving their escorting Whippets far behind; inevitably, when enemy machine-guns were encountered they were themselves forced to retire and wait until the Whippets arrived to deal with the problem. But the Tank Corps had been overruled and their own plans for a sweep by both Whippet battalions through the German rear was dismissed as being too ambitious. Fuller later wrote that if the Whippets had been accompanied by lorried infantry, whose vehicles could have been towed over the trench lines, far better results could have been achieved.[15]

One Whippet did penetrate deep into the enemy's rear areas, although ironically the extent of the chaos it caused was not revealed until after the war. The tank concerned was named *Musical Box* and was commanded by Lieutenant C.B. Arnold of 6th Battalion, with Driver Carney and Gunner Ribbans making up the crew.

By 0620 *Musical Box* was 2,000 yards in advance of the start line and was beginning to catch up with the Mark Vs and the Australian infantry. Between Abancourt and Bayonvillers the tank came under fire from a four-gun battery, which had already knocked out two Mark Vs nearby. Using a belt of trees for cover, Arnold swept round behind the battery. The gunners abandoned their weapons and fled only to be cut down by Arnold and Ribbans, and the Australians came forward to occupy the site while *Musical Box* set off again, running parallel with the railway.

By now the cavalry were hunting down the parties of fugitives that seemed to be everywhere. Arnold caught up with two patrols, which were suffering casualties from rifle fire and killed most of their opponents before continuing on his way.

He was now completely on his own. His map showed a German bivouac area in a small valley between Bayonvillers and Harbonnieres and he drove into this to find the inhabitants hastily packing their kit. *Musical Box* opened fire at once, putting them to flight and killing about sixty, many of whom had tried to escape over the railway embankment.

Arnold now swung left across country. He soon encountered files of enemy infantry retreating through the standing corn. They were engaged at ranges between 200 and 600 yards and went to ground at once. *Musical Box* remained for more than an hour in this area, cruising up and down and shooting at any sign of movement.

Conditions inside the vehicle were now all but intolerable. Tins of petrol stowed on the roof for replenishment purposes had been punctured by the incessant fire directed at the tank, and the contents were running down the inside walls of the fighting compartment. The fumes meant that the crew, already suffering from the effects of heat and cordite smoke, were compelled to breathe through the mouthpieces of their respirators. Nonetheless, in spite of this and the ever-present danger of fire and explosion, Arnold decided to continue the advance.

Soon *Musical Box* found herself in the midst of the retreating army. On all sides were columns of horse and motor transport, and marching men. These were engaged at close range, heavy casualties being inflicted. The tank's sudden appearance in what was regarded as a relatively "safe" area caused complete panic until it was realised that the Whippet was operating alone. A field gun was brought to bear and quickly scored three hits at the very moment Arnold was instructing Carney to turn for home.

The tank burst into flames. Arnold dragged his semi-conscious crew out and the three men rolled on the ground to extinguish their blazing clothes. Enraged Germans swarmed round, one shooting Carney dead while Arnold and Ribbans were hammered with rifle butts and kicked all but senseless. Some were for killing them outright, but calmer views prevailed and they were marched off to spend what remained of the war in prison camp. Only on Arnold's release did the full story become known; he was awarded the DSO.

So ended one of the most remarkable runs in the history of armoured warfare. *Musical Box* had been in action for more than ten hours and had advanced eight miles since crossing the start line, causing chaos and confusion wherever she went. One can but speculate on what might have happened had both Whippet battalions been present instead of a single tank.

A little to the north, Lieutenant-Colonel E.J. Carter's 17th Battalion had embarked on an even more wide-ranging career of destruction and disruption. The battalion's sixteen Austin armoured cars had been towed across the captured trench lines by tanks. They had advanced along the main Amiens – St Quentin road, which was found to be partially blocked by fallen trees.

These were removed with assistance from a tank, and the cars then passed through their own infantry and out into the country beyond. They then fanned out along the side roads to the north and south, raiding into the villages of Framerville, Harbonnieres, La Flaque, Chuignolles, Proyart and Foucaucourt.

Throughout the morning they chased lorries, destroyed convoys, killed mounted staff officers, shot up troops in their billets, exploded the boilers of several steam wagons with their fire, disabled a train and ambushed crowds of fugitives streaming back from the broken front. The most significant achievement of the day was the capture by Lieutenant E.J. Rollings' section of a hastily evacuated corps headquarters in Framerville, over which the Australian Corps flag was promptly hoisted. The headquarters contained a complete set of plans of a twenty-mile stretch of the Hindenburg Line, which was put to good use the following month.

Between them, Carter's armoured cars and Arnold's *Musical Box* had demonstrated the obvious validity of Fuller's Plan 1919 and all that it implied. But for all that and the fact that the British line had been advanced more than six miles by the end of the day it appeared at first as though Amiens, like Cambrai, was going to be another "might-have-been" victory. On the morning of the 9th only 145 tanks were fit for action and German divisions were being rushed in from all quarters to seal off the gap. By 11th August it was clear that the offensive was over.

In fact, Germany had been dealt a mortal blow. The German report on the battle, subsequently quoted in the British Official History, gives clear evidence of the mood of despair which pervaded all echelons of the command structure.

As the sun set on 8th August on the battlefield, the greatest defeat that the German Army suffered since the beginning of the war was an accomplished fact. The total losses of the units employed in the Second Army sector can be put down as from 650 to 700 officers and 26,000 to 27,000 men. More than 400 guns and an enormous quantity of machine-guns, mortars and other war material were lost. More than two thirds of the total

German losses were due to prisoners. Almost everywhere it was evident that German soldiers had surrendered to the enemy or thrown away rifles and equipment, abandoned trench mortars, machine-guns and guns, and sought safety in flight.

The statistics tell their own story. The German soldier was now more interested in survival than fighting, and was not prepared to sacrifice himself in a cause in which he had lost belief. At home there was political unrest and a population on the verge of starvation; in the field, the Allies seemed to grow stronger with every month that passed. The sheer weight of the tank attack had broken his nerve at last, and he knew that he had no effective defence to offer.

Discipline too was severely strained. Divisions moving up to fill the gap were hailed as "blacklegs" and accused of prolonging the war. Ludendorff recalled 8th August as "the black day of the German Army", and frankly admitted to the Kaiser that the war could now only be ended by negotiation and that a German victory was no longer possible. His primary concern now became the preservation of the German Army as a bargaining factor at the conference table.

The effect of Amiens was therefore more psychological than physical. Slowly the Allies began to scent victory as a series of sharp attacks along the entire front resulted in a uniform German withdrawal to the Hindenburg Line.

By the end of August three weeks fighting had resulted in the capture of more than 70,000 prisoners. A month later the Hindenburg Line was stormed and the German Army committed to the retreat that would continue until the Armistice came into effect on November 11th. By then the Imperial Navy had mutinied, Germany was racked by revolution and the Kaiser had been forced to abdicate.

Of the part played by the Tank Corps during the last weeks of the war, Sir Douglas Haig wrote: "Since the opening of our offensive on August 8th, tanks have been employed on every battlefield, and the importance of the part played by them in breaking the resistance of the German infantry can scarcely be exaggerated. The whole scheme of the attack on August 8th was dependent on tanks, and ever since that date on numberless occasions the success of our infantry has been powerfully assisted or confirmed by their timely arrival. So great has been the effect produced upon the German infantry by the appearance of British tanks that in more than one instance, when for various reasons real tanks were not available in sufficient numbers, valuable results have been obtained by the use of dummy tanks painted on frames of wood and canvas."

More than 2,000 miles away the now half-forgotten Palestine campaign confirmed the lessons of the Western Front. In August 1915 a Turkish attempt on the Suez Canal had been defeated and throughout the following year the British, under General Sir Archibald Murray, had slowly advanced across the Sinai while their water-supply pipeline was extended from Egypt.

In March 1917, Murray attacked the main Turkish position, situated along a series of ridges between Gaza and Beersheba, but made very little progress. Unfortunately, the action was represented as a success, and Murray was ordered to advance on Jerusalem. He attacked Gaza again in April, supported by a handful of tanks, which inspired local panics, but were too few in number to affect the main issue, and was again checked, this time with heavy loss. He was removed from command and replaced by General Sir Edmund Allenby, a former Inspector-General of Cavalry whose handling of the Cavalry Corps during the First Battle of Ypres had played a critical part in halting the German advance on the Channel ports.

Tall, heavily built and given to explosive outbursts of rage, Allenby was known as The Bull, but had the ability to inspire enthusiasm and was determined to lever the Turks out of their position and fight a mobile war; almost his first act was to remove General Headquarters from the comforts of Shepheard's Hotel in Cairo and re-establish it close to the front.

About one-fifth of his army was mounted, consisting of British Yeomanry and Indian cavalry regiments, a regiment of French Spahis, and a large contingent of Australian and New

Zealand Light Horse. The last-mentioned usually fought as mounted infantry, riding big, hardy animals known as whalers, which were less affected by the climate than other breeds. Their tremendous *elan* and total ferocity in the attack was something the Commander-in-Chief prized highly, so much so that when occasionally hailed as "mate" by down-under troopers sublimely indifferent to rank, he affected a convenient deafness.

The various cavalry formations, 4th and 5th Cavalry Divisions, Australian Mounted Division and Anzac (Australian and New Zealand) Mounted Division, together with some Camel Corps battalions, were formed into the Desert Mounted Corps, commanded by Lieutenant-General Sir Harry Chauvel, an Australian regular officer who has been described as the greatest leader of mounted cavalry in modern times. In the months to come the Corps' operations would be supported by, and frequently led by, Light Armoured Motor batteries, equipped with Rolls Royce armoured cars, and Light Car Patrols with Model T Fords.

Throughout the hot summer months, Allenby planned what was to be the third and last Battle of Gaza. The Turkish right flank was to be pinned down by a heavy diversionary attack on Gaza itself, while Chauvel with the Australian and Anzac Mounted Divisions moved out into the desert and then attacked Beersheba from the east and north-east, thus turning the enemy's line.

The battle began on 31st October. Chauvel's brilliant approach march was consummated by an astonishing 7,000-yard charge made by the Australian 4th Light Horse Brigade in loose order, the troopers jumping two lines of trenches, some galloping on into Beersheba while others dismounted to wade into the Turks with rifle and bayonet. At a cost of thirty-one killed and thirty-six wounded the brigade had captured Beersheba, taken 800 prisoners and nine guns.

At Gaza the diversionary attack had achieved better results than had been anticipated, the tanks all but breaking the enemy line between the city and the sea. Allenby decided to reinforce success and increased the pressure. The Turks' German Commander-in-Chief, General Kress von Kressenstein, conscious of Chauvel's indirect pressure inland, ordered a general withdrawal that was immediately followed up.

The Turks committed their last reserves, but were unable to establish a new line and on 8th December evacuated Jerusalem. Allenby entered the Holy City on foot through the Jaffa Gate, the first Christian commander to do so since the days of the Crusades, curiously fulfilling the ancient prophesy that when the waters of the Nile flowed into Palestine the long Turkish rule would end; The waters, in fact, flowed through an unglamorous pipeline, but they had arrived. To simple men, the significance of the event was appropriately confirmed by the local corruption of Allenby's name into *Allah en Nebi*, the Prophet of the Lord.

The disaster cost von Kressenstein his job. He was replaced by General Erich von Falkenhayn, who managed to construct a new front stretching from the Jordan valley to the sea in torrential winter rain that almost brought movement to a standstill. There the line remained for nine months, Allenby's capacity for a further advance having been curtailed by the need to provide substantial drafts to meet Ludendorff's spring offensives in France. However, by September he had been reinforced and was ready to go over to the attack again.

What he planned was a break-through on the coast, following which the whole army, led by the Desert Mounted Corps, would pivot on the Jordan and wheel to the east like a gate, crushing the Turkish front. An elaborate deception plan, involving the construction of dummy camps and simulated troop movements, was designed to convince the Turks that the main thrust would be made up the Jordan valley, while out in the desert Lawrence and his Arabs prepared for a final orgy of destruction on the enemy's lifeline, the Hejaz Railway.

On the vital fifteen-mile coastal sector Allenby concentrated 35,000 infantry, 9,000 cavalry and 383 guns against 8,000 Turkish infantry supported by 130 guns. Along the remaining forty-five miles of front the British had only 22,000 infantry, 3,000 cavalry and 157 guns in the line as against the Turks' 24,000 infantry and 270 guns. Secrecy was the keynote of the plan, and brigade and battalion commanders received a personal briefing from Allenby himself when he visited their divisional headquarters only two or three days before the operation was due to start.

Falkenhayn had now left the theatre, his place being taken by General Liman von Sanders, whose headquarters were at Nazareth. Under command he had three armies, the Eighth on the coast under Djevad Pasha, the Seventh in the centre under Mustapha Kemal, the hero of the Dardanelles, and the Fourth on the left under Djemal Kucuk, their activities being controlled through a main telephone exchange at Afula, south of Nazareth.

At 0430 on 19th September the British artillery began a whirl-wind bombardment of Eighth Army's positions, reaching a crescendo of 1,000 rounds per minute, following which three infantry divisions stormed the Turkish front line. The Desert Mounted Corps immediately began to pass through the gap.

Meanwhile, the Royal Air Force was having a profound effect on the conduct of the operation. Armed with Bristol fighters, SE5As, DH9s, some Nieuports and a single Handley Page bomber, it bombed and strafed the headquarters of the Seventh and Eighth Armies, situated respectively at Nablus and Tul Karm, and the telephone exchange at Afula, cutting communication and leaving von Sanders groping in a fog of war at Nazareth. Contact with Tul Karm was lost at 0700 and never regained; it was re-established with Nablus about noon and only then did the Turks' Commander-in-Chief learn from Kemal that Djevad's army had been routed and that cavalry were pouring onto the Plains of Esdraelon. Much of Eighth Army had surrendered; what remained was caught by the RAF retreating along the Tul Karm – Mas'udiye road, and bombed and machine-gunned to destruction.

Von Sanders was not prepared for the speed with which Chauvel's men would exploit the break-through. At 0530 the next morning the 13th Cavalry Brigade galloped into Nazareth almost capturing the general, who was forced to make an undignified exit in his pyjamas while his staff and GHQ clerks held off the pursuit. Elsewhere on the 20th the Australian Mounted Division took Jenin and the 4th Cavalry Division Beyt Shean on the Turkish line of retreat.

Kemal had tried hard to preserve a coherent front, but with his right flank turned and his rear menaced, he could only do what he could to extricate Seventh Army from its predicament. During the night of 20th/21st September, his artillery and transport began moving back along the Wadi Far'a, only to be discovered by the RAF shortly after dawn and subjected to four hours' continuous air attack. First, the head of the column was halted; the vehicles behind, unable to by-pass the obstruction because of a ravine, were then attacked by two aircraft every three minutes with an additional six every half-hour. Total chaos and confusion produced a hopeless tangle of ninety guns and limbers, fifty-five motor lorries and ninety-two supply wagons. It took days for the British to sort out the mess, yet oddly there were few dead horses and even fewer dead men. The Seventh Army had simply disintegrated when its men bolted for safety, straight into the arms of Chauvel's waiting cavalry.

Thus, two days after the offensive had begun, the Turkish Seventh and Eighth Armies had been reduced to several hundred frightened stragglers, without direction from above. Kucuk's Fourth Army, isolated and alone, did not survive them long. Only the two regiments of the German Asia Corps preserved their discipline and integrity to the end.

The pursuit by Chauvel's Corps faced only local opposition. Damascus was entered on 1st October, Beirut on the 8th, Tripoli on the 13th and Aleppo on the 25th. Five days later the Turkish government concluded an armistice with the Allies. In the thirty-eight days since the Battle of Megiddo, as the break-through operation was to become known, Allenby had advanced 360 miles, destroyed three Turkish armies, taken 76,000 prisoners and captured 360 guns. The cost was 853 killed, of whom only 125 belonged to the Desert Mounted Corps, and 4,482 wounded.

Between the wars, Allenby's feat was often quoted as a justification for the retention of mounted cavalry; in fact, the arm has never really disappeared. The Red Army, as will be seen, used its Cossacks to deadly effect as late as 1944, and later on the Portuguese and Rhodesian armies both used mounted troops in the antiterrorist role in the African bush.

Many decades later, perspective enables us to look on Megiddo and its aftermath as the first *Blitzkrieg* of modern times. The fact that armoured vehicles were only present in small numbers is not really relevant. Having concentrated a superior force opposite the sector chosen for the break-through, Allenby achieved complete surprise and then used his cavalry's mobility to strike across the Turks' lines of communication at the strategic objective of the Jordan valley, while von Sanders' command network was paralysed by air attack. This combination of mobility and air power destroyed the Turkish Army within forty-eight hours.

Serving on Allenby's staff was a taciturn, thoughtful officer of the Black Watch who had lost an eye as a result of wounds received on the Western Front. He greatly admired Allenby, whose biography he later wrote, together with a study of the Palestine campaign. His name was Archibald Wavell and in later years, using the principles of Third Gaza and Megiddo, he would win an astonishing series of victories over an enemy who outnumbered him by ten to one.

Chapter 2: New Weapons, New Ideas

"The tank proper was a freak," said Major-General Sir Louis Jackson in a lecture given to the prestigious Royal United Services Institution in November 1919. "The circumstances which called it into existence were exceptional and are not likely to occur again. If they do, they can be dealt with by other means."

In one sense the general was right; the very existence of the tank made the digging of trench lines a fruitless exercise. But in his reference to "other means" can be detected an echo of the desire expressed by many of the pre-1914 generation of officers to get back to some "real soldiering", whatever that was, after the nightmare of the Western Front.

There were, however, officers who appreciated that the battles of 1918 pointed the way to the future and that there could be no turning back. They had seen shock action, by tanks on the Allied side and by massed artillery and gas on the German, break through successive defence lines; they had witnessed the disruptive influence of ground-support air operations; and they had observed the paralysing effects of infiltration and exploitation on static command structure. They understood that the results were primarily psychological and that it was now preferable to destroy an army's will rather than embark on the piecemeal destruction of the army itself. Equally important, they realised that the primitive fighting vehicles and aircraft of 1918 would inevitably give place to more sophisticated machines with greater mechanical endurance and destructive capacity.

Each of these strands confirmed in some measure that the next major war would be one of mobility. Woven together they would form the fabric of a technique designed to save life by achieving a lightning victory – the technique of *Blitzkrieg*.

The immediate post-war climate was not one in which the seeds of new military ideas could have been expected to germinate. The Great War had been a People's War and the suffering inflicted was written large on memorials in even the smallest villages of the land. Perspective had not yet defined the essential difference between 1918 and the earlier years; men thought only of the horror of trench warfare and of the lost generation of fathers, brothers and friends. Understandably, there was a revulsion against the whole concept of war and this, together with a deepening world economic crisis, ensured not only the contraction of armies but also that military spending was constrained by a financial strait jacket, which prohibited all but the simplest experiments with new weapon systems and techniques. By 1921 the Tank Corps, which had numbered twenty-five battalions in November 1918, had shrunk to a mere five battalions and a dozen armoured car companies, which were scattered throughout the Empire.

In fact, the Corps was lucky to survive as a separate arm of the service. Elies, Fuller and Martel, who had been the Corps' Brigade Major on its creation, continued to advocate the tank's potential in an autonomous role, particularly in operations that involved deep penetration of the enemy's rear areas, fighting an up-hill struggle against a conservative Establishment dominated by cavalrymen who were naturally prepared to resist any threat to their own arm. Fuller in particular continued to produce books and papers on the subject, all of which demonstrated an almost prophetic insight into the shape of things to come.

The Twenties has been quoted as the decade in which the British Army obstinately continued to pay more for its fodder than for its fuel. On the other hand, it was (and indeed remains) a fair-minded institution and by 1927 had decided to let the enthusiasts put their theories to the test. In that year an Experimental Armoured Force was briefly established on Salisbury Plain, consisting of a medium tank battalion, a mixed battalion of armoured cars and tankettes,[16] a motorised artillery regiment and machine-gun battalion, a motorised engineer squadron and various RAF fighter and bomber units.

Some enthusiasts would have preferred a larger mechanised infantry element while others pointed out that the Force could have achieved greater flexibility if its components had been controlled by radio. In spite of this the experiment greatly impressed foreign military observers and received very favourable coverage from Captain Basil Liddell Hart, military correspondent of the *Daily Telegraph*.

Liddell Hart had served with the King's Own Yorkshire Light Infantry and had been severely gassed on the Somme. Since then, he had written a number of infantry training pamphlets, including one that recommended what he termed the "expanding torrent" method of attack, which bore great similarity to that used by Ludendorff's *Stosstruppen*. As a professional infantryman he remained firmly convinced that his own arm of service was the dominant factor on the battlefield until the events of 1918 and the writings of Fuller converted him to an enthusiastic advocacy of the tank as a battle-winner in its own right. In 1927, he was invalided out of the army and took up the pen as a way of life, his newspaper articles and books constantly commending the joint use of armour and air-power to achieve strategic paralysis by deep penetration, and exhorting the benefits of the indirect as opposed to the direct approach to a strategic objective. His work was eagerly read abroad, especially in Germany, where General Heinz Guderian later conferred on him the title "creator of the theory of the conduct of mechanised war".

Some may argue that the title more properly belongs to Fuller, but by the early thirties, Fuller's influence had begun to wane. The opinions expressed in his works, at times needlessly sharp in tone, had not endeared him to the Establishment, and in 1927 he had been on the brink of resigning over the question of command of the Experimental Armoured Force, which was eventually given to another officer. In 1933, his resignation became a reality when, as a major-general, he was offered what he personally considered to be an insultingly junior appointment, the command of the Bombay Military District. He devoted the rest of his life to the writing of military history, a task for which his keenly analytical mind made him brilliantly equipped.

The lessons learned from the Experimental Armoured Force were confirmed in 1931 when for six months a Tank Brigade was established under the command of Brigadier Charles Broad. The brigade's medium tanks were fitted with radios, which permitted orders to be given by voice over the air and thus removed the need for detailed pre-exercise briefings. This enabled the formation to operate with a flexibility unequalled anywhere in the world, and in 1934 it was re-established on a permanent basis as the 1st Tank Brigade, Royal Tank Corps.

Together, the Experimental Armoured Force and 1st Tank Brigade can be regarded as the direct ancestors of the armoured division, but it was not until 1938 that the British Army set about producing its own formations of this type. Prior to this, the War Office had supported in general terms the philosophy that the tank was an infantry support weapon, but practical experience had now confirmed that armoured formations, including a balanced infantry and artillery element, *could* operate autonomously as the Army's major striking force in exactly the manner prescribed by Fuller and Liddell Hart.

Two such divisions, known then as Mobile Divisions, were established, one in the United Kingdom and the other in Egypt, but neither was properly equipped when war broke out. This was due in part to Britain's late start in her re-armament programme, and in part to the diversity of equipment required by the newly created Royal Armoured Corps to fulfil its tasks.[17] In addition to the Cruiser tanks, which would form the principal weapon of the Mobile Divisions, slow but heavily armoured Infantry tanks were needed for the Army Tank Brigades whose function was direct infantry support, while the infantry's own divisional cavalry regiments were to be equipped with fast, machine-gun armed Light tanks. Such a procurement programme took time to implement, time that was simply not available; the net result of a generation's political parsimony was that in September 1939 the British Army had no offensive capability whatsoever in the purely European context.

Great Britain, while still regarded as a seed-bed of interesting ideas, was in fact no longer considered by the majority of the international community to be a major factor in the field of armoured warfare. The French, who had finished the Great War with several thousand two-man Renault FTs and a few hundred mediums, were considered to be the experts, and the French said that the tank's function was infantry support, actually transferring responsibility for the arm from the artillery to the infantry itself.

The French system of attack involved two types of tank. The leading wave consisted of well-armoured mediums or heavies – the huge Char 2C or *Char de Rupture* was specifically designed for this role – which would smash their way into the enemy's defences, to be followed by the main infantry assault wave, which would be accompanied by a large number of smaller tanks whose task was to eliminate remaining pockets of resistance.

During the Thirties some consideration was also given to the role to be played by the mechanised cavalry regiments and by the outbreak of war three Divisions Legeres Mechaniques (DLMs) had been formed. However, these formations were never intended for use in the manner of the armoured division and their duties simply duplicated those of the old horse cavalry in that they provided a screen for the main body of the army, carried out reconnaissance *en masse* and were available to exploit a victory when the moment arrived.

Seriously alarmed by the resurgence of Germany, France had begun to renew her stock of tanks in 1931 and for the next nine years continued to turn out a wide variety of vehicles for both infantry and cavalry use. Many, like the Char B and the Somua, were well armoured and satisfactorily armed for their time, but all suffered a most serious disadvantage in that they carried one-man turrets. In practice this meant that a vehicle commander was simultaneously employed in directing his driver; choosing ground for tactical advantage; loading, aiming and firing his guns; possibly using his radio; and trying to control the other tanks under his command if an officer. To ignore any of these functions was to court disaster, yet their combined pressure was such that none could be adequately performed.

The French Army did not lack officers of imagination but the General Staff turned a deaf ear to the pleas of pioneers such as Estienne for the formation of armoured divisions. In 1934 Colonel Charles de Gaulle produced a book called *Vers l'Armee de Metier* in which he advocated the idea of a fully armoured army as France's principal weapon in a future war. He might as well have asked for the moon, for French politicians of the left had a deeply ingrained mistrust of the Army dating back to the bloody days of the Commune of 1871, and the creation of a potentially dangerous elite within an elite was not something that could be countenanced. Three years later a left-wing Popular Front itself seized power after several days of rioting, introducing one crack-brained economic measure after another. The inevitable consequences included inflation, unemployment and widespread industrial unrest. The deep rifts in French society had not healed by 1939 and although the Army was not directly affected its substantial reserve classes were, with results that were to become apparent later.

A further development that influenced military thought in France was the Maginot Line, built at a cost of billions of francs as a defence against possible German aggression. The Line's steel and concrete casemates, manned by specially trained troops, incorporated underground railways, hospitals, anti-gas devices and air-conditioning, and ran from the Swiss border along the common frontier with Germany as far as the mountains of the Ardennes, which were considered to be tank-proof; from the Ardennes to the Channel coast the Line did not exist at all, as it was felt that the construction of fixed defences might be construed as a hostile act by the Belgian government.

So much treasure and ingenuity had been poured into the completed section of the Line that it was held to be virtually impregnable. This created a climate of complacency in which the traditional French spirit of the offensive was allowed to wither and die. Such complacency was ill-founded, for the Ardennes remained an open door in spite of theories to the contrary; Liddell Hart, visiting the area in 1935, agreed that it was difficult country for conventional forces but was convinced that tanks were quite capable of forcing their way through.

Notwithstanding French prestige, it was the Soviet Union that owned the largest tank fleet in the world. After the Civil War the Red Army could muster only a handful of British Mark Vs and French Renault FTs, which it had captured from the Whites, and since the Bolsheviks were regarded as international pariahs it was unable to supplement its stock by purchasing additional machines from the industrialised nations. In an attempt to overcome this difficulty, the 1922 Rapallo Agreement was signed with Germany, who found herself in a similar situation, both nations undertaking to pool their tank experience at a secret experimental station deep inside Russia.

Only on completion of her compulsory industrialisation programme was Russia able to commence the manufacture of tanks on her own account. Foreign prototypes were purchased, modified and put into mass production, little attention being paid to finish but a great deal to the fitting of a powerful main armament – at a time when most western medium tanks carried 37-mm guns the Red Army was installing high-velocity 76.2-mm weapons as a matter of course. This apart, the prime requirement of any Russian design was that it should be simple and soldier-proof, very necessary elements where a mass of recruits with virtually no technical education had to be trained quickly in the basics of driving, maintenance and gunnery.

Russian designers were, however, only too willing to learn and to incorporate foreign expertise in their own work. By the end of 1939 the team of Alexander Morozov and Nikolai Kucherenko, led by the brilliant Mikhail M. Koshkin, had completed the design of a new medium tank, which employed the American Christie high-speed suspension system and which was driven by a 500-h.p. aluminium diesel engine. The tank, designated T34, was a balanced combination of the three classic elements of tank design, firepower, protection and mobility, and was an ideal tool for *Blitzkriegs* it has, in fact, influenced tank designers ever since.

It was ironic that such a vehicle should have been produced when morale in the Red Army had reached its lowest ebb, especially in the armoured corps. The Russian High Command, STAVKA, had always favoured the French doctrine and methods of infantry support for its tanks but some officers, notably Marshal Mikhail Tukhachevsky, were impressed by the writings of Fuller and Liddell Hart and possessed sufficient influence to be allowed to put their theories into practice.[18] Mechanised brigades were formed, each consisting of three battalions equipped with fast BT tanks (which also employed the Christie suspension), and an assault infantry battalion. Two or three such brigades, grouped with a mechanised infantry brigade and a motorised artillery regiment, formed a mechanised corps, the intention being to use these formations in deep penetration operations against the enemy's rear areas. Unfortunately, radios were in chronically short supply in the Red Army and because of this the mechanised brigades and corps lacked any real flexibility as each phase of an operation required careful briefing and rehearsal instead of being talked through on the command wireless net, as in the west; moreover, once a formation had been committed to a particular course of action it was difficult to control and almost impossible for it to react quickly to an unforeseen change in circumstances.

Tukhachevsky and his like-minded colleagues did, however, represent a progressive school of thought within a traditionalist Red Army, and this professionalism naturally tended towards the development of military theories and philosophies that did not have their roots firmly planted in the central councils of the Communist Party. The party had always regarded the Army as an extension of its own will and was seriously alarmed at what seemed like an attempt to remove it from political control; Stalin in particular, supported by a clique of Civil War cavalry officers, saw what he fancied to be the stirrings of an infant Praetorianism in the armoured corps and decided that it must be strangled at birth.

On 9th June 1937, Tukhachevsky and his two principal supporters were relieved of their posts. On the 11th they were court martialled, found guilty and shot at dawn the following day. In the months that followed the Army was mercilessly purged from top to bottom of any who were even suspected of having been remotely contaminated by the disease. The full extent of the slaughter will probably never be known but estimates suggest that some 35,000 officers were murdered, disappeared without trace or sent to labour camps. During the Great Purge the Red Army lost three of its five marshals, thirteen of its fifteen army commanders, fifty-seven out of eighty-five corps commanders, nine of every ten divisional and brigade commanders and eight of every ten colonels. Deprived of most of its keenest minds, the Army was totally cowed, its surviving officers being literally unable to issue the simplest orders without direct approval from their attached political commissar.

The Stalinist justification for this further lapse into barbarism relied heavily on an ill-conceived and illogical attack on the theories of the western tank experts, which, it was claimed, were representative of a decadent society that was forced to rely on machines for its defence; the real strength of Soviet Russia, the argument continued, lay with the rifle-carrying mass of its armies of workers and peasants. The mechanised formations were broken up and their tanks dispersed to infantry support battalions.

For the next three years the newly purified STAVKA ate little but crow. The presence of Russian tanks failed to affect the outcome of the Spanish Civil War and Soviet prestige suffered. The tiny Finnish Army inflicted defeat after defeat in the Winter War, while the 1939 advance across the eastern Polish frontier revealed alarming discrepancies between German and Russian operational procedures.

Only in distant Mongolia was there cause for satisfaction. Japanese ambitions having resulted in a shooting war along the disputed border.

In August 1939 these ambitions were sharply curbed by a severe defeat on the banks of the Khalkhin-Gol, and it is interesting to note that while the Russian commander, General Grigori Zhukov, was a prominent member of Stalin's cavalry clique, his methods were those of Tukhachevsky, an independent armoured brigade being used to break through the Japanese flank and establish a block behind the enemy's line, which was then assaulted by the main Russian force.

In the light of these experiences and the example provided by the German panzer divisions STAVKA was compelled to reorganise the armoured corps on Tukhachevsky's principles. Tank divisions were established and the mechanised corps reintroduced; given time, the Red Army would certainly have eliminated the various imperfections and incompatibilities that characterised these formations, but its political masters had forced it to change horses in mid-stream once too often and far, far too late in the day for the consequences of this further upheaval to be anything less than horrendous.

Across the Atlantic the United States' small but enthusiastic Tank Corps had been disbanded as a separate entity in 1919, the General Staff taking the view that "the primary mission of the tank is to facilitate the uninterrupted advance of the rifleman in the attack". This view was given statutory force by the National Defense Act of 1920, which decreed that in future tanks would operate solely under the direct command of the infantry.

A very few voices were raised in dissent but among them, significantly, were those of General John J. Pershing, former commander of the American Expeditionary Force in France, Major George S. Patton, Jr, a cavalry officer with personal experience of tank warfare on the Western Front, and Major David Dwight Eisenhower; Patton and Eisenhower actually went into print on the subject and were told in positive terms to shut up or suffer irreparable damage to their careers.

It was in fact in the U.S. Cavalry that the most progressive schools of thought on armoured warfare were to be found in America. Under the urgings of Colonel Adna Chaffee its armoured cars were eventually supplemented with light tanks (which it was forced to call Combat Cars to circumvent the National Defense Act) and with these it demonstrated successfully the possibilities of wide-ranging operations in armour.

The interest generated by the British Experimental Armoured Force led directly to the American Army establishing its own comparable Mechanised Force at Fort Eustis, Virginia, in 1928. When the Mechanised Force moved to Fort Knox, Kentucky, in 1932 it became the responsibility of the cavalry and gradually evolved into the 7th Cavalry Brigade (Mechanised), the United States' first operational armoured formation.

The parallel development of the infantry and cavalry tank arms continued until 10th July 1940 when the establishment of a joint Armored Force put an end to sectional interests. However, for twenty years the Army had been so starved of funds that it had been able to do little more than produce one or two experimental prototypes per year, accompanied by relatively short production runs of designs that had been standardised. With a world war raging the Armored Force found itself in possession of about 500 machines, the majority of which were quite obsolete, although the recently standardised M3 Light Tank (Stuart) was a good design for its weight and the M2 Medium Tank was developed into the 75mm-armed M3 Medium (Lee) at very short notice while design of a main battle tank, the M4 Medium (Sherman), was well in hand.

The true potential of the Armored Force lay, in fact, not only in the United States' enormous industrial capacity, but also in the American genius for organisation, which by the time the Army was committed to active service had produced balanced armoured divisions with arguably the most flexible command structure in the world.

The Italian Army also supported the idea that the tank was primarily an infantry support weapon, but from 1936 onwards experimented with various armoured formations and in 1939 actually formed three armoured divisions, the tank element of which consisted nominally of one four-battalion regiment, although in practice an acute shortage of machines reduced this to one light and one medium battalion, each of two companies. To add to the difficulties facing the Italian tankmen, their own designs were the most backward in Europe, the tankette being used both in the infantry support role and in the light companies of the armoured divisions, while a new medium, the M11/39, can lay some claim to the title of being the worst tank ever built.

In Japan the situation was only marginally better, for the Japanese Army was by tradition an infantry army and its infantry dominated hierarchy made no bones about the fact that its tanks existed for the benefit of the foot soldier. Some attention was paid to western ideas in that a small spearhead formation known as the Independent Mixed Brigade was introduced in 1933, but in general the tanks remained firmly tied to infantry requirements.

From 1931 onwards the Japanese were continuously involved in operations on the mainland of China. The Chinese had virtually no armour and very little in the way of effective anti-tank artillery, so that the Japanese tanks were generally successful in their limited role. This led to a complacent satisfaction with machines that were adequate in the purely local context but which were rapidly becoming obsolete by western standards. A further factor that inhibited tank development in Japan was a shortage of steel, the majority of which was needed for naval construction.

On the eve of World War II, the Japanese tank park could muster a series of tankettes, light and medium tanks, all of which were thinly armoured, under-gunned and badly arranged, although they were powered by trouble-free air-cooled diesel engines, which had been specifically designed for the environments in which they were to operate. Training was confined to simple sub-unit tactics directed at specific objectives, either in line across open country or in column along a road, and use of ground for cover was ignored; so, too, was the prospect of having to fight against other tanks.

Thus, after a generation of comparative peace, none of the world's major military powers – with one exception – were able to carry out the sort of armoured operations advocated by Fuller and

Liddell Hart, the reasons being economic, political or psychological. The exception was Germany, and in this there was a certain historical inevitability.

On conclusion of the Great War the Allies had done everything in their power to humiliate Germany, imposing a crippling indemnity and stripping her of territory both at home and overseas. There was also a consensus among the victorious partners that the German capacity for waging war must be reduced to impotence and the Treaty of Versailles therefore contained a number of military clauses that provided, *inter alia*: that the new republic's Regular Army should not exceed 100,000 men; that the possession of military aircraft was forbidden; and that, with the exception of some armoured cars for internal security, Germany was strictly prohibited from building, acquiring or using any form of armoured fighting vehicle.

The effects of all this were as counter-productive in the military sphere as they were in the political. Under General Hans von Seeckt, sometimes called the Scharnhorst of the Twentieth Century, the Reichswehr chose only the fittest, most intelligent men and trained them to a level one or two steps above their actual rank so that when the time for expansion arrived the enlarged army would be of a uniformly high quality. Each unit was intentionally linked to a unit of the old Imperial Army, whose traditions and customs it assiduously maintained. The Army itself was restored to its honoured place in German society, partly as a result of clever disseminations that it had not been beaten in 1918, but betrayed by politicians.

At the more professional levels the reasons for the 1918 defeats were subjected to searching analysis and the conclusions reached all pointed in one direction – towards the tank. In the immediate post-war years there was nothing the Reichswehr could do about this, but the Treaty of Rapallo with Soviet Russia and some technical assistance provided by Sweden enabled it to keep abreast of developments in tank technology.

A large country with a small army must of necessity think in terms of a fully mobile defence and its mechanised transport department is naturally one of particular importance. A specialist in this field was a former Jager officer, Lieutenant-Colonel Heinz Guderian, who read everything he could find on armoured warfare and who later wrote:

> "It was principally the books and articles of the Englishmen, Fuller, Liddell Hart and Martel, that excited my interest and gave me food for thought. I learned from them the concentration of armour, as employed in the battle of Cambrai. Further, it was Liddell Hart who emphasised the use of armoured forces for long-range strokes, operations against the opposing army's communications, and also proposed a type of armoured division combining panzer and panzer-infantry units.
>
> "Since nobody else busied himself with this material, I was soon by way of being an expert. A few small articles that I contributed to the Militar-Wochenblatt served to enhance my reputation: its editor, General von Altrock, visited me frequently and encouraged me to write more on the subject. He was a first-class soldier and was anxious that his paper should publish material dealing with contemporary problems."[19]

One aspect of the subject that especially impressed Guderian was the perfectly tenable theory that having penetrated an opposing front, an attacker's best protection lay in continuous movement, since the enemy would be unable to execute effective counter-measures against a force the precise location of which remained uncertain. There was nothing new in this; it was simply the maxim of the cavalry raider reapplied after a long era of static defensive warfare and implemented by machine rather than muscle.[20]

Guderian's ideas were opposed by the more conservative members of the German officer corps, but he also received every encouragement from a number of highly placed individuals including Generals Lutz, von Blomberg and von Reichenau. Exercises were carried out with dummy tanks and a few prototypes were built under a thin-cover story that they were tractors.

On Hitler's coming to power, Guderian's career received rapid advancement, for the new Chancellor was fascinated by weapon systems. Even before the military clauses of the Versailles Treaty were formally repudiated on 16th March 1935, Guderian was serving as Chief of Staff to the Armoured Troops Command, and when the first three panzer divisions were formed on 15th October the same year, he was appointed to command one of them while still a colonel. Promotion to major-general followed in August 1936 and to lieutenant-general in February 1938. On 20th November 1938 he was appointed Chief of Mobile Troops and simultaneously promoted General.

The panzer divisions of which Guderian was the principal architect were the best balanced armoured formations of their day, consisting of a two-regiment panzer brigade, each regiment possessing two battalions; a motorised rifle brigade containing one two-battalion rifle regiment and a motor-cycle battalion; an artillery regiment of three battalions, two of which had three four-gun batteries while the third was equipped with twelve howitzers; an armoured reconnaissance battalion and a reconnaissance flight of nine light aircraft; a thirty-six-gun anti-tank battalion; an anti-aircraft battalion; engineer and signal signals battalions; and divisional services.

The theoretical establishment of the panzer battalions provided for three Light/Medium companies and one Heavy company, but a general shortage of equipment meant that most battalions operated with only two Light/Medium companies and a Heavy company that was well below strength. The Light/Medium companies were equipped with the PzKw I, intended originally as a training vehicle, the PzKw II, which had been designed primarily for reconnaissance, both of which were armed exclusively with machine-guns, and the PzKw III, which mounted a 37-mm gun with an armour-piercing capability. The Heavy company was equipped with the PzKw IV, armed with a short 75-mm howitzer, its role being to suppress the fire of hostile anti-tank gun screens and static strong-points that were holding up the advance. However, despite the German rearmament programme, tank production lagged far behind anticipated requirements and had the rape of Czechoslovakia not resulted in a substantial rein-forcement of 35T and 38T light tanks, both armed with 37-mm guns, the *Panzerwaffe* would have been hard pressed to fulfil its commitments in 1939.

In addition to his wide experience in mechanisation, Guderian had specialised in wireless communication and between 1914 and 1917 had held appointments as Signals Officer with various higher formations. He was therefore in a better position than most to confirm the real flexibility conferred by good communications and it was at his insistence that every tank was fitted for radio and armoured command vehicles, mounting the requisite number of sets, provided for the divisional commanders and their operational staffs.

The panzer division was purely offensive in concept. With its tank brigade spearheading the assault, and with close co-operation from the Luftwaffe (q.v.) it would attack a sector of the enemy front not more than 5,000 yards wide. The tanks' firepower was concentrated into a *keil* or wedge, each wave of which would deal with a particular aspect of the defence. The sheer weight of the attack would generally take it right through the defended zone and then the panzer brigade would accelerate towards its strategic objective, avoiding centres of resistance whenever possible.

Through the gap created by the tanks would pour an appar-ently endless stream of vehicles; the motor rifle battalions, who would deal with isolated areas of opposition along the divisional centre-line and hold selected areas of captured ground; the mech-anised artillery batteries ready to support tanks or riflemen as and when required; the anti-tank gunners, capable of deploying their weapons rapidly into screens with which to beat off an armoured counter-attack; and finally the divisional service units with their facilities for replenishment, supply and maintenance.

The whole operation would be controlled by the divisional commander, not from the rear as in the past, but from his command vehicle that travelled just behind the leading ranks of the *Panzerkeil* This enabled him to make his decisions on the spot in the light of his own observations, while his units would respond immediately to orders given over the command net.[21] His sole concern was to maintain his formation's momentum and direction towards the strategic objective he had been set, and to achieve this he was prepared to by-pass towns and other known defended localities, leaving them to be reduced by the conventional infantry divisions that were marching in the panzers' wake.

Concentration being the keynote of all panzer operations, an efficient command apparatus was also established for two higher formations: the Panzer Corps, which controlled from one to three divisions, and the Panzer Group, which controlled a variable number of corps. Since the German Army took a justifiable pride in its staff work, these headquarters operated with smooth efficiency even in the most testing circumstances; the only possible source of friction lay in the personalities of the various formation commanders and since they were men of will some conflict of opinion was inevitable.

However, as the Thirties drew to their close, men were beginning to have second thoughts about the tank's real potential. The Spanish Civil War had provided an opportunity for modern theories of war to be tested and its lessons seemed to suggest that tanks were not, after all, capable of fighting as a separate arm of service.

Soviet Russia naturally supported the communist Republicans, supplying tanks, aircraft and technical assistance.[22] Germany and Italy did the same for General Franco's Nationalists. On 29th October 1936 Russian BTs and T26s won an easy victory over Nationalist cavalry in the streets of Esquivas, which they then exploited in the manner suggested by Tukhachevsky; but having left their infantry far behind in the hot pursuit, they found themselves unable to hold their ground in isolation and were forced to turn back when their fuel ran out. Some weeks later lightly armoured German PzKw Is attacked Republican positions near Madrid, but after some initial success were shot to pieces by anti-tank guns and then driven off the field by a Russian counterattack. On 8th March 1937 the Italian Black Flames Division, a mechanised formation composed of lorried infantry, supported by tankettes and armoured cars, led an assault on Guadalajara, advancing twenty miles in five days. Once again, the Russians counter-attacked and the wretched tankettes, unable to engage on equal terms, were faced with an alternative of taking to their heels or being blown apart. The Republican tanks advanced twenty-five miles, but were again forced to turn back, having repeated the same mistakes they had made at Esquivas. The battle ended with a slight territorial advantage in favour of the Nationalists.

The Russian commander, General Pavlov, had used his tanks with greater imagination than his opponents, but after Guadalajara he reported that the new ideas did not work and that in his opinion the correct use of armour was in support of infantry operations. On the other side of the lines Franco tended to agree, although the view was sharply contested by his German tank expert, Colonel von Thoma.

Many foreign observers felt that the tank had more than met its match in the anti-tank gun; even Liddell Hart wrote that it had failed to fulfil its early promise. Guderian, on the other hand, remained unmoved, pointing out that the mountainous nature of the country predictably channelled thrust lines along valleys that deprived armour of its principal asset, the ability to manoeuvre freely; that the scale of operations had been too small for any firm conclusions to be drawn; and that Spain should be regarded as a test-bed for equipment and not as a school for tacticians. The real test was still to come.

Armour, of course, is only one component of the *Blitzkrieg* technique, albeit the most important. Its partner, air power, had also been the subject of conflicting theories in the twenty years since the end of the Great War. Of these, that put forward by the

Italian General Guilio Douhet in his book *The Command of the Air*, published in 1921, received most attention.

What Douhet suggested was an attack on an opponent's will to fight by terrorising his civil population. Air fleets would bombard his cities, industrial plants and commercial centres with a rain of high explosive, gas and incendiary bombs until morale cracked. The damage inflicted would be psychological as well as physical and the conventional ground forces would simply have the task of mopping up.

In spite of the lessons of the Western Front and Palestine the Royal Air Force enthusiastically adopted this philosophy and, apart from Imperial policing, more or less ignored the question of tactical ground support for the Army. Indeed, some officers felt that the Army was moribund as an institution and that any future war would be won by the bomber alone. There was, however, an initial revulsion at actually putting such a policy into effect, for when it was suggested to Sir Kingsley Wood, the Secretary of State for Air, that the Black Forest be raided with incendiary bombs in reprisal for the ferocity of the German air attack on Poland, he recoiled in horror. "Are you aware it is private property?" he exclaimed. "Why, you will be asking me to bomb Essen next!" Essen was the home of Krupps, the privately owned heavy engineering concern that supplied the German Army with much of its equipment, including tanks.

The French air arm, the *Armee de l'Air*, became an independent service in 1934. It too supported the Douhet theory and in the event of war planned an all-out attack on the enemy's material supply and distribution centres; when this phase had been completed it would be concentrated for ground-support tasks on the decisive sector of the battlefront. The problem was that the majority of the machines available in 1939 were obsolete, and even the performance of the more modern designs fell short of the Luftwaffe's. Further, "One of the most serious faults of French pre-war air policy was its complete inability to appreciate the importance of dive-bombers. As early as the Riff War in Morocco in the 1920s, French airmen had recognised the potentialities of this weapon, and others had fully comprehended the importance of the German dive-bombers in Spain later; but they were in a minority. In his memoirs General Gamelin claims that the Army was in favour of dive-bombers, but that the Air Force opposed them on technical grounds."[23] Equally important, in view of the knowledge that the Luftwaffe possessed dive-bombers, was the failure to study the effect on the morale of those who had been their targets in Spain, and to provide an adequate number of high-angle heavy automatic weapons, which would be the ground troops' only effective counter. It is also worth mentioning that in 1939, with production of German combat aircraft all but reaching 3,000 a year, the troubled French industry was turning out about 600 machines – in contrast to the 5,000 man-hours needed to build a Messerschmitt 109, a Morane 406 fighter required 18,000.

For a while, Russia dabbled in the development of a strategic bomber force, but after the experiences of the Spanish Civil War decided that her air arm should be devoted exclusively to the tactical support of the Red Army. Each Military District was allotted its own air command, while in reserve was a Long Range Air Force, consisting mainly of medium bombers, which operated under the direct control of STAVKA against targets in the enemy's immediate rear.

The Soviet ground-attack armoury included both dive- and fighter-bombers, the most notable types being the tubby little Polikarpov 1-16, the Sukhoi Su-2 two-seater, the Ilyushin 11-2 (otherwise known as the Stormovik), and the sleek Yak-1 and Mig-3 single-seater fighters, both of which entered operational service in 1940. In the field of air-to-ground weapon systems the Russians were ahead of western air forces and were, in fact, already using heavy automatic cannons and rockets as well as a variety of bombs.

The Red Air Force's major deficiency mirrored that of the armoured corps in that it lacked the most elementary tactical flexibility. An almost complete absence of ground-to-air radio equipment meant that once a formation was in the air it could not be controlled by the troops it was supposed to support, while the rigid discipline imposed after the Great Purge ensured that pilots obediently attacked their designated targets even if they were no longer relevant, ignoring more significant battlefield developments that might be in clear view.

In America the US Army Air Corps tended to follow the British lead and concentrated on bomber development at the expense of ground-attack techniques, although the Navy and Marine Corps both used dive-bombers because of the need for pinpoint accuracy when engaging maritime targets.

Italy was in fact the first country to employ its air force, the *Reggia Aeronautica*, in direct support of a mechanised army. When she invaded Abyssinia in 1935 her ground troops were aided by Caproni and Savoia bombers and Fiat fighters, which strafed the poorly armed Ethiopians whenever they concentrated in sufficient numbers, provoking an international outcry by the use of mustard gas bombs. It was, perhaps, in the field of supply that the Italian airmen showed most imagination, using their Ca 101 tri-motor bomber-transports to maintain troops in a country where distances were great and roads few. The technique was used again in 1939 during the invasion of Albania when a mechanised column advancing on the capital, Tirana, was re-supplied by parachute drop.

In Spain the Italians provided the Nationalists with greater assistance in the air than did the Germans and formed their own *Aviacione Legionaria*, which operated in the tactical bombing and ground support role. Nonetheless, when Italy entered World War II the *Reggia Aeronautica* was neither a strategic nor a tactical air force in the true sense of either, and to its other duties was added that of maritime air warfare in the Mediterranean.

Like America, Japan formed separate military and naval air forces. Both services used a variety of interceptors, bombers and fighter-bombers, although the Navy possessed more vertical-attack aircraft. In China the Japanese showed themselves to be whole-hearted adherents of Douhet's theories, bombing cities without mercy. However, in common with the French, they were prepared to fly tactical missions once the strategic air offensives had done their work, although the question of close co-operation with mechanised forces did not, of course, arise.

Germany had managed to circumvent the aviation clauses of the Treaty of Versailles in a number of ways. The Rapallo Agreement enabled her designers to pursue their work in Russia, while in return for technical assistance the Russians set up a flying training school at Lipetsk for Reichswehr personnel. At home the enthusiasm of an air-minded general public was exploited by the formation of numerous gliding schools set up by the *Luftsportverband*, which provided a thin cover for the German War Ministry. By 1926 this organisation had 30,000 members who were receiving flying training both practical and theoretical. In that year also the Allies lifted restrictions on commercial flying and the founding of a national airline, Deutsche Lufthansa, meant that Reichswehr officers could be seconded for aircrew training. Thus, on the formation of the Luftwaffe in 1935, 20,000 qualified personnel were available for immediate duty.

Chief of the new service was Hermann Goering, the last commander of Richthofen's famous squadron and an intimate of Hitler's, much given to bombast and the wearing of exotic uniforms. His Deputy Air Minister was Field Marshal Erhard Milch, a capable and energetic officer who, while completely dedicated to his work, was utterly ruthless and a very bad choice of enemy. In control of administration and Chief of Air Staff from 1936 to 1937 was General Albert Kesselring, while commanding the important Development Section of the Technical Branch was Colonel-General Ernst Udet, another World War I fighter ace with a record of kills second only to Richthofen's.

Personal relationships between these men were bad. Goering lacked the wide organisational experience that Milch had obtained as Lufthansa's chief executive, and since he was uncomfortable in such matters, he tended to distrust his Deputy's motives, with some reason. He also had reason to dislike Udet, who had once thrown him out of the Richthofen Veterans' Association on the grounds of falsification of his war record. Milch, for his part, despised Udet's easy-going and slightly bohemian life-style. Kesselring disagreed violently with Milch on a number of professional and personal issues, and soon left the Air Ministry for the less heated atmosphere of an operational command. Yet surprisingly as a team they produced the most balanced air force in existence, capable of both strategic and tactical employment.

The Luftwaffe's policy was that while terror bombing should be used to weaken an enemy's resolve (and, incidentally, choke the roads in his rear with refugees, so inhibiting troop movements), wars would be won by the Army to whose operations the most immediate battlefield support must be given. In the latter context, the German concept of ground-attack fell into two categories, close tactical support and interdiction.

Close support was considered to be particularly important for the panzer divisions because it was thought that their artillery regiments, which, while mechanised were not yet self-propelled, would find difficulty in keeping up with the tank spearhead; in such circumstances ground-attack aircraft would serve as flying artillery and deal promptly with any source of opposition: remarkably, enemy formation headquarters held a low priority in the overall close-support attack plan. Interdiction meant the bombing of communications, assembly areas, troop concentrations and airfields, isolating the battlefield and preventing reinforcements from reaching the front.

Control of close-support operations was facilitated by efficient radio links and the siting of Air Fleet headquarters close to those of the Army Groups with which they were to co-operate. The procedure was slightly over-organised in that the Luftwaffe's forward air controller, positioned among the Army's most advanced units, would signal his requirements back to Air Corps, which would then detail squadrons by radio or telephone links to their airfields. As the aircraft approached the front, they became the responsibility of the forward air controller who would talk them onto their targets, assisted by ground markers and the release of coloured smoke. In spite of its complexity the system worked well.

In 1933, Udet was in America and was sufficiently impressed by a demonstration of Curtiss F8C Helldivers to order two for Germany. Trials revealed that with these dive-bombers it was possible to land a bomb within 30 yards of its target and the Junkers Organization was asked to design a similar machine. The result was the Ju 87 Stuka, a name that has become almost synonymous with *Blitzkrieg*.[24] The prototype flew in late 1935 and soon the first production models were on their way to Spain to supplement the German Kondor Legion's vulnerable Henschel Hs 123 biplanes in the ground-attack role.

The Stuka had a maximum speed of 250 m.p.h., a ceiling of 26,000 feet and, with a full bomb-load, a range of 373 miles. It was armed with two fixed machine-guns in the wings and a third manually aimed machine-gun in the rear cockpit; one 1,102-lb bomb was slung beneath the aircraft's belly and four 110-lb bombs attached to wing racks.

Capable of an almost vertical dive onto its target, the Stuka was intended to induce terror as well as inflict damage, and the rising whine of its accelerating engine was supplemented by a high-pitched siren fitted, it is said, at Hitler's personal suggestion. When pulling out of his dive the pilot was subjected to tremendous G-forces and could black out for several seconds; during this period the plane was controlled by a specially fitted auto-pilot.

The Stuka remained Germany's principal close-support air weapon during World War II, while interdiction tasks were carried out by the level bomber fleet of Dornier Do 17s and Heinkel He 111s, joined later by the Junkers Ju 88. Protection for the ground-attack aircraft was provided by the Messerschmitt Me 109 and 110 fighters, the former having already proved itself a decisive influence in aerial combat over Spain; during the Battle of Britain its performance was barely equalled by the Hawker Hurricane and barely exceeded by the Supermarine Spitfire.[25]

Yet, while the Luftwaffe approached World War II with good equipment and carefully conceived policies, it remained an air force designed for short wars. No provision was made for a second generation of aircraft and this, among other things, contributed to its eventual defeat.

A further factor of relevance to the *Blitzkrieg* technique, not always mentioned, is the airborne operation. Here two types of formation are involved, parachute and air-landing. Parachute troops drop onto their objective as individuals and form into tactical units on the ground; airlanding formations arrive by transport or glider and are already formed and ready for action at the sub-unit level.

The use of such formations to seize bridges and other features in the path of an advancing armoured spearhead is, of course, obvious; so too, is their potential for disrupting an enemy's command structure by eliminating his headquarters. Arguments against the use of airborne forces are that, like any air operation, their success is contingent upon good weather and accurate navigation; that operations must, of necessity, be of limited duration and the troops involved be relieved before they are overwhelmed by the enemy's counter-measures; and that while the dividends produced by a successful operation can be of critical importance, there is little margin for error or ill-luck and virtually no chance of remedying a difficult situation that has arisen in the early stages.

Few nations had taken the trouble to produce a viable airborne force between the wars. The Italians air-landed infantry reinforcements to bolster the last phase of their advance on Tirana, and the Russians staged huge parachute drops for propaganda purposes, the men emerging precariously from hatches in the hull of a TB 3 bomber, clinging to the wings and roof until instructed to free-fall by the despatcher.

Germany, on the other hand, developed a small but fully operational airborne force, which included both parachute and airlanding troops. Much importance was placed on *Fallschirmjager* units landing on the objective itself instead of on a nearby dropping zone, it being considered that the additional risk of injury was more than outweighed by the tactical advantages.

The German airborne force operated, logically, under Luftwaffe control, and its workhorse was the tri-motor Junkers

Ju 52 transport, which had been designed during the early days of Lufthansa. In July 1936 twenty of these aircraft ferried more than 13,000 Nationalist troops from Morocco to Spain, ensuring the success of the revolt against the Communist government.

War has been defined as an extension of politics by other means; every politician forced to employ such an extension prays that the war will be short and victorious. By 1939 Germany's generals had provided her with the weapons, organisation and methods for just such a Lightning War, while Adolf Hitler possessed the political will to use them. The rest of the world lacked the means, and frequently the will as well.

Chapter 3: The Matador's Cloak

In August 1914 the nations had gone willingly to war, cheering their men to the echo as they marched away. In September 1939 they were sadder and wiser and embarked reluctantly upon the task that had been forced upon them. Even in re-armed Germany there was little joy at the prospect, for the memory of the country's two million dead was still comparatively fresh. Indeed, the consensus among senior German officers was that the Wehrmacht was not ready and that, for once, Hitler had miscalculated. Poland had stubbornly resisted his demands, her frontiers guaranteed by the British and French governments, which had recovered their self-respect following years of appeasement. The prospect of war on two fronts, for generations the nightmare of the German General Staff, had again become a reality, mitigated to some degree by the conclusion of a non-aggression pact between Hitler and Stalin, thus removing the possibility of Soviet intervention in the east.

The term *Blitzkrieg* had yet to be conceived. What Hitler demanded of his generals was a quick victory, a long campaign and large casualty lists being politically unacceptable. Every effort had to be made to conquer Poland *before* the western allies could mobilise their strength. "Should England and France open hostilities against Germany," ran his War Directive No 1, "It will be the duty of the Armed Forces operating in the west to maintain conditions for the successful conclusion of operations against Poland."

Failure against the Poles was never contemplated. The Polish Army, though numbering 800,000 men, was extremely old-fashioned and emotionally wed to the tactics that had defeated

Tukhachevsky's cavalry at the very gates of Warsaw in 1920. Its main strength lay in its thirty infantry divisions, but its pride was its eleven mounted cavalry brigades. There were also two lorried infantry brigades and a single armoured brigade equipped with two battalions of 7-TPs (a local version of the Vickers Six-Tonner) and one battalion of French R35s. Tankette companies were also available to support both infantry and cavalry formations. The Polish Air Force had 159 bombers of various types and 154 fighters, mainly of the high-wing monoplane PZL 11 class, which was no match for the Messerschmitt 109.

Geography has never been a friend to Poland and has often led to her dismemberment among acquisitive neighbours. In 1939 she began her war strategically outflanked by East Prussia in the north and by German-occupied Czechoslovakia in the south. Her armies, disposed around the 1,750-mile common frontier in a half circle, could not hope to be strong everywhere; moreover, their lines of communication, radiating from the centre of the country, were thus infinitely more vulnerable than those of armies deployed in a straight line, and any penetration of the front, if made in sufficient depth, was bound to have most serious consequences.

The total German force available was forty infantry, six panzer, four light and four mechanised divisions, and one cavalry brigade, tank strength amounting to 1,445 PzKw Is, 1,223 PzKw IIs, 98 PzKw IIIs and 211 PzKw IVs.[26] Flying in support of the ground operations were two Air Fleets, Kesselring's 1st and Loehr's 4th, equipped with 1,300 machines including He 111 bombers, Me 109 and Me 110 fighters, Ju 87 and Hs 123 ground-attack aircraft.

The details of the German offensive, known as *Fall Weiss* or Plan White, had been prepared as long ago as June by Field Marshal von Brauchitsch, Commander-in-Chief of the Army. Two Army Groups, North under von Bock and South under von Rundstedt, would penetrate the Polish cordon; then, spearheaded by their panzer and motorised divisions, they would swing together first in an inner and then an outer encirclement. The Poles would then be destroyed in detail.

The invasion began at 0445 on 1st September with an attempt by the Luftwaffe to destroy the Polish Air Force on the ground. The Poles had, however, foreseen this move and had moved their aircraft to secondary airfields, and little damage was done. Later in the day they responded by bombing German troops crossing the frontier, and continued to fight hard throughout the campaign although technically outclassed and frequently engaged by their own anti-aircraft batteries.

The Luftwaffe, for its part, while providing limited ground support, concentrated on interdiction tasks, the results of which were soon felt in the line.

It took two days of hard fighting to break the Polish Front. The one thing the Poles were not short of was courage. Anti-tank gunners and artillerymen took their toll of the panzers, while cavalrymen charged not only German infantry but armour as well. By 3rd September, however, the panzer divisions were through and driving for the Vistula, which was crossed two days later, forcing the frontier armies into a concentric retreat as the jaws of the inner pincer closed.

In part the German success had been due to the penetration of densely forested zones that the Poles considered impassable. Once the front had been ruptured, however, the pace of events accelerated so sharply that the Polish High Command, thinking as it did in the rhythm of 1920, was unable to react with the necessary speed. A French observer, General A. Armengaud of the *Armee de l'Air*, noted exactly what was taking place and incorporated his conclusions in a report that he submitted to General Headquarters on his return to France later in the year.

> "The German system consists essentially of making
> a breach in the front with armour and aircraft, then
> to throw mechanised and motorised columns into
> the breach, to beat down its shoulders to right and
> left in order to keep on enlarging it, at the same
> time as armoured detachments, guided, protected
> and reinforced by aircraft, advance in front of the

supporting divisions in such a way that the defence's manoeuvrability is reduced to impotence."[27]

"It would be madness," said Armengaud, "Not to draw an exact lesson from this pattern and not to pay heed to this warning."

On 9th September the 4th Panzer Division, spearheading Army Group South's drive on Warsaw, entered the outskirts of the capital only to be violently ejected with the loss of sixty of its tanks. Simultaneously the Poles launched a counter-offensive against von Rundstedt's northern flank along the River Bzura. By committing his reserves and diverting his armour from other missions Rundstedt was able to hold the attack, but fierce fighting continued on this sector until the 15th.

Elsewhere the jaws of the outer pincer were beginning to form as List's 14th Army crossed the San and swung north to meet Guderian's XIX Panzer Corps coming south along the Bug from East Prussia. By the 16th the Polish armies had been effectively defeated.

The following day the Red Army crossed the frontier into eastern Poland. Stalin's transparent excuse was that as a true friend of the Polish people, he intended to put an end to the fighting. He was, of course, simply after a share of the spoils, which Hitler willingly gave him, the country being dismembered into German and Russian zones of influence. What remained of the Polish Air Force flew out to internment in Rumania, where it was joined by those troops able to fight their way to the border.

Warsaw and other isolated garrisons continued to resist. On 24th September the Luftwaffe used 1,150 aircraft in a terror attack, which turned the capital into an inferno. Three days later the city surrendered and by 3rd October all fighting had ended.

The speed with which their victory had been obtained surprised even the Germans. Not since the Six Weeks War against Austria in 1866 had there been such a *Blitz Krieg*, or Lightning Campaign. The Polish Army had been destroyed at a cost to Germany of 8,000 dead and 32,000 wounded.

The system seemed to have operated with almost total efficiency, but this was not the case. For the panzer divisions, it was their first time out under active service conditions (excluding the bloodless invasions of Austria and Czechoslovakia) and their performance was inevitably sluggish in comparison with their subsequent achievements; even after the Polish cordon defence had been broken their initial daily advances averaged only eleven miles, less than that required of marching infantry, although this improved towards the end. There was, too, a notable reluctance among commanders and crews alike to embark on apparently dangerous and certainly unprecedented drives deep into the enemy's heartland. Guderian had to apply considerable stick to get what he wanted out of his divisions, as did other panzer leaders, although this entirely understandable nervousness became less evident as the campaign progressed.

Germany admitted the loss of 218 tanks, or 10 per cent of the total employed, most of these being the thinly armoured PzKw Is and IIs. There are grounds for believing that this figure is artificially low, reinforced by post-war Polish estimates of losses inflicted. Only a few weeks after the campaign had ended Hitler was told that an immediate offensive in the west was out of the question as half the tanks were still in workshops. What is certain is that by May 1940 some 826 PzKw Is and 268 PzKw IIs had disappeared from the German order of battle; obviously part of this deficiency was absorbed by the diversion of machines for training or the conversion of their chassis for other roles, or simply for scrapping if they had outlived their useful lives, but as Germany needed every tank she could muster this still leaves a wide margin for doubt. Very possibly Dr Goebbels, Hitler's propaganda expert, was well aware that a 10 per cent loss ratio would attract little professional attention in international military circles since the Polish Army was notoriously ill-equipped, whereas disclosure of a higher, more accurate figure would blunt the moral edge that the Panzerwaffe had attained. Temporary loss of tanks due to mechanical failure was later revealed as being 25 per cent at any one time, a high proportion for such a short campaign.

The importance of Poland, therefore, is that it served as a proving ground for the new theories of war just as Spain had provided a technical laboratory for the new weapons. Those theories had been demonstrated as being valid and the lessons learned enabled senior commanders in both the panzer arm and the Luftwaffe to improve their operational methods, and bring their commands to the pitch of efficiency in time for the next offensive, which would be directed against the western Allies.

Hitler had long dreamed of "one last decisive battle against France", the result of which would end once and for all a century of Franco-German rivalry, and he wanted it to be fought as soon as possible. On 5th November, he summoned the Army's Commander-in-Chief to his Chancellery to discuss the matter. Brauchitsch, intelligent, highly strung and painfully reserved, had an instinctive horror of violent public scenes and was thus vulnerable to bullying by Hitler, whose street-brawling background had left him with no such reservations. He began by expressing the collective view of the Army that it was not yet ready to take on the French, whom the Fuhrer should not underestimate. Hitler immediately cut him short.

"I hold quite different views. Firstly, I place a low value on the French Army's will to fight. Every army is a mirror of its people. The French people think only of peace and good living and they are torn apart in Parliamentary strife. Accordingly, the Army, however brave and well trained its officer corps may be, does not show the combat determination expected of it. After the first setbacks it will swiftly crack up."

Brauchitsch attempted to counter by suggesting that the performance of certain infantry divisions in Poland was not all it might have been and that the Army might not react well to the pressures of a major campaign in the west. Hitler flew into such an uncontrolled rage at this criticism of the Army that *he* had created that when Brauchitsch arrived back at his headquarters, he was shaking and completely incoherent.

Later that month, Hitler assembled all his generals down to the level of corps commander, together with their Navy and

Luftwaffe equivalents, and treated them to a similar tirade for their lack of resolve to get to grips with the French. It was a taste of things to come, but for the moment the Fuhrer was still prepared to listen to professional advice and the effects of the disease that was affecting his brain were not yet so pronounced that he was quite blind to logic.

The problem was how to get at the French. An attack on the Maginot Line was not even worth considering and the only alternative lay in an approach through neutral Holland, Belgium and Luxembourg. A number of drafts were drawn up before the details of the operation were incorporated into a document known as *Fall Gelb*, or Plan Yellow. There was some superficial resemblance between *Gelb* and the opening moves of the 1914 Schlieffen Plan, but the former was far more modest in its aims, and sought only to separate the British Expeditionary Force from the French and to secure Ghent by means of a double envelopment.

On 22nd October, Hitler, Brauchitsch and the latter's Chief of Staff, General Franz Halder, had met to discuss *Gelb*. Taking a red map marker, Hitler had quite unexpectedly drawn a line between the Meuse south of Namur and the Somme estuary. Perhaps thinking of Ludendorff's failed *Michael* offensive, he had then turned to Brauchitsch and asked whether a thrust along this axis might not cut off and destroy those Allied forces north of the line. Brauchitsch had not committed himself, but had redrafted *Gelb* so as to incorporate a stronger left wing. Hitler had not pressed the point.

However, serving as Chief of Staff to von Rundstedt's Army Groups A, which faced southern Belgium and Luxembourg, and had its headquarters at Koblenz, was General Erich von Manstein. A former Guards officer, Manstein was known as a strict disciplinarian who was respected if not loved. Totally dedicated to his profession, he was not without humour or finer feelings; once told to get rid of two Jewish officers, he had tartly and successfully retorted that the men were German officers first and Jews second. In General Staff circles he had acquired a reputation for brilliant operational planning but, like Fuller and other men of genius, had the unhappy knack of speaking truths that were not immediately apparent to lesser mortals, thereby incurring resentment.

Without knowing what was in Hitler's mind, Manstein's thoughts were also turning to *Michael* and the Somme estuary. He saw that *Gelb*, suitably modified, could be used to draw the British and French north into the Low Countries like a matador's cloak; also that a major thrust through the Ardennes, across the Meuse and on to Amiens and the sea would have the effect of trapping and ultimately *annihilating* the Allied forces north of the Somme instead of merely defeating them as envisaged in the original *Gelb* concept. Indeed, the more troops sent north to aid the Dutch and Belgians the better; therefore, the modified *Gelb* must have real weight and not be treated simply as a feint. An added bonus was that when the French High Command was faced with the real thrust on the Meuse, it would still be unable to identify its destination in time to react. In fact, the French would have to allow for three possibilities, namely that the Germans could swing south, *behind* the Maginot Line; march directly on Paris; or continue in a westerly direction towards the sea. It was considered unlikely that sufficient reserves would be available to the French for them to cover every contingency.

The drive to the coast would be led by the panzer divisions, but Manstein was not certain whether they could be passed through the Ardennes. In November, he asked Guderian to visit him and advise on the problem. Guderian said that it could be done, adding that for the sort of operation Manstein was considering only the maximum possible concentration of armour would suffice. Manstein then committed his plan to paper, obtained Rundstedt's approval, and despatched it to Halder, as etiquette demanded.

Like Brauchitsch, Halder was an artilleryman. He had a sharp, analytical mind which took its relaxation in the study of mathematics. He was essentially an academic and indeed his highly polished *pincenez* produced a startling impression of his holding a senior chair at some august seat of learning. In common with many academics, he was prone to professional jealousy and resented Manstein's reputation for brilliance.

He turned down the plan out of hand. Manstein submitted it again and continued to submit it until on 12th January it arrived on Halder's desk for the sixth time, accompanied by a note from Rundstedt requesting that it be placed before the Fuhrer. Halder suggested that Rundstedt should mind his own business.

Brauchitsch, well aware of what was going on, visited Koblenz on 25th January. Manstein, coldly hostile, made reference to "the well known negative attitude of OKH", and virtually accused the Commander-in-Chief of deliberately half-hearted planning. Brauchitsch was prepared to take bullying from Hitler, but not from his own subordinates. Two days later Manstein was told to relinquish his post with Rundstedt and assume command of an infantry corps based on Stettin, just about as far away from the operational zone as it was possible to get.

At this point Fate intervened. A few days before Manstein left Koblenz Colonel Schmundt, Hitler's military adjutant, paid a routine visit and was struck by the parallel between his plan and the Fuhrer's ideas. On return to Berlin, he informed an intensely interested Hitler of what had taken place, and Manstein was summoned to the presence on 17th February.

The original *Gelb* plans had been compromised on 10th January when a light aircraft carrying two officers was forced down by bad weather at Mechelen, just inside Belgium. In their possession was a briefcase containing details of the offensive, which the Belgian authorities duly passed on to the French. *Gelb*, already the subject of endless postponements because of unpreparedness or poor flying conditions, was virtually dead on its feet.

Hitler therefore listened to Manstein with rapt attention for several hours before dismissing him to his command at Stettin. The following morning, he sent for Brauchitsch and Halder, presented them with Manstein's plans as being his own, and ordered them to draft a new directive forthwith. Recent war games had inclined OKH towards a more sympathetic view of the concept and the directive, known as *Sichelschnitt* (Sickle Cut), had been completed by the 24th February. For it Manstein received no credit whatsoever.

The Allied strategy could not have fitted the German more perfectly. On land France was the senior partner and the only decision that counted were those of her 68-year-old Commander-in-Chief, General Maurice Gamelin, who had served under the legendary Joffre and actually drafted the orders that led to victory on the Marne in 1914. Reserved, given to deep thought and with a passion for art and philosophy, he disliked the hurly-burly of active daily command and instead preferred to determine general lines of policy, leaving the detailed implementation to his subordinates; his orders, it was said, were issued as a basis for intellectual discussion rather than as executive commands. His headquarters, located in the ancient castle of Vincennes, lacked modern signals equipment, and relied on the public telephone system and despatch riders for communication with his field commanders.

From the outset, he was concerned with the preservation of French manpower, for the terrible losses of the Great War had been compounded by a falling birth-rate. For this reason, he had made no move against Germany while she was engaged in Poland, although the Rhine could have been reached against negligible opposition. If Germany attacked France, he was certain that she would employ a mechanised version of the Schlieffen Plan, sweeping round through the Low Countries. In that case the Allies would race north to join the eleven Dutch and twenty-three Belgian divisions, which would swell his army to the level at which he felt ultimate victory was attainable, first halting the German advance along the line of the River Dyle. His best troops, including the BEF, were earmarked for this role, leaving the rest of the front, including the sector opposite the Ardennes, to be held by a cordon of second- and third-line formations. Thus, at the point where the German *Sichelschnitt* offensive was to be at its strongest, the French defences were at their weakest. In fairness to Gamelin there was nothing he could have done to fortify the

Ardennes, since most of the area lay in Belgium and Belgium was committed to strict neutrality unless attacked. The fact remained, however, that France had lost the first and all-important planning stage of the war long before the main issue was joined.

Hitler had been uncannily accurate in his assessment of the French Army's potential for war, even though the causes went rather deeper than his contemptuous analysis suggested. It was, in fact, an elderly army, which, because of the low birth-rate, made up its number by recalling to the colours men who had long since passed their physical peak. Of the two million who had been mobilised, only 600,000 were between the ages of twenty and twenty-five, the ideal years for active soldiering; in 1914 the figure had been 1,250,000. Even its commanders were far older than the majority of their British and German counterparts. Many of the older reservists, known as *crocos* to the rest of the Army, belonged to Class B Reserve divisions, which were low on the priority list for supporting artillery, armour and transport, and which were intended for employment on the less active sectors of the front.

In 1914 the French soldier had gone to war impelled by his frightening capacity for *La Rage*; in 1939 he was not an angry man, but for a short time internal differences were set aside in pursuance of the common aim. As the winter progressed, he was compelled to live in discomfort, which neither his officers nor the government did a great deal to alleviate. Since there was no fighting, and little prospect of any, the whole thing began to seem pointless and his goodwill drained slowly away. He spent much of his time digging defence lines and not a lot in training, and in consequence became bored and resentful: in particular he resented the fact that British pay and allowances, niggardly in themselves, actually exceeded his own by a very wide margin. He began to absent himself in large numbers, with or without leave, to attend to family and business matters. His standards of discipline and dress began to deteriorate; drunkenness increased and the simple compliment of the salute was frequently ignored. Apathy became the order of the day and too often the first response of staffs at all levels was to temporise. This state of affairs by no means applied to the Army as a whole, but it was prevalent enough to raise serious doubts in the minds of many British officers serving in France.

However, in the light of the Polish experience and as a result of reports submitted by officers such as Armengaud, the Army had begun forming heavier armoured divisions than the Divisions Legeres Mecaniques (DLM), which were discussed in the last chapter. Known as Divisions Cuirassees (DCR), they consisted of two demi-brigades, each equipped with one battalion of thirty-four heavy Char B tanks and one battalion of forty-five Hotchkiss H 35s (giving a total tank strength of 158), a motor-rifle battalion and two motorised twelve-gun artillery battalions. By the end of April three DCRs were operational while a fourth was in process of forming.

Unfortunately, the move had come too late, for the various component units of the new divisions were as yet unused to working together and had hardly begun their training schedules before being pitched into action.

In practical terms neither the DCR nor the DLM fulfilled the flexible concept of the German panzer divisions. The former, with its heavy Infantry Tank element, was best suited to the break-through role, while the latter, as already mentioned, performed in armour several aspects of the cavalry's function. Nor was any real form of flexibility to be attained, since only one vehicle in five was fitted with a radio.

In April, the Allies were jerked sharply awake by the sudden German invasion of Denmark and Norway, undertaken by Hitler to safeguard his supply of iron ore from Swedish Lapland, which travelled by sea down the Norwegian coast and was, therefore, vulnerable to disruption by the Royal Navy. Codenamed *Weser-ubung*, or Exercise Weser, the operation was characterised by the use of parachute drops on selected airfields, which, once secured, enabled follow-up troops to be air-landed very quickly. These were accompanied by amphibious landings at strategic points around the Norwegian coast.

Denmark, incapable of defending herself, surrendered at once, but the Norwegian armed forces offered fierce resistance and Allied troops were hastily despatched to their aid. The most important sector of operations was the valley of Gubrundsdalen, leading north from Lillehammer into the heart of the country, and on this axis the Germans employed a single tank battalion, supported by the Luftwaffe, which effectively ruled the skies. Without tanks and virtually without anti-tank weapons, the Allies were unable to prevent the German armour breaking through their defensive road-blocks, and by the end of the month had cut their losses and re-embarked, although fighting continued in the far north until June. The combined morale effect of the Luftwaffe and the tanks had determined the outcome of the short campaign from the beginning, and although the latter's parent formation, 35 Panzer Regiment of 4th Panzer Division, devoted a mere one-and-a-half lines of their official history to the subject, their presence had frequently been decisive.

It was true that the success of *Weserubung* had been achieved at the cost of half the German surface fleet, either sunk or out of commission undergoing major repairs, and that whatever Hitler's real intentions towards the British Isles may have been, the Kriegsmarine was under no illusions that an invasion was not a practical possibility. Conversely, Allied prestige had suffered a damaging blow. The imaginative use of airborne troops had come as something of a surprise, and the expert German propaganda apparatus turned the knife in the wound by hinting that part of the tank battalion's equipment had consisted of new and powerful PzKw Vs. The "PzKw Vs" that had been encountered were three rather elderly prototypes of a heavy tank design, which had been abandoned some years earlier, and the real PzKw V, known as the Panther, had yet to be conceived.[28]

Thus, as well as having lost the planning war, the Allies were now morally behind on points as well, having failed to influence events either in Poland or Scandinavia. It was beginning to look very much as though Germany had something that they did not.

In May, the French *Deuxieme Bureau* suggested that she had between 7,000 and 7,500 tanks, a wild exaggeration even allowing for the integration of the Czech tank fleet. There were, in fact, now ten panzer divisions, the light divisions having been converted after the Polish campaign, and these possessed between them 523 PzKw Is; 955 PzKw IIs; 349 PzKw IIIs; 278 PzKw IVs; 106 Czech 35Ts and 228 Czech 38Ts – a total of 2,439 battle tanks discounting a small mechanical reserve and 135 PzKw Is and IIIs converted to armoured command vehicles.

The French Army, on the other hand, could field about 3,000 machines, 500 in the newly raised DCRs, 800 with the DLMs and mounted cavalry divisions, and the remainder dispersed among infantry support battalions. In addition, the BEF could supply the 210 light tanks of its divisional cavalry regiments and 100 Infantry Tanks serving with 1st Army Tank Brigade, while in England the 1st Armoured Division, with a further 174 Light and 156 Cruiser tanks, could be made available at short notice.

The *Panzerwajfe* was, therefore, substantially outnumbered in every class save that of light tanks, which were of no value in the tank battle. It was also at a qualitative disadvantage in that its thickest armour was only 30-mm while that of the 800 modern Char Bs and Somuas alone was 60-mm and 55-mm respectively, with the little British Infantry Tank Mark I weighing in with a remarkable 80-mm; and its standard armour-defeating weapon, the 37-mm, could not compare with the 47-mm gun carried by the Char B and Somua, as well as being inferior to the British 2-pounder. This was balanced to some degree by the French having diverted so much of their armour for infantry support, by their lack of experience in handling modern armoured formations *en masse*, by the poor internal layout and limited operational radii of their vehicles, and by the limited provision of radios.

In the air, however, the Luftwaffe had a distinct and decisive superiority, being able to put up 1,268 fighters (Me 109 and 110), 1,120 level bombers (He 111 and Do 17), 350 Stukas and a large transport fleet of Ju 52s, against which the *Armee de l'Air* could oppose only 700 inferior performance fighters (Morane, Potez,

Bloch and Dewoitine) and 150/175 Breguet and Leo bombers; nor was the gap bridged by the BEF's Air Component of 500 fighters and light bombers, many of its types such as the Gladiator and Defiant fighters and the Battle light bomber being obsolete, and only the few Hurricane squadrons being able to compete on even terms, although reinforcement from the United Kingdom was possible.

The stage was now set for the execution of Manstein's dramatic *Sichelschnitt*, delayed by Hitler until the Scandinavian diversion had been brought to a satisfactory conclusion. The Matador's Cloak, which would draw the Allies into the Low Countries, was von Bock's Army Group B (6th and 18th Armies) led by two Panzer Corps, Schmidt's XXXIXth with a single panzer division, the 9th, which would operate in Holland, and Hoepner's XVIth, consisting of 3rd and 4th Panzer Divisions, destined for central Belgium. Bock's task was to be eased by the widespread use of airborne troops and a heavy Luftwaffe involvement.

The main thrust, as Manstein had planned, would be delivered through the Ardennes by von Rundstedt's Army Group A (4th, 12th and 16th Armies) with no less than three Panzer Corps converging on the Meuse. On the right, Hoth's XVth, with 5th and 7th Panzer Divisions under command, would cross near Dinant; in the centre, Rheinhardt's XLIth (6th and 8th Panzer Divisions) would cross at Montherme; on the left Guderian's XIXth (1st, 2nd and 10th Panzer Divisions and the elite *Grossdeutschland* Regiment would cross at Sedan followed immediately by Wietersheim's XIVth Motorised Corps, which would cover the left flank after the French Front had been broken. Together, Rheinhardt, Guderian and Wietersheim operated under the control of a Panzer Group Headquarters commanded by General Ewald von Kleist, an appointee of Halder's known for his conservative views who, it was hoped, would be able to keep Guderian's furious energy within bounds.

The Luftwaffe's tasks on Army Group A's front would include the provision of blanket cover during the advance through the Ardennes, effectively concealing the size of the operation from the

Allied air forces; maintaining air superiority over the battle zone; a heavy ground-attack programme during the Meuse crossings; and extensive interdiction behind the French lines.

On the left of the German offensive the nineteen divisions of von Leeb's Army Group C would be confined to making local demonstrations between the Siegfried and Maginot Lines, and along the upper Rhine.

During the early hours of 10th May the Luftwaffe bombed Dutch, Belgian and French airfields with limited success. In Holland these raids were followed by parachute drops near Rotterdam, The Hague, Moerdijk and Dordrecht and the arrival of air-landing divisions once suitable bases had been secured. The effect was to paralyse the interior of the country and spread terror and confusion. In the Maastricht Appendix, separating Belgium from Germany above their common frontier, Trojan Horse parties of German soldiers dressed in Dutch uniforms or as civilians seized and held bridges over the Maas (the Dutch continuation of the Meuse) until relieved, so opening the door into Belgium.[29]

The Belgian Army had planned to fight defensively along the line of the Albert Canal until joined by its British and French allies. Its flank was turned immediately by a spectacular glider-borne operation that landed *on top of* the allegedly impregnable Fort Eban Emael, dominating the junction of the canal with the Meuse; after several hours of being attacked at close quarters with explosive charges and flamethrowers, the garrison surrendered.

Everywhere, Army Group B flooded across the frontiers. At Vincennes, Gamelin was delighted. "On *les aura!*" he exclaimed on hearing the news, little realising that Army Group A was already moving into the Ardennes. His Dyle Plan was implemented at once, Giraud's 7th Army racing north along the coast towards Antwerp with Lord Gort's BEF and Blanchard's 1st Army swinging right to join the Belgians. Conforming to the move, Corap's 9th and Huntziger's 2nd Armies pivoted on Sedan, and closed up to the Meuse, thus completing a solid front facing east.

However, the speed of the German advance in Holland had isolated the tiny Dutch Army before help could reach it. It fought bravely on, inflicting startling loss and opening dikes to deny territory to the enemy, but after the centre of Rotterdam had been razed by terror bombing on the 14th it surrendered, having been threatened with the similar destruction of all Dutch cities if it did not do so.

Gamelin's opinion that the main German thrust was being made through Belgium seemed to be confirmed when the French 1st Cavalry Corps (2nd and 3rd DLMs), screening the advance of 1st Army, fought an encounter battle with XVI Panzer Corps in the good tank country of the Gembloux Gap on 12th and 13th May. Fighting was severe and the panzer crews found the Somuas to be formidable opponents even though their own efforts were assisted by Stukas. The overworked French commanders tended to fight as individuals against whom teams of German tanks combined but losses were about 100 vehicles on each side; the difference was that when the Cavalry Corps retired, having fulfilled its mission of allowing 1st Army to settle unmolested into the Dyle position, its casualties were abandoned on the battlefield, whereas those of the Germans were mostly repaired by recovery teams. One result of this hard-fought action was that Gamelin maintained his policy of committing his reserves, including 1st and 2nd DCRs, to the north.[30]

Meanwhile, Army Group A, whose columns stretched back as far as the Rhine, was beginning to emerge from the Ardennes and was approaching the Meuse. Its passage had been trouble-free and the hardest-worked troops were the engineers who had to deal with blown bridges and other obstacles created by the retreating Belgian Chasseurs Ardennais. French cavalry that made contact with the heads of the columns were fiercely repulsed and thrown back across the Meuse without discovering the scale of the German effort, while the ever-vigilant Luftwaffe also prevented the Allied air forces from obtaining a clear picture of what was taking place. However, by the morning of the 13th, the day on which Army Group A was scheduled to cross the

Meuse, enough evidence had been collected for Gamelin to have second thoughts about the strategy with which he had begun the campaign, although the Commander-in-Chief of the North-East Front, General Georges, continued to send him optimistic situation reports.

There were few grounds for optimism for lying directly in the path of Panzer Group Kleist and straddling the 2nd/9th Army boundary were four Class B Reserve divisions, 55th, 61st and 71st Infantry and 102nd Fortress, while opposite Panzer Corps Hoth the troops had not yet finished moving into their positions. At 0900 the Stukas and level bombers of General Hugo Sperrle's Third Air Fleet, escorted by a swarm of Messerschmitts, arrived over these unfortunate formations to commence a continuous six-hour attack, which paid particular attention to their supporting artillery batteries. The incessant howling of the dive-bombers, the scream of their bombs and the endless explosions, accompanied by blinding smoke and the shrieks of the wounded, would have strained the nerves of hard-bitten regulars let alone those of these middle-aged and rather unwilling soldiers who thought only of returning to their families. For the infantry, cowering in trenches and bunkers, it was an ordeal that induced deep shock, but for the artillery in their wider gun-pits it was infinitely worse.

Shortly after 1500 the last of Sperrle's bombers droned away to the east and the Germans began their assault crossing. Incredibly, the despised *crocos* fought back, sending the first waves of rubber assault boats drifting downstream in tatters. As a result of the energy of such commanders as Guderian and Major-General Erwin Rommel, the commander of the 7th Panzer Division, tanks and 88-mm anti-aircraft guns were brought down to the eastern bank to systematically reduce by direct gunfire the bunkers that were spitting fire from the French side of the water. Little by little the defence was eaten away and the trickle of men reaching the far shore increased to a steady flow. By dusk, all three panzer corps had secured a footing, although for the French there was as yet nothing irremedial about the situation; in fact, at 1800 General

Georges despatched a further report describing the air attack but confirming that the situation was under control.

The old saw tells how for want of a nail the shoe was lost; for want of the shoe the horse was lost; for want of the horse the rider was lost; and for want of the rider the battle was lost. There were many suspect nails in the French Army's shoe, and one finally tore loose in the 55th Division, covering Sedan, just as Georges was sending his signal. An artillery officer, his judgement impaired by shock, suddenly reported German tanks near the village of Bulson. The rumour spread like wildfire. More German tanks were spotted elsewhere. Soon the guns were limbered up and heading for the rear. Left unsupported, the infantry streamed away from their positions. The flood gathered momentum as the 71st Division, on the right, became infected. Headquarters were swept up by the tide and carried away to the west. The troops themselves did not understand what was going on and there were none to tell them; their officers swore they had received orders to withdraw, and in many cases this was true. In some places there arose the dreadful panic cry of "*Sauve qui peut!*" In others the more muted "*Nous sommes trahis*" of men who have endured much and fought hard to no avail. And yet this frightened stampede had been provoked by a collective hallucination of greater proportion even than the celebrated Angels of Mons. Tanks *had* been seen, but they were French, moving into their counter-attack positions; not one German tank crossed the Meuse at Sedan on the 13th, although as darkness fell the panzers' divisional engineers were working hard to complete the bridges that would allow them across.

The news that a yawning gap had opened between 2nd and 9th Armies brought Georges to the brink of emotional collapse. When General Aime Doumenc arrived at his headquarters during the early hours of the 14th he found it necessary to restore his composure before himself detailing the counter-measures that he deemed to be necessary.[31] The Allied air forces would concentrate on the destruction of the German bridges while the three DCRs were to converge on the bridgeheads and wipe them out; the

1st would be brought down from central Belgium and attack from the north; the 2nd, actually in transit, would be halted and come in from the west; and the 3rd, lying close to Sedan, would attack from the south. If the French war machine had been as well equipped and operated at the same speed as the German, the plan might have succeeded. As it was, the 14th May can be identified as the date upon which France lost the war.

The Germans had, of course, predicted that their crossing sites would come under heavy air attack. The banks of the Meuse bristled with anti-aircraft guns and the sky above was controlled by a protective umbrella of Messerschmitts. Guderian admired the suicidal bravery of British and French pilots who forced their way through the fighter screen and flew on into the teeth of the anti-aircraft fire to drop their bombs, but the bridges remained intact and the panzers continued to roll across to the west bank, beating off local counterattacks by French infantry tank battalions on arrival.

Rundstedt, in process of moving his headquarters to Bastogne, arrived at Sedan at the height of an air raid. In such circumstances it is incumbent upon senior officers to put on a little show for the benefit of their men and, with Guderian, he walked out into the centre of one of the pontoon bridges to survey the whole scene of barking AA guns, falling bombs, and smoking aircraft reeling towards the horizon.

"Is it always like this here?" he asked dryly.

"I can honestly say that it is!" replied Guderian, equally dryly.

The attempt to remove the Meuse bridges cost the RAF seventy and the *Armee de l'Air* forty aircraft, so weakening them that several British squadrons, officially reserved for home defence, had to be despatched from the United Kingdom the following day.

The great armoured counter-stroke envisaged by Doumenc never really got moving. It might have done if the three DCRs had been administratively grouped into a corps and their movements controlled by a single commander and staff, but this was not to be. Instead, each division was to fight under the command of an infantry corps, a decision that was to have disastrous consequences.

Thus, although 1st DCR was alerted during the morning of the 14th, its commander was not required for briefing until 1330; then, instead of being briefed on the spot (let alone on the move), he had to travel twenty miles to XI Corps Headquarters to receive the simple order to attack towards Dinant as soon as possible. The greater part of the day had been frittered away before the division set out for its objective along roads choked by refugees and fugitives from Corap's 9th Army, which, like Huntziger's 2nd, was on the verge of disintegration. Progress was painfully slow and the tanks began to run out of petrol. The time of the attack was postponed from dawn until noon on the 15th while refuelling took place.

However, at first light Hoth's Panzer Corps, led by Rommel's 7th Panzer Division, broke out of its bridgehead and caught the French tanks in close leaguer, replenishing. Calling up his Stukas to batter them, Rommel closed in to fight at close range before swinging away to the west, leaving the thoroughly ruffled 1st DCR to be dealt with by 5th Panzer, following in his wake.

During the ensuing tank battle the French fought hard and claimed a slightly exaggerated total of 100 German vehicles knocked out. 5th Panzer found the armour of the Char Bs, which they called *Kolosse*, quite impervious to their fire but manoeuvred skilfully into positions from which they could send their shots through the vulnerable radiator louvres or shoot off the tracks. 1st DCR withdrew slowly during the night, abandoning many of its vehicles for want of fuel. By dawn on the 16th it had been reduced to a mere seventeen tanks and was no longer a force to be reckoned with.

2nd DCR was removed from the board by inept staff work without having fired a shot. The division's tanks were travelling north by rail and its wheeled transport by road when Doumenc's redeployment, of which its commander was not advised, took place. When he reported to his original destination, HQ 1st

Army, on the morning of the 14th, he was told that the division had been re-allocated to 9th Army. Corap, however, informed him that the division now belonged to a short-lived blocking force known as Army Detachment Touchon and its various units, now spread over a wide area, were ordered to converge on Signy L'Abbaye throughout the following day. Meanwhile, Rheinhardt's Panzer Corps had also broken out of its bridgehead and at about 1700 on the 15th overran part of the divisional artillery. The rest of the wheeled transport took refuge south of the Aisne, leaving the tanks to the north. 2nd DCR, cut in two, was never reunited, although its tanks continued to fight under local control.

3rd DCR arrived at the Sedan bridgehead at dawn on the 14th and was ready to attack at 1600. At this point General Flavigny, commanding XXI Corps, intervened with sorry consequences. The counter-attack was cancelled and the tank battalions broken up to form an eight-mile line of static pillboxes along the southern flank of the bridgehead. A golden opportunity to strike at Guderian at the very moment he was preparing to break out was thus irretrievably missed. When Guderian did break out he was faced with the shaken survivors of the previous evening's rout; faced this time with *real* German tanks, they broke again, this time beyond recall. Significantly, when Huntziger asked Georges whether he should deploy what remained of his army to cover the Maginot Line or Paris, he was told to use his own judgement; Georges could not decide and he would have been wrong had he chosen either alternative.[32]

Seven panzer divisions were now roaring through a forty-mile gap in the French line, followed by the motorised troops and the marching infantry divisions that would line the flanks of the corridor they would carve across France. Retreating French troops and reinforcements trying to reach the front alike surrendered *en masse*, bemused by the sudden appearance of the panzers in their midst and demoralised by the Luftwaffe's constant attacks. Once through the forward zone, the German armour motored across a sunlit, deserted landscape as though on summer manoeuvres.

By the 16th the French acknowledged that they had lost a decisive battle. Deeply worried, Winston Churchill, Britain's newly installed Prime Minister, flew to Paris to meet his opposite number, Paul Reynaud. When Gamelin explained the position to him he was horrified.

"But where are your strategic reserves?" he asked.

"There are none," said Gamelin.

They had already been sent to Belgium.

Reynaud had already decided to replace Gamelin with the seventy-three-year-old General Maxime Weygand, summoned from Syria. On the 20th, Weygand, brisk and energetic for all his years, arrived at Vincennes to assume command.

"I have the secrets of Marshal Foch!" he explained confidently, tapping his notebook.

"I could have retorted," wrote Gamelin in his memoirs, "that I had those of Marshal Joffre and they had not sufficed."

The only secrets that mattered on 20th May were those of Erich von Manstein, for on that day Guderian reached the sea and the trap clanged shut on all Allied troops north of the Somme. On the way he had bickered interminably with the cautious von Kleist, even tendering his resignation on one occasion, and had fended off several attempts by Major-General Charles de Gaulle's new-born 4th DCR to break in on his line of march. He had also secured bridgeheads over the Somme at Peronne, Amiens and Abbeville, which would serve a useful purpose later in the campaign. Fuel had always been a worry but the Luftwaffe had flown supplies to captured airfields whence they had been delivered by lorry to the panzer spearheads, and, if these were insufficient, vehicles had filled up at civilian pumps.

In Germany, official reaction was varied. Halder, the professional analyst, had shed his doubts and was now confident of victory. Hitler, the visionary who claimed the scheme as his own, was permanently worried by the prospect of a counter-stroke isolating the panzer divisions in the west, his anxieties being shared by the majority of conservative-minded generals who viewed what was taking place as something quite unorthodox and fraught with risks.

On 21st May there were nine panzer divisions in the corridor, Hoepner's XVI Panzer Corps having now joined Army Group A. Echeloned back to the right they now turned north to drive into the rear of the Allied Northern Army Group, already under fierce pressure from von Bock's Army Group B. Tough resistance was encountered everywhere for these troops were a very different proposition from those that had been met on the Meuse.

South of Arras, 7th Panzer Division moved off at 1500, led by its armoured regiment. Rommel, as was his custom, travelled with the tanks, but found to his annoyance that his Rifle Regiments had fallen behind and hurried back to chase them along. He found them under heavy attack from Brigadier Douglas Pratt's 1st Army Tank Brigade. The German 37-mm anti-tank guns were quite useless against the stout armour of the Infantry Tanks, which rolled contemptuously over their screen to disperse one Rifle Regiment and start a panic in the other, which in turn communicated itself to the nearby SS Motorised Division *Totenkopf.* Only the combined fire of 7th Panzer's divisional field, medium and anti-aircraft artillery, personally directed by Rommel and supplemented by the ubiquitous Stukas, brought the advance to a halt. The division's panzer regiment, hurrying towards the fray, ran into a British anti-tank gun screen and the remnants of 3rd DLM, covering the right flank of the operation, and received an unexpected beating.

During the evening the British withdrew and Rommel concentrated his scattered units. While displaying his characteristic drive he was obviously shaken by the fact that for a while 7th Panzer had been cut in two, and his report reflected this; he had, he said, been attacked by "hundreds" of British tanks. In fact, 1st Army Tank Brigade's strength on 21st May amounted to fifty-eight Infantry Tanks Mark I, sixteen Infantry Tanks Mark II (better known as Matildas), and a dozen or so Light Tanks Mark VI.

At the higher German headquarters the report was received with horror. This was the news that the optimists had been dreading, the pessimists expecting. The northward advance was immediately stopped in its tracks and Rheinhardt's Panzer Corps ordered to retrace its steps towards the seemingly dangerous situation developing around Arras. It was twenty-four hours before the panzer divisions were set in motion again, and in that time the British had reinforced the vital coastal sector.

The Arras Counter-Attack was the only Allied riposte considered worth mentioning in the German strategic history of the campaign, and actually formed the northern prong of an attempt by Weygand to cut the panzer corridor in two; the southern prong, mounted from the Somme, never really got moving. In its planning stages it was one of the few occasions when the BEF was consulted about anything; Gamelin had treated Lord Gort as a sort of senior corps commander.

The failure of Weygand's scheme left Gort with only one alternative – evacuation via Dunkirk following the fall of Calais on the 25th after a heroic defence that bought the time for a defensive perimeter to be established. But a further factor was working in favour of the trapped Allied armies. On the 24th, Hitler personally ordered the panzer divisions to halt on the line of the River Aa; Guderian was not alone in being flabbergasted by the decision, the precise reasons for which have led to intense speculation ever since.

It has been suggested that Hitler wished to save British face by permitting the evacuation, a political move that might pay a dividend at a subsequent peace conference; or that he wished Goering's Luftwaffe to have the glory of giving the *coup de grace* to the shrinking pocket, a task that it failed to fulfil largely because of the intervention of the RAF, flying from airfields in England. Neither suggestion has the ring of truth and it seems far more likely that Hitler was influenced by the pragmatic Rundstedt, who recognised that the reduction of the pocket was now of secondary importance to the destruction of the remaining French armies lying south of the panzer corridor. For this, the panzer divisions must be allowed a breathing space to collect the break-downs that had been shed along the way and which were now starting to catch up, to do some overdue maintenance, and to unravel their tangled lines of communication. As if to confirm Rundstedt's view the exhausted Belgian Army surrendered on the 27th, making the position of the trapped French and BEF even more untenable.

The Dunkirk evacuation continued from 28th May to 4th June, 226,000 British and 112,000 French and Belgian soldiers being shipped across the Channel. They owed an immense debt to the Royal Navy's organisational ability, to the bravery and patriotism of the civilian volunteers manning the hundreds of little ships, and to the dogged tenacity and courage of the French rearguard, which sacrificed itself on their behalf. None of this had been foreseen in Manstein's plan but, as Churchill put it, "Wars are not won by evacuations," and the BEF had left behind all its heavy equipment.

While the majority of the British Army was awaiting evacuation from Dunkirk, other British troops, including the 1st Armoured Division, were landing at Cherbourg. 1st Armoured was a mere shadow of what it should have been. Its field artillery, motor battalions and one armoured regiment had all been removed for service elsewhere and what remained was badly equipped, being short of guns, ammunition, sights and much else besides. "It was with this travesty of an armoured division," wryly commented Major-General Roger Evans, its commander, "A formation with less than half its proper armoured strength, without any field guns or a proper complement of anti-tank and anti-aircraft guns, without bridging equipment, without the bulk of its ancillary services, and with part of its headquarters in a three-ply wooden 'armoured' command vehicle – that I was ordered to force a crossing over a defended, unfordable river (the Somme), and afterwards to advance some sixty miles, through four *real* armoured divisions, to the help of the British Expeditionary Force."

On the 27th the division took part in Weygand's attempt to reduce the Somme bridgeheads, together with de Gaulle's 4th DCR and the remains of several other French armoured formations that had survived the disaster. After some initial success the Allied attacks were held and finally abandoned. The lightly armoured British Cruisers, used incorrectly as Infantry Tanks, suffered heavily at Abbeville.

With the limited resources now remaining at his disposal, Weygand could only prepare for the renewal of the German onslaught once the northern pocket had been eliminated. He proposed to meet this with a defence in depth, based on artillery, and constructed a zone of fortified villages, woods and dominant features several miles wide, the areas between being carefully registered as artillery killing grounds.

By 5th June, the German dispositions for the second phase of the Battle of France, known as Fall *Rot* (Plan Red) had been completed and once more the panzers rolled to the attack. On the coast was von Bock's Army Group B, led by Panzer Group von Kleist (XIV, XV and XVI Panzer Corps); in the centre, Rundstedt's Army Group A, whose Panzer Group (XXXIX and XLI Panzer Corps) was led by Guderian. Both were to exploit as hard as possible once they were through the French line, while to the east Leeb's Army Group C increased its pressure on the Maginot Line.

To their surprise the Germans encountered a French Army that, if infinitely weaker than at the start of the campaign, possessed a revitalised fighting spirit. Attacks stalled in front of the defended areas, and when the panzer adopted their well-tried tactics of working round them, they were hammered by artillery and anti-tank guns. For several days progress was both painfully slow and costly and it was not until the Luftwaffe finally wrote down the French artillery that break-throughs were made. Thereafter, France had nothing to offer and the panzer divisions raced on, unopposed, leaving an entire army group trapped against the Maginot Line. The British 1st Armoured Division re-embarked at Cherbourg and Brest in the nick of time, but most of the 51st

(Highland) Division was surrounded by Rommel at St Valery and forced to surrender.

France capitulated on the 21st June, the instrument of surrender being signed by Huntziger on the same spot Foch had dictated terms to Germany in 1918, and in the same railway coach. Outside, in full view of the newsreel cameras, Hitler danced a little jig of uncontrolled joy. Fighting was not to cease until the 25th; by then the panzers had overrun three-fifths of the country.

It had taken a mere six weeks to defeat the two Great Powers of Western Europe and their allies. Germany lost 27,000 men killed, 110,000 wounded and 18,000 were missing, or about one-third of the casualties she had incurred at Verdun alone in 1916. Total British losses came to 68,000, Belgian 23,000 and Dutch 10,000. France had borne the main burden of the war and had suffered 90,000 dead and 200,000 wounded, while 1,900,000 of her soldiers had been taken prisoner or were missing.[33]

The Luftwaffe lost 1,284 aircraft, the RAF 931 and the *Armee de l'Air* about 560; success in the air had by no means been one-sided, although in the areas that counted the Germans' technical superiority had given them victory. The British lost all their tanks and artillery, the French all but a small proportion of theirs.

When the campaign ended the *Panzerwaffe's* strength had been reduced by half, most of the loss falling on the light PzKw Is and IIs and the thinly armoured Czech vehicle. Average daily runs for Guderian's XIX Panzer Corps during the dash to the Channel were nineteen miles per day, the best day's performance achieving fifty-six miles. The break-down rate remained steady at 30 per cent but would have risen had fighting continued any longer. The recovery and repair services had coped well enough although latterly vehicles had a lengthy and time-consuming journey from the heavy repair workshops in Germany to the panzer spearheads.

In general, it was easier and less wounding to the pride for the British and French public to accept the *Deuxieme Bureau's* estimate of German strength and believe that their armies had simply been overwhelmed rather than paralysed by a superior technique; it would be many years before the true facts were released.

For the victorious Wehrmacht there were promotions, decorations and parades. Many units returned to barracks in their pre-war stations, and the Army was partially demobilised. In Berlin strollers filled the leafy Unter den Linden and the Tiergarten, and at weekends families enjoyed the summer pleasures of the Grunwald or boated on the Havel. The war, it seemed, was over.

It was not over. Luftwaffe casualties actually increased as a result of heavy air fighting over southern England. At sea the total blockade continued to damage business interests. And in North Africa a tiny British force was squaring up to a large Italian army with results that were both startling and embarrassing; but North Africa was far away and the Italians were apparently in no immediate danger.

Chapter 4: North Africa

To anyone not born and brought up in the Imperial era it is, perhaps, difficult to understand the importance placed upon the security of the Middle East in general and the Suez Canal in particular, not merely by Service Chiefs, but also by the entire British public, since the area was not simply a vital link in the Imperial defence chain, but an essential ingredient in the Empire's commercial infrastructure.

It was not therefore surprising that in 1939 the only truly viable British armoured formation outside the United Kingdom was the so-called Mobile Division (Egypt), commanded by Major-General P.C.S. Hobart. This formation was, in fact, an under-strength armoured division, consisting of a Light Armoured Brigade (7th and 8th Hussars) equipped with light tanks, a Heavy Armoured Brigade (1st and 6th Royal Tank Regiments) with a mixture of light and cruiser tanks, a Pivot Group (3rd Royal Horse Artillery with field and anti-tank guns, and 1st King's Royal Rifle Corps), a divisional armoured car regiment, the 11th Hussars, manning ancient Rolls Royce and Morris armoured cars, a single RASC supply company and a field ambulance.

Hobart brought this small force to a high pitch of efficiency and instilled into it the basic concepts of fast-moving armoured operations. Equally important, he trained it hard for the demanding conditions of desert warfare, teaching his men to fight, maintain and supply themselves in one of the harshest environments on earth. In the months to come, while the Italian enemy hugged the coast or remained behind fixed defences, the

British armour would roam the desert almost unchecked, and propagandists would boast a natural British affinity for the desert; save in the case of individuals, no such affinity existed, but it was a nice compliment to Hobart's training methods.

It was unfortunate that the combination of Hobart's ungovernable temper and his too-oft stated conviction that only armour counted on the modern battlefield cost him his job. Neither General Sir Archibald Wavell, GOC-in-C Middle East, nor Lieutenant-General Maitland Wilson, GOC Egypt, felt that they could employ such an intolerant and intolerable subordinate, and he was relieved of his command and prematurely retired. The Mobile Division, now re-styled 7th Armoured Division, was taken over by a cavalryman, Major-General Michael O'Moore Creagh, but remained very much Hobart's creation throughout the opening months of the Desert War.[34]

It was not that Wavell was in any way reactionary or unreceptive to Hobart's theories; he was, on the contrary, a quiet, deeply thoughtful man who knew that when the time came it would be necessary to fight a hard-hitting, mobile war to balance the immense forces arrayed against him, and he simply could not afford to have friction among his senior commanders.

His responsibilities were immense, stretching from Syria to Somaliland and from Palestine to the Libyan frontier. To cover this vast area, he had only 50,000 troops, of whom 36,000 were immediately available in Egypt, the remainder being dispersed thinly across the Sudan, Kenya and British Somaliland. Apart from 7th Armoured Division, his only other major formations in Egypt were the incomplete 4th Indian Division and two British independent infantry brigades, although the 6th Australian Division was beginning to assemble in Palestine. At sea, the British Mediterranean Fleet could match the Italian Navy in battleships, but was dwarfed in all other classes of warship save aircraft carriers, of which it had two and the Italians none, a fact that worried the latter scarcely at all, since their intention was to support their naval operations with land-based aircraft. In the air, the Royal Air Force could put up a few hundred obsolete Bombay and Blenheim bombers, and Gladiator fighters against the 2,000 aircraft, many of the most modern type, available to the *Reggia Aeronautica*.

On 10th June 1940, Mussolini, jealous of Hitler's easy victories in Poland, Scandinavia and France, declared war on Great Britain, claiming that he "needed a few thousand dead so that he could sit at the conference table as a man who has fought". The announcement was not entirely unexpected and the prospects for Wavell's tiny force seemed bleak, faced as they were by an army of 250,000 men in Libya and a further army of 200,000 in Italian East Africa. Moreover, for the British cause a defeat in the Mediterranean could spell extinction since the Spanish dictator Franco, anxious to repay the debts he had incurred during the Civil War, was teetering on the brink of joining the Axis, and did in fact occupy the International Zone of Tangier on the 12th, while in the Levant itself Turkey was being assiduously wooed to break her strict neutrality and join in the dismemberment of British interests in the area. Faced with such mounting odds even Churchill might have felt compelled to conclude a negotiated and inevitably humiliating peace.

The threat, however impressive, contained less substance than was at first apparent. Mussolini's decision had been a political one, made against the advice of his Army Chief of Staff, Marshal Pietro Badoglio, who had warned him that at least two years would be needed to train and equip the Army to the standard required to tackle a mechanised European enemy, and that in its present condition it was only capable of engaging in short-term hostilities. The fact was that the Italian Army, while it had formed or was forming several armoured divisions, was essentially an infantry army, and since it was short of mechanical transport in practical terms that meant a marching army which relied to a substantial degree on pack animals for its supplies. This was particularly true of troops serving in the overseas colonies.

In North Africa the only Italian formation worthy of note was the two-battalion Libyan Tank Group, equipped with seventy M11/39 medium tanks. Although protected by 30-mm armour, average for a medium tank of the period, the M11/39 was a badly designed fighting vehicle in which the 47-mm main armament was mounted in the front plate of the fighting compartment while the turret contained two machine-guns, such a layout making for difficult communication between the vehicle commander and gunner. The vehicle was also unreliable and at any one time a high percentage of the Group's tanks was in workshops being overhauled. Again, the restriction of radio sets to company commanders and above denied the Italian armour of any capacity for tactical flexibility, so that of necessity armoured operations relied on adherence to plans made in advance and which might not fit altered circumstances. A further flaw in the Italian Armoured Corps' practice was that of firing on the move, which looked impressive but which produced little return for the ammunition expended.

Each infantry division also had its organic tank battalion, but this was equipped with L3 tankettes, which were little more than lightly armoured machine-gun carriers. They had been designed primarily for use in mountain warfare and had performed adequately enough in Ethiopia, Spain and Albania, but were quite useless in a tank battle and could barely cope with the British armoured cars.

By far the best element in the Italian Army was its artillery, which, although its guns were elderly, as indeed were many of the British, fought to the muzzle throughout the campaign, earning universal admiration. It was, however, hampered by lack of a good anti-tank gun, a factor that was to have a decisive bearing on the outcome of events.

Apart from its deficiencies in equipment, the Italian Army was flawed in other ways. Its senior commanders were capable and professional in their approach, but the officer corps as a whole was riddled by political preferment, and at regimental level relations between officers and men remained distant, the former receiving privileges that even extended to the issue of better rations when in the field. The ranks themselves contained many brave men who performed numerous acts of individual heroism, but in general their motivation and will to fight was far lower than that of Wavell's men.

For his part, Wavell refused to be intimidated by his huge opponent, and on the day following the declaration of war, 7th Armoured Division commenced harassing operations on the Libyan side of the frontier wire, its tanks and armoured cars striking deep at convoys and outposts, causing the abandonment of the border forts of Capuzzo, Sidi Omar and Maddelena, and obtaining a complete moral ascendency over the enemy. The Italians reacted by confining movement between their garrisons to large, well-protected groups, but not even these were safe and at Ghirba on 15th June an entire column was wiped out without loss to the British. During the first few weeks of the war 7th Armoured Division inflicted 3,000 casualties in exchange for only 150 of its own and made itself master of the desert. Attempts to control British incursions by using the *Reggia Aeronautica* produced little result, while in return the Royal Air Force continued to take a steady toll of enemy aircraft, some destroyed in combat, rather more on the ground. Visiting German liaison officers found their allies nervous and depressed, talking in terms of "the will to resist" rather than making plans for the destruction of Wavell's impudent intruders. Worse, a thoroughly bad start was aggravated by an incredible piece of *Schlamperei* on the part of an Italian anti-aircraft unit that shot down its own Commander-in-Chief, Marshal Italo Balbo, while he was flying over Tobruk on 28th June.

Mussolini was beginning to look slightly silly, and instructed Balbo's successor, Marshal Rodolfo Graziani, to prepare for an immediate invasion of Egypt. Graziani had acquired something of a reputation for dash in Ethiopia, but was actually a cautious general, sometimes given to bouts of intense depression, and was above all a realist. He fully appreciated that the key to successful desert warfare lay in the logistics of personal survival and that mere numbers in a partially mechanised army could prove to be a crippling handicap, since many mouths drink much water, of which there was never an adequate supply. He told Count Ciano, the Duce's son-in-law and Foreign Minister, that a defeat in the desert "must inevitably develop into a total disaster", and events were to prove him right. He temporised for as long as he could, until told by Mussolini that unless he obeyed his orders he would be relieved at once.

It was therefore with considerable aversion for the task ahead that he crossed the frontier at Solium on 13th September, and four days later occupied the little fishing village of Sidi Barrani, sixty miles further on. Mussolini had his triumph, and that night Rome Radio announced to the world and to the surprised inhabitants of the few mud huts that "all is quiet and the trams are running normally again!" The advance had been made cautiously in the hourly expectation that the elusive British armour, whose strength had by now been grossly overestimated, would suddenly materialise out of the desert to the south and fall on the marching columns, but in fact few British troops were encountered, and those that were succeeded in neatly disengaging and breaking all contact with the invaders.

Wavell had in fact ordered the bulk of 7th Armoured Division to withdraw from the frontier zone some time previously as continual hard usage was beginning to take toll of its vehicles and he had no wish to blunt the edge of his principal strike weapon before the main issue was joined. While Graziani's men were marching into Sidi Barrani, the division was completing some much-needed maintenance at the main British defence position at Mersa Matruh, which had been under construction for several weeks.

On 4th October, Hitler and Mussolini met at the Brenner Pass, the Duce being complimented on his obvious domination of the Mediterranean theatre of war, but being kept in total ignorance of the German occupation of Rumania, which was at that moment taking place. Only on his return to Rome was Mussolini informed of the event, and in a fit of rage at being treated by the Fuhrer as a stuffed shirt, announced that he was going to "occupy" Greece. It was the decision of a power-crazed *poseur*, devoid of either logic or necessity, and it involved the diversion of troops, armour and aircraft that might otherwise have altered the course of the war in North Africa. When Italian troops actually did cross the Greek frontier on the 28th they were subjected to a series of resounding defeats and pursued back across the border into Albania. As if this was not bad enough, on the night of 11th/12th November Swordfish torpedo bombers flying off HMS *Illustrious* crippled the Italian battle-fleet in Taranto Harbour, completely altering the balance of power at sea in favour of the Royal Navy.

Meanwhile, in Egypt, Graziani was obstinately refusing to proceed further than Sidi Barrani, although fully sixty miles now separated the two armies. He insisted that he required reinforcements, particularly of mechanical transport, and declared his intention of consolidating his gains until he was ready to pursue the next phase of his advance. He concentrated most of his strength close to the coast and constructed a chain of fortified camps stretching obliquely away south-westwards to the escarpment, thus refusing his right, the classic manoeuvre of a commander with an open flank; there was, however, a fatal flaw in his dispositions, and one that the British would not be slow to discover.

Wavell's position had been gradually improving as a result of reinforcements shipped round the Cape, and Hurricane fighters were beginning to arrive in Egypt by means of the West African ferry route, but his relationship with his political masters was a poor one. Churchill had been telling generals how to run their business since he had himself been a junior officer, but Wavell was not a man who took kindly to a stream of high-level signals criticising local deployments or allocating unwanted priorities, and made no bones about it. In August, he had been summoned to London and a very frank discussion, described in Churchill's own memoirs as "severe," had taken place. As a result of this the Prime Minister took the courageous step of detaching three armoured regiments from the scant resources available for the defence of the United Kingdom, and despatching them to Wavell's command.[35] Nonetheless, Churchill remained uneasy about his Commander-in-Chief's intentions and in October his Secretary of State for

War, Anthony Eden, was sent out to Middle East Headquarters with a watching brief.

Almost as soon as the Italians had settled into their camps reconnaissance revealed that the majority of these were incapable of providing each other with mutual support; in particular, between the camps of Nibeiwa and Rabia lay twenty miles of unoccupied desert known as the Enba Gap. In this area British light forces rapidly established the same sort of moral ascendency that had existed during the early days along the frontier, and it was quickly obvious that the Gap provided an ideal back door into the heart of the Italian position.

While Graziani temporised, both Wavell and Wilson saw the possibilities inherent in the situation, and began planning a spoiling attack that would disrupt such preparations as the Italians had been able to make for a further advance. The executive field commander of the Western Desert Force at Mersa Matruh, Lieutenant-General Richard O'Connor, was particularly enthusiastic about the idea, since he had fought alongside the Italians during World War I and knew how intensely they disliked being attacked from the flank or rear.

In outline the British plan called for both Western Desert Force's divisions to penetrate the Enba Gap by night while a diversionary attack was made on the coast against the enemy's advanced post of Maktila. Then, while one of 7th Armoured Division's brigades swept north to cut the coast road behind Sidi Barrani and the other acted as a screen against interference, 4th Indian Division, spearheaded by the Matildas of 7 RTR, would storm each of the fortified camps north of the Gap and then attack Sidi Barrani itself. Five days would be allowed for the operation, which would be called Compass, following which O'Connor was warned that 4th Indian Division would be removed from his command and sent to the Sudan, where its presence was urgently needed, and responsibility for following up the success would rest upon 7th Armoured Division.[36]

Training for Operation Compass went ahead in conditions of the greatest secrecy, the details being known only to the most senior officers and the commanders of certain corps troops, as Wavell felt that the best way to handle the politicians was to present them with a *fait accompli*. However, in November a signal arrived from Churchill insisting that priority be given to aiding the Greeks, and Wavell had little alternative other than to disclose his hand to Eden, who at once flew to London with the details. Notwithstanding his anger at being deliberately excluded from the planning, Churchill grasped the potential of Compass at once and eagerly urged Wavell to set his sights on more distant objectives still.

The administrative problem of getting both diversions simultaneously into the Gap after a sixty-mile approach march was brilliantly solved by staggering departure times and dates, the slow Matildas beginning their journey ahead of the rest. Incredible as it might seem, hundreds of tanks and guns, and several thousand wheeled vehicles crossed the desert completely undetected by the *Reggia Aeronautica* or the Italian ground forces. During the night of 8th/9th December the assault elements of the two formations were moving up to their start lines inside the Gap, the sound of their engines drowned by Bombay bombers droning low over the Italian camps, and it was only then that the troops were told that they would be going into action the following morning.

At first light on the 9th more than 200 guns, including the whole of the Corps and 4th Indian Divisional artillery, began battering Nibeiwa, supplemented by Vickers medium machine-guns combing the area of the defences in the sustained fire role, while 7th Armoured Brigade moved into position to screen the camps at Rabia and Sofafi.

By 0715, 4th Armoured Brigade was beginning its advance towards the coast. Its tank commanders, glancing over their shoulders at the embattled camp lying under its pall of dust thrown up by thousands of shells, could see the Matildas of A and B Squadrons 7 RTR grinding into the attack from the west, followed at a distance by the tracked carriers and lorries of 11th Indian Infantry Brigade.

Nibeiwa camp was an approximate rectangle measuring 2,500 by 2,000 yards and was held by a divisional sized force known as Gruppo Maletti after its commander. Aerial reconnaissance had shown that the perimeter was ringed by a minefield, but the presence of a tank leaguer slightly to the west betrayed the location of the garrison's supply corridor, and it was along this that the assault was made.

The Italian tanks, twenty-three M11/39s, belonged to 2nd Battalion 4th Tank Regiment, and represented the entire operational strength of the Libyan Tank Group, the regiment's 1st Battalion having been withdrawn to Tobruk for a refit. Their crews were caught scrambling aboard by the Seventh's leading squadron, and within minutes every tank had been knocked out; the engagement was conducted at point-blank range and in some cases the British 2-pounder shot passed straight through the enemy vehicles.

As the slow Infantry Tanks bore down on the camp itself the Italian artillerymen, frantically serving their pieces behind dry-stone hangars, were horrified by the discovery that the Matilda's 80-mm armour was quite impervious to their fire, but remained at their guns until shot down or crushed around them, those that survived watching the tanks sweep on past the gun positions and into the core of the defences.

The fate of their armour and artillery shocked many Italians into immediate surrender; others courageously tackled the tanks with machine-guns, small arms and grenades – one such was General Maletti himself, sprinting from his command bunker, machine pistol in hand, who died exchanging fire with one of his invulnerable assailants. Then the British infantry stormed into the broken defences, bombing, shooting and bayonetting their way through the camp until the last of the defenders had surrendered, yielding a total of 4,000 prisoners.

Throughout the day the combination of Major-General Noel Beresford-Peirse's 4th Indian Division and Lieutenant-Colonel R.M. Jerram's 7th Royal Tank Regiment proved to be unstoppable. Camp after camp fell to their joint assault – Tummar

West in the early afternoon, then Tummar Central and finally, as the light faded, Tummar East. In Sidi Barrani, General Gallina, commander of the Libyan Group, signalled Graziani to the effect that the whole desert to the south was crawling with British armour, that the road west and the vital water pipeline had been cut, and that he was losing contact with most of his major formations.

During the afternoon the *Reggia Aeronautica* appeared over the battlefield, only to find the RAF present at its maximum strength. To add to the difficulties of the Italian airmen, they had no way of knowing which of the camps were in friendly and which enemy hands, and this fog of war was compounded in a physical sense by the dust clouds of thousands of vehicles, all heading north, some from broken Italian units, but the majority belonging to Western Desert Force. Somewhere among the leading British elements of the apparently chaotic scene below was a little group of command vehicles manned by O'Connor and his staff, in constant wireless contact with their formations, monitoring and controlling the situation as it developed.

The following morning almost began badly when 16th British Brigade was caught leaving its lorries within range of the Sidi Barrani garrison's guns. The situation was retrieved by Jerram leading his Matildas in a 4,000-yard attack into the defences, in which they remained for an hour, destroying a considerable quantity of artillery and taking 200 prisoners. 4th Armoured Brigade was ordered east to assist, while the attack was replanned under cover of a sandstorm. When it was resumed at 1600, 2 RTR attacked the western defences while 7 RTR spearheaded the infantry assault as usual. Already shaken by the Matildas' dawn foray, the Blackshirt garrison quickly surrendered. Meanwhile, 6 RTR had skirted the battle and prevented 1st Libyan Division, withdrawing under pressure from the diversionary attack on Maktila, from reaching Sidi Barrani; the Libyans remained surrounded throughout the night, but gave up the following morning.[37]

Thus, by the evening of the second day's fighting, Wavell had achieved the primary object of Operation Compass, the virtual destruction of Graziani's army in Egypt. 4th Indian Division was withdrawn from O'Connor's command, although 6th Australian Division was promised in its place as soon as it could be brought forward from Palestine, and for a while Western Desert Force consisted solely of 7th Armoured Division and 16th British Brigade.

In his underground headquarters at Cyrene, Graziani went completely to pieces. On 11th December he advised Rome that four divisions had been utterly destroyed at Sidi Barrani, announcing the next day that he was considering a withdrawal as far as Tripoli since he could not be expected to "wage the war of the flea against the elephant". Mussolini refused to believe that the news could possibly be so bad, and commented that his North African Commander-in-Chief, whom he despised, was obviously out of his mind.

With the collapse of the entire Italian line north of the Enba Gap, the 63rd Division, manning the Rabia and Sofafi camps, was left in isolation and would have been attacked *in situ* on the 12th had it not evacuated its positions overnight and marched hard for the frontier along the escarpment. The 64th Division, which had been in general reserve east of Buq Buq, had the advantage of the coast road for its withdrawal, but was not quite as quick off the mark and became the target for 7th Armoured Brigade, hitherto scarcely involved in the fighting.

The brigade commander had intended to cut the road behind the retreating Italians, but his left hook landed short and he reached the coast to find the enemy gone. A tail chase ensued until the leading regiment, 3rd Hussars, ran into 64th Division's rearguard close to Buq Buq, being confronted by ranks of guns deployed along the crest of a semi-circular ridge behind a salt flat.

The "Galloping Third's" two light squadrons went into the attack at once, but sudden found themselves floundering as their tracks broke through the thin crust of the salt marsh. Quickly the Italian artillery registered onto its immobile targets, the shells blasting the Light Mark, VIs apart as they churned their way deeper into the morass.

It is probable that the two squadrons would have been annihilated had not the commander of the Third's cruiser squadron (actually B Squadron 2 RTR[38]), which had been giving covering fire, spotted a route forward onto the enemy's flank and drawn some of the fire onto his own vehicles as they moved out. Minutes later, the brigade's second regiment, 8th Hussars, arrived and after a brisk duel with the Italian guns, its cruisers worked their way onto the opposite flank. Once the tanks had got among the gun crews the action was soon over, but it had proved needlessly costly.

With its rearguard overrun and its artillery destroyed 64th Division stood little chance and was quickly rounded up, together with stragglers who had escaped the Sidi Barrani debacle. The growing throng of fugitives swelled throughout the day until any sort of headcount became impossible, senior officers being startled by reports that quantified the prisoners by the acre rather than by number. In fact, a total of 14,000 prisoners and sixty-eight guns were taken at Buq Buq.

Four days' fighting had produced a total capture of four generals, 38,000 men, 237 guns and seventy-three tanks. For the most part the prisoners, whose number wildly exceeded the rump of Western Desert Force, were passive and indeed co-operative, organising themselves into columns and using their own transport to convey themselves, virtually unescorted, to hastily erected compounds. Many men doubtless had no interest in continuing to fight, but for the majority surrender meant survival as an alternative to a hideous death from thirst. As Graziani had predicted, for an inadequately equipped army, defeat in the desert spelled disaster. For O'Connor, too, the scale of the victory was an embarrassment, since the British logistic planning had simply not allowed for the sheer numbers involved and without active Italian assistance would have been quite unable to cope with the situation.

Soon the 7th Armoured Division had re-established its former grip on the frontier, and as Major-General Iven Mackay's 6th

Australian Division began taking its place in the line, Wavell and O'Connor worked on the next phase of the campaign. While Operation Compass and its immediate sequel had succeeded in ejecting the enemy from Egypt, the poor showing made by the Italians thus far provided an incentive to exploit the victory in Cyrenaica, but before this could be done the stronghold of Bardia would have to be eliminated.

But Bardia was a much tougher nut to crack than had been the Sidi Barrani camps, being ringed by a permanent anti-tank ditch, minefields, deep barbed wire entanglements and concrete strong-points with interlocking arcs of fire, while the garrison, consisting of the 62nd, 63rd, 1st and 2nd Blackshirt Divisions, a total of 45,000 men, was supported by 400 guns and more than 100 tanks.

Christmas was spent by the Australians practising their assault technique on a full-scale replica of a sector of the perimeter defences, in conjunction with a composite squadron of Jerram's Matildas.[39] The penetration itself was to be made on a narrow front and expanded concentrically as more and more of the defenders' territory was captured. On 1st January 1941, Western Desert Force changed its title to 13 Corps, and two days later began its attack on the fortress.

At 0530 on the 3rd the entire Corps artillery thundered out, while from the sea the Italians were subjected to the nerve-shattering ordeal of a fleet bombardment by the battleships *Barham*, *Valiant* and *Warspite* and their escorting warships.[40] An infantry battalion stormed the nearest enemy posts by direct assault, covering Royal Australian Engineers who worked like beavers to clear lanes through the minefields and wire, throwing down the sides of the anti-tank ditch to form causeways for the tanks, which began entering the defences at 0630. The power of the terrible Matildas was already known to the enemy, but equally frightening was the sight of the Australian infantry looming through the morning mist, big men made larger by their bulky greatcoats, men who fought hard with a natural edge of aggression, probably the best assault troops in the world. In general, the

Italians were happy to surrender their fortified posts after their fire had been suppressed by the tanks and the infantry had begun to close in with bayonet and grenade; by late afternoon the defences had been cut in two and so many prisoners were streaming towards the gaps in the perimeter that they were mistaken by some officers for Australians rallying after an unsuccessful attack. In this manner fighting continued throughout the next day, the harbour falling at about 1600 hours, the last pockets of resistance being eliminated on the fifth.

Mussolini had entertained high hopes that a successful defence of Bardia would do much to restore his badly battered prestige, but instead the world's press was again treated to the spectacle of endless columns of trudging prisoners and parks of captured tanks, guns and equipment of all kinds; a tiny crumb of comfort was provided by the escape of the garrison commander, General Bergonzoli, a popular figure commonly known as Electric Beard, who succeeded in reaching Tobruk and passing through to fight again another day.

O'Connor was the last man to rest on his laurels, and even before the final shots had been fired inside Bardia he had despatched 7th Armoured Division to isolate Tobruk, this mission being accomplished by the evening of the 6th January. In the wake of the armoured brigades came the Australians and 7 RTR, tightening their grip around a garrison that already knew itself to be doomed.

The Tobruk defences were similar to those of Bardia and were manned by the 61st Division, a naval detachment of 2,000, and 9,000 stragglers who had found their way to the port. On 21st January the outer perimeter was breached by an identical battle drill, and by evening the attackers had reached the edge of the escarpment overlooking the town. After a night rent by explosions and tinged by fire as the garrison destroyed its stores, resistance collapsed rapidly throughout the following day and a further 25,000 prisoners began the long march to Egypt, leaving behind them more than 200 guns and eighty-seven tanks.

Graziani now abandoned his headquarters at Cyrene and left for Tripoli, ordering General Tellera to hold the line of the Wadi Dema, which offered a good defensive position between the sea and the foothills of the Djebel Akhdar, with what remained of Xth Italian Army. In Rome, Mussolini was apparently blind to the true significance of events, and continued to radiate false optimism until severely taken to task by Count Ciano, who pointed out that the Duce's illusions regarding Sidi Barrani, Bardia and Tobruk had each been shattered in turn and that there were scant grounds for pinning his hopes on the Wadi Derna. "The trouble," he concluded, "is grave, mysterious and deep."

In essence the trouble was that if the Italian Army chose to fight behind fixed defences, these were stormed by the Matildas and the Australian infantry; and if it chose to fight in the open it was cut to pieces by 7th Armoured Division. There were, however, various checks and balances at work in the opposing forces. Once the *Reggia Aeronautica* had lost its complex of tactical airstrips around Tobruk it was virtually out of the battle since, with the exception of the small civilian airport of Benghazi, its nearest bases were in Tripolitania and out of effective range. The RAF, too, was flying at the limit of its endurance, and it was clear that the next round of the campaign would be fought almost unaided by the ground forces alone. In 7th Armoured Division mechanical attrition was beginning to take its toll and O'Moore Creagh was forced to send two of his regiments, 8th Hussars and 6 RTR, back to Egypt in order to keep the others up to some sort of strength and to reduce the strain on his workshops and logistic support units. On the other hand, the Italians had never had so many effective tanks, Graziani having received a reinforcement of 100 Ml3/40 mediums, which had been formed into an armoured brigade under General Babini. The Ml3 corrected the major design fault of the M11 in that the 47-mm main armament was now located in the turret, where its commander also performed double duty as gunner, but the Babini Armoured Brigade, in addition to suffering from the general inflexibility inherent in

Italian armoured formations, was also inexperienced and quite unused to working together.

These things apart, Babini's men had not been in Africa long enough to be in awe of the Desert Rats'[41] reputation, and were quite prepared to make the most of their opportunities. On the morning of 24th January, the 7th Hussars' light tanks were covering the inland flank of the 6th Australian Division as it closed up to the Wadi Derna when they were suddenly assailed by fourteen Ml3s. The Hussars had only three cruiser tanks that could engage on equal terms, and one of these was quickly knocked out and a second damaged, while the light tanks began to suffer severely. The regiment was compelled to withdraw and 2 RTR's two cruiser squadrons were sent to its aid. In their eager pursuit the Ml3s rushed headlong into a carefully set fire-trap, and only five of their number succeeded in escaping from the cruisers' crossfire. If the skirmish had ended in favour of the British, it was also an indication that the Italian armour could no longer be dismissed out of hand.

Ironically, the Italians fought more stubbornly at the Derna defence line than at any other time throughout the campaign, and the Australians were unable to make any headway during their initial attacks. The slow Matildas were called forward from Tobruk, but in the event were not used, for on the 28th Tellera, anxious about the pressure being exerted on his right flank by 7th Armoured Division, decided to abandon the position and withdraw along the coast road through Benghazi to Tripolitania. Babini's retirement to the northwest to act as the army's rearguard, confirmed O'Connor's suspicions that the Italians were pulling out and presented him with an opportunity to employ the same sort of Indirect Approach that had worked so well at Sidi Barrani.

His plan called for Mackay to pursue Tellera along the road north of the Djebel Akhdar, while 7th Armoured Division would advance along the axis Mechnili – Msus – Antelat, cutting across the base of the coastal bulge and going into a blocking position astride the road at Beda Fomm, south of Benghazi, thus trapping Xth Italian Army between 13 Corps' two principal formations.

The division's advance guard, commanded by Lieutenant-Colonel John Combe, was composed of 11th Hussars' armoured cars, 2nd Rifle Brigade, C Battery 4th RHA with 25-pounders, and nine 37-mm *portee* anti-tank guns manned by 106th RHA, began to move off early on 4th February.[42] Behind came 4th Armoured Brigade, now consisting of 2nd RTR, 3rd and 7th Hussars, 7th Armoured Brigade, reduced to a single regiment, 1st RTR, and the Support Group. The going through the Djebel country was abominable, consisting of loose slab rock, which slowed down the pace, caused petrol consumption to rise alarmingly, and subjected vehicles and crews to a severe battering. The fuel and ammunition lorries found difficulty in keeping up with the tanks and began to fall steadily behind, but by midday on the 5th, Combe had reached Beda Fomm and begun to construct his roadblock. There was barely time for the infantry to dig basic slit trenches and lay a few mines before the first convoy began approaching from the north.

The leading vehicles were engaged by the armoured cars and artillery, their startled occupants tumbling out to take cover by the roadside. They were mainly administrative and line-of-communications troops, but were escorted by a Bersaglieri regiment, which launched a series of attacks on the block. These failed because of the absence of artillery or tank support, the majority of the Italians' fighting troops having only just left Benghazi. However, during the afternoon more and more vehicles began to pile up behind the trapped convoy and pressure against Combeforce began to grow.

By now, 4th Armoured Brigade was fast approaching the scene of action and Combe suggested to its commander, Brigadier J. Caunter, that the tanks should engage the flank of the lengthening column from a series of ridges to the east of the road. Caunter agreed, and shortly after 1700 his regiments were beginning to stream across the ridges to shoot up the endless line of vehicles halted on the road to the west. Only the arrival of darkness and the acute shortage of petrol saved the Italians from a sharper mauling than they actually received.

Eventually the column stretched for eleven miles and it was clear to Tellera that he was faced with much more than a simple roadblock. Babini was ordered to send down sixty of his tanks from the rearguard, while Bergonzoli worked on a plan to free the ensnared army. Under cover of massed artillery fire the Italian armour would attack eastwards from a point known as The Pimple and drive Caunter's tanks back from the ridges, then turn south and engage Combe from the flank and rear.

Amid the wind and rain of a grey dawn the M13s began to push out towards their first objective along which the artillery's bursting shells were already beginning to mushroom. Of the British cruisers there was little sign save occasional turrets rising above the crests to fire several shots and then disappearing as the tank commanders skilfully changed position: against such targets the Italian practice of firing on the move was of little use.

Again, Bergonzoli's attacks were poorly co-ordinated and launched piecemeal as contingents of tanks arrived, so that 2 RTR, fighting hull down, had no difficulty in holding them and inflicting mounting loss. The principal British worry throughout the day was the declining stock of 2-pounder ammunition, which had reached dangerously low levels by mid-afternoon. For Caunter this was the crisis of the action, although it passed unnoticed by the enemy and was quickly resolved when 1 RTR's cruisers, arriving from Antelat, came in alongside the Second and went straight into action. After a day-long tank battle, which had simply whittled down their armour for little return, the regiment's timely appearance convinced the Italians that the British had almost limitless reserves, and Bergonzoli discontinued his attacks; in fact, 7th Armoured Division's total tank strength amounted to only thirty-two cruisers and about fifty lights.

Further north, the light tanks of 3rd Hussars had harried the column in a series of dashing raids, while 7th Hussars had closed in around its tail. The Support Group had thrown an enemy battle group out of Scaledeima, and the Australians had entered Benghazi, a little puzzled at being hailed by the municipal authorities as "gallant allies".

During the night, Bergonzoli decided that he now had only one alternative – to batter his way past Combe. At dawn on the 7th, Babini's last remaining thirty tanks, supported by a heavy artillery preparation, launched a determined assault on the block, trading loss for loss with 106 RHA's *portees*, and forced their way into the position. The situation was saved by the 25-pounders firing directly into the area held by the Rifle Brigade, with the latter's full consent, and by the solitary surviving *portee*, manned by the battery commander, his batman and a cook, which drove out to a flank and destroyed the last five M13s on their objective with five successive shots.

Bergonzoli had played his last card and it had not been quite high enough. He came in to surrender to Combe, who gave him breakfast, and remarked to his captor that the ambush had taken Xth Army completely by surprise, as the staff had calculated that 13 Corps was not less than two days' march behind. Tellera had died among his troops, of whom 25,000 were taken prisoner. 216 guns were also captured, and sufficient tanks in working order to re-equip 6th RTR. Wavell received a short signal from O'Connor informing him that the Italian Army in North Africa had ceased to exist; it read: "Fox killed in the open."

In two months, O'Connor's small corps had advanced 500 miles; inflicted 100,000 casualties; taken 130,000 prisoners; destroyed ten Italian divisions; and captured 380 tanks and 845 guns. The cost to the British had been a mere 500 dead, fifty-five missing and 1,373 wounded, plus a handful of tanks. In the wider sphere, the campaign convinced Franco that full neutrality was a better policy than "non-belligerence", and he refused to sanction Hitler's plan for an attack on Gibraltar by way of Spain, although he did send a volunteer formation to fight on the Russian Front. Equally important, the Wehrmacht was now committed irrevocably to bolstering the shaky Italian forces. It was ironic that O'Connor, who had brought all this about by his brilliant application of the *Blitzkrieg* technique, was not particularly influenced by the Armoured Idea and in fact had not read the works of the theorists; his tactics, he commented in later years, had been dictated by simple common sense.

It has often been said that Wavell should have permitted O'Connor to continue his advance as far as Tripoli and so conclude the war in North Africa once and for all. The Italians could have offered virtually no resistance and O'Connor was convinced that he could have got there, using captured stores if necessary. But the fact was that Wavell had achieved his object, the destruction of Graziani's army, and an advance on Tripoli would have lengthened the distance between 13 Corps and his own operational hub to little apparent purpose without diminishing his overall responsibility for the Middle East; further, Churchill had once again turned his eyes towards Greece, to whom Wavell was ordered to render every possible assistance. In this light, therefore, the decision to leave only a small covering force at El Agheila was entirely justified from the military viewpoint, and there were few complaints at the time.

It would have required a high degree of clairvoyance to predict that two months after Beda Fomm, Lieutenant-General Erwin Rommel, former commander of 7th Panzer Division, would actually disobey his orders and undertake an offensive with very limited resources. The success of that offensive was equally unpredictable, since it led to the British abandoning all of Cyrenaica save Tobruk, and falling back to the frontier.[43]

The subsequent Desert War has been called many things: an ideal laboratory for armoured warfare; a tactician's paradise and a quartermaster's hell; and even the last of the gentlemen's wars. All of this may have been true, but it contained no further examples of a successful *Blitzkrieg* since each side fully understood the other's technique and although each in turn suffered defeats, these never approached the proportions of a rout. The decisive Battle of Alamein was fought on the principle of attrition, but Rommel's army remained in being to fight a long rearguard action all the way to the Tunisian border, the war in Tunisia being ultimately decided by a series of set-piece infantry/tank battles, which broke the Germans' mountain defences and permitted the Anglo-America armoured divisions to be unleashed onto the empty coastal plain beyond, so capturing the vital ports of Tunis and Bizerta.

Chapter 5: Directive No 21

As the short midsummer night drew to its end and the sky began to lighten in the east Russian sentries at airfields from the Baltic to the Black Sea detected the hum of approaching aircraft engines. Puzzled, they looked up as the hum became a roar and wave after wave of black-crossed Junkers, Dorniers and Heinkels appeared overhead; then the sound was blanketed by the scream of bombs, the rattle of automatic weapons and explosion after explosion among the neatly parked ranks of Polikarpovs, Ilyushins, Tupolevs on the ground.

Away to the west the horizon had suddenly flared in flickering light as thousands of guns opened fire simultaneously from the German side of the frontier in a long rumbling drumfire, and soon field-grey infantry in rubber assault boats were swarming across the border rivers to establish bridgeheads for the pontoons that were already being driven into position. On the River Bug the PzKw IIIs of 18th Panzer Divisions, trailing long schnor-kelling hoses developed for the cancelled invasion of England, were submerging and driving across the river-bed to appear on the far bank and commence the first panzer thrust into the body of Soviet Russia.

The date was 22nd June 1941 and the time 0315 hours, which had been chosen specially so that the Wehrmacht would enjoy the maximum possible daylight for the opening stages of Operation *Barbarossa*, the codename for Hitler's most supremely arrogant folly.

His motives for initiating a train of events that would ultimately lead to his own death and the dismemberment of Germany are beyond the scope of this book, and it is sufficient to say that whatever grand strategic illusions he laid before his General Staff for so gigantic an undertaking, he regarded the destruction of the cradle of Bolshevism and the subjugation of the Slavonic *Untermensch* (sub-humans), as he called them, as being the culmination of his life's work. The full scope of his intentions was summarised in two paragraphs of Operational Directive No 21, issued by Fuhrer Headquarters on 18th December 1940:

"The bulk of the Russian Army stationed in Western Russian will be destroyed by daring operations led by deeply penetrating armoured spearhead. Russian forces still capable of giving battle will be prevented from withdrawing into the depths of Russia.

"The enemy will then be energetically pursued and a line will be reached from which the Russian Air Force can no longer attack German territory. The final objective of the operation is to erect a barrier against Asiatic Russia on the general line Volga – Archangel. The last surviving industrial areas of Russia in the Urals can then, if necessary, be eliminated by the Luftwaffe."

Why, it might be wondered, should a former company runner, albeit a very good one, hope to succeed in such a design when professionals such as Charles XII of Sweden and Napoleon had failed in less ambitious schemes? The answer was that his rapid and total victory in France had so impressed upon him the Wehrmacht's capabilities that he did not see how he could fail. It was true that the Luftwaffe's feathers had been singed during the Battle of Britain, but it was still a formidable force highly tuned to support all operational requirements. It was also true that the German Army of 1941 was the best in the world, riding high on the crest of a wave of spectacular achievements, and that its panzer divisions were instruments of penetration honed to the keenest edge.

What Hitler forgot in his euphoria was that even the best armies do have limitations to what they can perform. His logic was simple; the panzer divisions had won the Battle of France, therefore he would double their number for the much larger campaign in Russia. This was achieved by reducing the number of tank regiments in each division from two to one and forming new divisions around the second regiments. It would have been most surprising if he had not been advised against this dilution of unit strength, as one of the most evident lessons of the French campaign was the steady erosion of the numbers of vehicles available in proportion to the ground covered. Thus, after 200 miles' running, a divisional commander might have only 50 per cent of his combat vehicles immediately available for action. Under the old establishment this was still the equivalent of one tank regiment, but for the new divisions it meant that after a comparable run their strength would consist of about four companies, or 25 per cent of what the divisional establishment had been at the start of the 1940 campaign in the west, a situation that would reduce their potential to a dangerously low level; and in Russia the distances involved would be infinitely greater than those in France. Again, as each panzer division retained its full quota of supporting arms and services, the logistic requirement for the *Panzerwaffe* as a whole was doubled, although the total number of tanks remained approximately the same.

A further point that was not fully taken into account was that the rest of the army moved at a slower pace than the panzer divisions. For the most part the infantry marched while much of the artillery and supply echelons were horse-drawn and remained so throughout the war. This incompatibility had not revealed itself to any grave disadvantage during the short campaigns of 1939 and 1940, but for the sort of deep encirclements envisaged in Operational Directive No 21 there were worrying implications, since gaps would inevitably open and widen between the fast-moving armoured formations and the slower mass of marching infantry, which would complete the reduction of the pockets formed.

In addition to the immensity of the Russian hinterland, the Wehrmacht would be facing tremendous odds. Against the four Air Fleets, containing a total of 1,280 serviceable aircraft, which the Luftwaffe had available for Operation *Barbarossa*, the Red Air Force could put up approximately 15,000 machines, of which some 7,000 were deployed in 23 Air Divisions within range of the frontier. In terms of tanks, too, the numbers were equally daunting. The *Panzerwaffe* could muster 3,200 vehicles, of which only the 1,440 PzKw IIIs and 515 PzKw IVs really counted, the remainder being various types of light tank. Opposing these would be no less than 20,000 fighting vehicles ranging from monoliths such as the T100 and T35, through the thin-skinned BT series and T26s to the little amphibious T37 and T38 tankettes; there were also available, in small numbers as yet, two designs of which the Germans knew nothing, the KV Heavy and the T34/76 Medium, both mounting a 76.2-mm gun, which was far more powerful than anything carried by their own tanks. The KV (Klimenti Voroshilov) was protected by 75-mm armour (90-mm on the mantlet), thus making it as deadly an opponent as the British Matilda, while the T34's 45-mm glacis was angled back at thirty degrees, thus providing the equivalent ballistic protection of 90-mm plate. Both vehicles were powered by a robust and uncomplicated V12 diesel engine producing over 500 b.h.p., and were equipped with wide tracks, which enabled them to cope with the vagaries of the Russian climate better than the German machines; nor could the German vehicles hope to equal the T34's high speed cross-country performance, provided by a Christie suspension developed in the BT series.

It is doubtful whether foreknowledge of these formidable vehicles would have caused Hitler more than a few moments' hesitation, so great was his contempt for all things Russian. "We have only to kick in the door and the whole rotten house will come tumbling down," he announced; and indeed the Red Army's record since the Civil War was not impressive. Its fallibility had been revealed by the Poles in 1920, it had failed to influence events in Spain, and it had been very roughly handled by the tiny Finnish Army during the Winter War. It was true that there had been successes against Japan in the Far East, but of these little was known at the time, and in any event the Japanese were considered, with some justification, to be a race of military illiterates as far as armoured warfare was concerned.

The Red Army was, in fact, flawed to a greater degree even than the French. Soviet Russia was ruled on the communist principle of "All power to the Centre", and it was at the Centre that all decisions, both civil and military, were made. From subordinates all that was required was unquestioning obedience; personal initiative was considered to be rather more of a vice than a virtue, as its implementation could disrupt details of some grand design of the Supreme Soviet's, from whom all wisdom must be seen to flow. In such a climate those senior and middle-rank military commanders who had survived the Great Purge of the officer corps were certainly not going to place themselves in jeopardy by initiating some move of their own devising when it was so much safer to wait for orders from above. The inevitable result of such suffocation was that Russian planning tended to be overtaken by events, in sharp contrast to the *modus operandi* of the German panzer leaders who made rapid decisions in the forefront of the battle and who relied on verbal orders broadcast over a radio net embracing every fighting vehicle under their command.

Even if the Russian command system had been more flexible and less turgid, execution of its orders still could not have matched that of the Germans for speed, since the issue of tank radios only went down only as far as battalion commanders' vehicles. Russian armoured operations tended to rely on detailed briefing and careful rehearsals, both of which took time, time that the very nature of *Blitzkrieg* would deny. Once an armoured formation had been committed to action, the only control that its commander could exercise was by means of hand or flag signals, which might or might not be seen by his subordinates amid the dust, smoke and terror of battle. Any major redeployment once in contact with the enemy was a virtual impossibility.

It was not that the German successes in Poland and France had gone unnoticed in Russia. On the contrary, STAVKA was forced to admit that the late Marshal Tukhachevsky's ideas had obviously been valid and had begun to group its armour in divisions in the German manner. A Russian armoured division consisted of two tank regiments, each with 200 tanks, a motor rifle regiment and an artillery regiment. Two such divisions and a mechanised (i.e. motor rifle) division formed a tank corps, an organisation that looked well on paper but which, because of the command-and-control difficulties described above, was unwieldy and impractical. Moreover, in June 1941 these formations, equipped with a dog's breakfast of tanks, including many obsolete types, had not been formed long enough for tactical theories to be fully developed and tested in large-scale manoeuvres.

Concerning this period, the Soviet Official History comments with an apparently engaging honesty on the abysmally low standard of individual crew training, and remarks that at the time of the German onslaught only 25 per cent of the Red Army's tanks were in an operational state. One can accept the first point on the understanding that it is a sweeping generalisation, but the second requires some examination, since Russian history is written under strict Party supervision and the choice of words is often made more for their underlying than for their literal meaning. If we accept the Official History's figure, it seems as though only 5,000 or so tanks took the field, a figure not greatly in excess of the strength of the *Panzerwaffe*. However, we are intended to understand that these vehicles could not all have been present in the forward zone at the outset, but were distributed in formations throughout Russia. Having been led this far, we are therefore invited to draw the conclusion that it was the Germans who possessed the overwhelming numbers during the early months of the campaign, and so to join in the general recriminations on Stalinist inefficiency. The actual German experience indicated a far greater involvement than is suggested, and even allowing for the lower standard of technical training among Russian tank crews, the idea of three out of every four vehicles being off the road in a peacetime situation, with every opportunity for maintenance, is not one that is easily digestible.

Barbarossa should have begun earlier than it did, but Hitler felt compelled to remove all potentially hostile threats to his southern flank. In Albania the Italians were still suffering defeat at the hands of the Greeks, who were now receiving active British assistance, and would have to be rescued from the embarrassing predicament in which they found themselves. Planning for this was well in hand under the codename *Marita* when on 26th March an anti-Nazi coup took place in Yugoslavia, altering the whole political complexion of the Balkans.

Hitler was furious and gave instructions that the new regime was to be crushed "with merciless brutality". Like the well-oiled machine that it was, OKW smoothly and in a remarkably short space of time laid the groundwork for the deliberately named Operation *Punishment*, and on 6th April the whole apparatus of *Blitzkrieg* was hurled at the ill-equipped Yugoslav Army, already torn by political and racial schisms, while simultaneously Greece was invaded from Bulgaria. On 17th April the Yugoslav government capitulated and the Greek armies in Albania were isolated, surrendering three days later. The British troops holding the line at Thermopylae suddenly found their left flank hanging in the air and were forced to evacuate the country. On 24th April Greece surrendered.

The outcome of these operations was never in doubt and they added little to what was already known of the *Blitzkrieg* phenomenon, although they were remarkable for the determination of the panzer crews in forcing their vehicles through some of the wildest and most difficult mountain country in Europe. Whether they were strictly necessary is another matter, for neither Yugoslavia nor Greece had the potential to pose a serious threat to *Barbarossa*, and the situation in Albania could have been controlled by the despatch of German reinforcements, in much the same manner as the Afrika Korps was sent to assist the Italians in Tripolitania. However, they did have the effect of postponing by five weeks the start of the invasion of Russia, and since OKW had allowed only nineteen weeks for the establishment of the Archangel – Volga line, with no margin for error, *Barbarossa* had already suffered its first serious dislocation.

At midnight on 21st June the armies of Germany and her allies were disposed as follows:

On the right flank and with an operational front stretching from the Black Sea to a point level with the Pripet Marshes was von Rundstedt's Army Group South, led by von Kleist's *Panzergruppe* I and consisting of three German and two Rumanian armies, and a Hungarian corps.

In the centre, where the principal thrust was to be made, was von Bock's Army Group Centre, with two armies and two *Panzergruppen* (IInd and IIIrd, commanded respectively by Guderian and Hoth) at its disposal.

In East Prussia was von Leeb's Army Group North, also with two armies, and Hoepner's *Panzergruppe* IV.

This produced a total of 133 divisions, of which seventeen were armoured, with a further twenty infantry and two panzer divisions in reserve.[44]

In immediate opposition were 132 Russian divisions, of which thirty-four were armoured, organised in four military districts, which would become Fronts as soon as hostilities began.[45] In reserve were the apparently limitless resources of the largest army in the world. However, the Germans received an unexpected bonus in that although Soviet Intelligence had provided ample warning of the Wehrmacht's preparations and intentions, Stalin absolutely forbade any move to reinforce his troops along the frontier on the grounds that it might be construed as provocation; even movement of forward supply and ammunition dumps, which it was known would lie directly in the path of the German assault, was strictly prohibited.

When the storm broke, therefore, neither the Red Army nor the Red Air Force were prepared physically or psychologically for it. During the first day 1,489 aircraft were destroyed on the ground by the Luftwaffe, and 322 shot out of the sky. Within a week the Russian loss had soared to 4,990 machines at a trivial cost of only 179 German aircraft, and the Luftwaffe was able to give its entire support to the slender tank spearheads pushing on ever eastwards.

Never had German tanks and aircraft worked so closely together. The ground controllers now rode in their own tanks well up with the leading vehicles, ready to bring down their flying artillery onto stubborn knots of resistance, while pilots provided ample warning of any developing Russian counter-thrust. Meanwhile the medium bombers continued to pound enemy communications, concentrations and reinforcement columns.

Once it had overcome its initial shock the Red Army began a series of local counter-attacks. These were poorly co-ordinated at the higher levels, while on the ground the Russian tanks frequently advanced too far ahead of their infantry support and either drove into well-laid anti-tank gun ambushes or were roughly handled and brushed aside by the infinitely more manoeuvrable panzer divisions. The survivors of these encounters often found themselves bereft of their supply echelons, which had been destroyed by enemy air action, and were forced to abandon their vehicles for want of fuel. Breakdowns, too, took their toll, particularly among the large multi-turreted but mechanically sensitive T35s, dismissed contemptuously by the panzer crews as *Kinderschrecke*,[46] very few of which came into action. Soon western Russia was dotted with the funeral pyres and abandoned carcasses of hundreds of BTs, T26s and T28s, which had striven bravely but ineffectively to stem the tide.

For the Germans, Russia was full of surprises. First, the endless landscape that rolled on and on, changing little but closing round them and seeming to swallow them in its immensity. Then, with the exception of the Moscow – Warsaw highway, the almost complete lack of metalled roads and the realisation that the country's network consisted of good-weather earthen tracks. Next, the warm welcome they were accorded as liberators by the people of the Ukraine and Belorussia, tired of living under the rule of an avuncular mass-murderer and his local Party tyrants, unexpected goodwill soon to be squandered and turned to hatred by the sadistic cruelties of the SS *Einsatzgruppe*. For the generals, mounting operations against the enemy's lines of communication, came the startling discovery that with the exception of the armoured formations, about one quarter of the whole, these barely existed in the western sense since the Russian soldier could virtually live off the land; but without doubt the unpleasantest surprises of all were the KV and T34, since it had never been considered possible that the despised Soviets could actually be ahead in the field of tank technology.

When confronted by either tank the panzer crews found themselves in a situation where they could be destroyed at a range at which they could not hit back.[47] Both vehicles could shrug off the impact of the German 50-mm tank guns, and the infantry's 37-mm anti-tank gun was so useless that the troops called it the Door Knocker. The 88-mm dual purpose gun could, of course, deal killing blows at long range, and medium artillery could act as a deterrent, but in closer combat only explosive charges placed under the turret overhang, or a point-blank shot into the rear of the engine compartment, would knock out either tank. The T34 in particular, however ineptly handled, upset the morale of the *Panzerwaffe*, and was described as a wonder weapon, which should immediately be copied by the German tank industry. Naturally, this would have entailed enormous loss of prestige, but a more practical difficulty lay in copying the aluminium diesel engine; Germany's ultimate answer would be the PzKw V Panther, but this vehicle would not be available for two years, and then be plagued in its early service by numerous mechanical problems.

Alarming though the checks imposed by the KVs and T34s might have been, they were only temporary. On 27th June, 200 miles after crossing their start lines, the spearheads of Guderian's and Hoth's *Panzergruppen* swung inwards to meet east of Minsk, effectively surrounding the Soviet West Front in two pockets, one at Minsk itself, and another further west at Bialystok. As the German infantry arrived these were squeezed to destruction and eventually surrendered on 3rd July, yielding 290,000 prisoners, 2,585 tanks and 1,449 guns. The Front commander, Pavlov, was regarded as something of an expert in armoured warfare since he had commanded the Red Army's tanks during the Spanish Civil War; having avoided personal encirclement, he was summoned sharply to Moscow by Stalin, and shot.

This traditional communist remedy cured nothing, although the Front's new commander, Marshal Semen Timoshenko, was more cautious about pushing reinforcements forward into potential German traps, and concentrated on establishing a defence line based on the Dniepr River, behind which reserves could concentrate for a possible counter-blow. He was too late, for Army Group Centre's *Panzergruppen* were on the move again.

Guderian and Hoth were technically under the command of Field Marshal Gunther von Kluge of 4th Army, who was somewhat more traditional in his outlook than the two thrusting panzer leaders. Kluge wished the advance to continue at a more measured pace, but his orders were mysteriously side-tracked or overtaken by events. Suspecting some form of conspiracy, the Field Marshal threatened Court Martial proceedings, but both men managed to talk their way out and still have a good deal of their own way. By 7th July they were a fortnight ahead of 4th Army's infantry and were preparing to cross the Dniepr. Kluge, angry and alarmed, arrived at Guderian's headquarters to be told that preparations were too far advanced to be cancelled and that the operation "would decide the Russian campaign in this very year, if such a decision was at all possible". Reluctantly, Kluge gave his permission to proceed, commenting to Guderian that "Your operations always hang by a thread." By 11th July the panzers were across the river and the so-called Stalin Line had been broken with little loss.

Five days later, Hoth and Guderian joined hands at Smolensk to form another huge pocket. Timoshenko, now desperate, launched a relief operation, but his counter-attack was broken up without difficulty and the ring of steel around the trapped Russians resisted all attempts to break out. On 8th August the pocket surrendered and 185,000 men marched into captivity, leaving behind 2,030 of their tanks and 1,918 guns.

Army Group Centre's tanks had now advanced more than 400 miles, and although the losses incurred had been 50 per cent higher than in previous campaigns, the road to Moscow was now virtually open and the weather remained good. A chance of victory definitely existed, but at this point Hitler took a hand.

During the planning phase the whole scenario of *Barbarossa* had been played out in an elaborate series of war games under the direction of General von Paulus, later to achieve unhappy fame at Stalingrad. The war games had predicted, accurately, that at this phase Army Groups North and South would request armoured assistance from Army Group Centre to achieve their own objectives. The Directing Staff's recommendation had been that these requests should be ignored and that the whole of Army Group Centre's weight should continue to be directed at Moscow, the centre of the Soviet administrative machine and the hub of the railway system upon which so much of the Russian war effort depended. The capture of Moscow would paralyse the nervous system of Communist Russia, while any delay on the central sector would work to the Russians' advantage and permit them to strengthen the capital's defences.

Hitler chose to disregard these recommendations. He wanted the industrial wealth of the Ukraine and the political prize of Leningrad *as well as* success in the centre. On 19th July, he issued Operational Directive No 33, the principal effect of which was to break up the team of Hoth and Guderian, the former being sent north to sever communications between Moscow and Leningrad, and the latter south to assist in sealing off a pocket that was forming near Kiev. Both Brauchitsch, the Commander-in-Chief, and Halder, his Chief of Staff, protested strongly and even went so far as to put their objections in writing, but to no avail. Hitler had decided, and from that moment the German Army ceased to be governed by reasoned professional considerations; its actions henceforth would be controlled almost exclusively by a diseased mind.

It did not seem so at first. On 16th September Guderian's tanks met von Kleist's, coming up from the south, at Lokhvitsa, a village 100 miles east of Kiev, and the pocket was closed. It is quite probable that if they had acted immediately the Russians could have broken out, for the additional track mileage had severely weakened Guderian's Panzergruppe and one of his divisions could muster only ten fit tanks. However, STAVKA had played into German hands by ordering that Kiev should be held at all costs, and by the time the encircled troops realised their terrible danger the moment had passed. The commander of South-West Front and his staff died while leading one of a number of frenzied attacks against the walls of the pocket, but by 26th September it was all over.

Russian losses dwarfed anything that had gone before and included 665,000 prisoners, 900 tanks and 3,719 guns. For the ordinary German soldier at the Front and for the private citizen at home there seemed to be every cause for rejoicing and men began to wonder how much longer the Red Army could absorb such hammer blows. Such general enthusiasm was not shared at the highest professional levels. Halder, who regarded the Kiev diversion as "the greatest blunder of the eastern campaign", was already aware that the Red Army's capacity for punishment was apparently infinite; his original estimates for the campaign had allowed for 200 divisions, but by mid-August alone 360 divisions had been identified and fresh formations were arriving all the time.

Hitler, well satisfied with the result of his strategy in the Ukraine, was balked at the northern end of the line by the obstinate defence of Leningrad, and decided that the city should be closely invested and systematically destroyed by heavy artillery and bombing. He was now convinced that operations against Moscow held absolute priority and insisted that they should recommence at the earliest possible moment.

The plan for the capture of the capital was codenamed *Typhoon* and required a further redistribution of the four *Panzergruppen*. Kleist would remain with Army Group South while Guderian retraced his steps and moved into position on the right of Army Group Centre; Hoepner and Hoth also joined Army Group Centre, the former in the middle of the line and the latter on its left wing. The last reserves of tanks were distributed, bringing the strength of the panzer divisions to something like a workable level again.

Timoshenko had done what he could to salvage the wreck of his armies and form a fresh defence line, but his troops were not of the same quality as the regulars who had been destroyed in the battles to the west and when *Typhoon* opened along a 300-mile front on 30th September the panzer spearheads experienced no difficulty in breaking right through and out into the country beyond.

Once again, the pincers closed shut behind the lines, Guderian and Kluge meeting at Briansk, and Hoepner and Hoth at Viazma further north. By the time the twin pockets formed were eliminated on 20th October a further 663,000 Russians had been taken prisoner, 1,242 tanks captured together with 5,412 guns, and Guderian and Hoth had already moved off, as they hoped, to encircle Moscow in a huge double envelopment. The campaign of 1941 was approaching its high-water mark.

A Tsar once remarked that two of the best generals in his army were named January and February. If he had lived to see the era of mechanised war, he might have commented that October and March were pretty impressive fellows too, for in October the first torrential winter rains reduced the roads to bottomless quagmires, while the spring thaw had precisely the same effect. Wheeled vehicles sank above their axles, tracked to their belly plates, and movement of any kind became a virtual impossibility. Where it still existed, tanks towed lines of lorries, further straining their already worn engines and transmissions.

In such circumstances, Hoth and Guderian crawled painfully forward, short of petrol, of vehicle spares, of food even, leaving a trail of broken-down vehicles along the roads. By 14th November, Guderian had only fifty tanks left out of the 600 with which he had begun *Barbarossa*, and none of the other *Panzergruppen* were in much better shape. Understandably, orders from the Fuhrer to seize particular objectives with "fast-moving" units were greeted with jeers of derision, since they bore no relation to the reality of the situation.

With the first frosts the ground hardened and movement was resumed for a while, but the damage had been done; the panzer divisions were now too weak to break through the stiffening opposition. As blizzards that were born in the heartland of Asia started to howl across the landscape, the mercury in thermometers continued to plunge well below zero, men died of exposure or suffered extreme frostbite, since many were still wearing the cotton denims in which they had begun the campaign, and no winter clothing was available. At temperatures that were well below the average German's experience, nature began playing cruel tricks on the panzer crews; metal became brittle and track-pins snapped without warning, fuel froze, oil turned to treacle, and ammunition refused to fire. The only way an engine could be kept operational overnight was by keeping a slow fire under its sump and starting it at least twice and hour, as no anti-freeze was available for the coolant systems.

Guderian eventually reached Vanev and Hoth Dmitrov, and there their advance ended. Immediately they were faced with fierce counterattacks mounted by the newly arrived regular Siberian divisions, composed of tough men of largely Tartar stock who seemed unaffected by the cold but who were in any case clothed and equipped for it. All along the front the story was the same.

The German Army was used to easy victories, and now it suddenly found itself flung onto the defensive in the most appalling conditions. In some cases, commanders had withdrawals forced on them, in others morale came dangerously close to cracking. Brauchitsch, recognising the danger signals, recommended a general withdrawal of ninety miles and was instantly dismissed by Hitler, who assumed his post personally and absolutely forbade any retreat whatever.

The Germans survived the terrible winter by retiring into the shelter of towns and villages, letting the Russian counter-offensive roll past until its potential had been dissipated. Several garrisons that had been cut off were supplied from the air by the Luftwaffe. Later, Hitler would boast that it was his No Withdrawal order that saved the Wehrmacht, and indeed would repeat the same order many times in totally inappropriate circumstances on the strength of this imagined success. In reality the German tactics were largely dictated by the need for self-preservation.

Blitzkrieg had failed and naturally recriminations followed. Two of the original Army Group Commanders, Rundstedt and Leeb, were sacked. Bock of Army Group Centre went on sick leave in the nick of time and was replaced by Kluge, who promptly accused Guderian of a premature withdrawal. Inevitably, Guderian argued and an acrimonious exchange took place; Kluge had him removed from his command and for the next fourteen months Germany was denied the services of her most brilliant panzer leader. Hoepner was also dismissed, as were a large number of corps and divisional commanders. Everyone was to blame but the Fuhrer himself.

The principal reasons for the failure can be summarised as follows. The Balkan campaigns dangerously reduced the time available for the completion of *Barbarossa* before the close of the campaigning season. This in itself was not fatal, but it left no margin for error. A gross error of judgement *was* committed following Smolensk in failing to maintain pressure along the Moscow axis; this not only absorbed what good weather remained but also added to the severe wear and tear already sustained by the tanks after several hundred miles running. The rate at which mechanical attrition would erode the panzer divisions' strength on a 600-mile run had been badly underestimated, and the centralised German repair organisation was unable to cope with the demands made upon it in view of the ever-widening distances between the workshops and the front. Again, the logistic burden was latterly insupportable for the same reasons and supply echelons were in any case becoming subject to ever-increasing attacks by partisan groups formed by Russian soldiers left behind in the retreat.

Five months fighting had cost the Wehrmacht 742,000 men killed, wounded or missing and, for the moment, the *Panzerwaffe* had been run into the ground. More significantly, *Barbarossa* had destroyed the German Army's confidence in its own ability to secure lightning victories, and it never quite recovered the old *elan* with which it had begun the campaign.

True, the Red Army had been terribly mauled, losing 2,500,000 men, 18,000 tanks and a comparable number of aircraft; but it was not enough. The chance of victory had gone. It was going to be a very long and bloody war, and beyond the Urals the Russian armaments industry, moved to safety lock, stock and barrel as soon as the invasion had begun, was starting to turn out fighting machines in numbers that Germany could never hope to equal. At sea, too, convoys were on their way to Murmansk and Archangel from Britain, America and Canada, bringing tanks, guns and aircraft that would make good much of Russia's apparently catastrophic losses.

Like the Chinese sentry of old, Hitler had caught a Tartar; the question was, what to do with him.

Chapter 6: Kaukasus – Hin und Zuruck!

It is strange to reflect that one of the major contributory causes of the destruction of the Third Reich was the very professionalism, patriotism and sense of personal honour of the German Officer Corps. In Germany, the Army had traditionally kept itself apart from politics and regarded itself as the shield and servant of the State, to whom it swore allegiance. The soldier's oath was solemnly binding upon those who took it, but in the case of Nazi Germany the Army as a whole swore loyalty to a single individual, Adolf Hitler, the Fuhrer, the embodiment of the State *in personam*. That this departed from the accepted practice was, in the opinion of many officers, disturbing, but the fact that they had accepted it at all bound them as honourable men to its strict observance.

But by 1942 some were beginning to question whether the values of a more gentlemanly age bore any relation to present circumstances, for Hitler was clearly exhibiting signs of the madness that many now believe to be the final symptoms of tertiary syphilis. This was particularly apparent to those who, in the nature of their duties, were forced to present him with unpalatable facts. Halder, Chief of General Staff, recalled that in the spring of 1942 an officer attempted to provide the Fuhrer with an accurate intelligence assessment of Russian strength, commenting that the Red Army had available approximately one-and-three-quarter million front line troops, and that Soviet factories were turning out some 1,200 tanks per month, well in excess of the German output. In a paroxysm of rage, Hitler all but physically attacked the unfortunate man with clenched fists and, literally foaming at the mouth, screamed that he would not tolerate further discussion based on such idiocy; the truth did not happen to coincide with his "unalterable will", therefore it did not exist.

Hitler was fond of commenting that his generals had no understanding of the economic aspects of war, although in fact it had been Halder himself who had pointed out as early as November 1941 that possession of the Caucasian oilfields as far south as Baku would not only provide the Reich with all the oil she needed, but also deal the Soviet war effort a probably mortal blow. The truth of this was sufficiently evident for it to become the principal element of the German master plan for 1942, as set out in Fuhrer Directive No 41, issued on 5th April.

"Our aim is to wipe out the entire defence potential remaining to the Soviets, and to cut them off, as far as possible, from their most important centres of war industry...

"First, therefore, all available forces will be concentrated on the main operations in the Southern sector, with the aim of destroying the enemy before the Don, in order to secure the Caucasian oilfields and the passes through the Caucasus Mountains themselves."

From the outset it was appreciated that lying on the left flank of this very deep penetration would be the city of Stalingrad, sprawling along several miles of the west bank of the Volga, and of this the Directive had this to say: "In any event, every effort will be made to reach Stalingrad itself, or at least to bring the city under fire from heavy artillery so that it may no longer be of any use as an industrial or communications centre."[48]

Thus, while the directive is open to interpretation in that it is unclear whether the primary objective was the destruction of the Russian armies west of the Don, *or* the seizure of the Caucasus oil, there can be no doubt whatever that Stalingrad itself was of secondary importance and could, if necessary, simply be screened off from the main operational zone.

On the Russian side of the hill, planning was also taking place for the coming campaign season. The movement of the heavy armaments industry to the Urals and beyond was beginning to pay dividends and T34s were rolling off the assembly lines at an ever-increasing rate, offsetting the disastrous losses of the previous year. Aircraft, too, were being manufactured at a rate that exceeded the German capacity, with heavy emphasis on the Yakolev single-seater fighter, which had a top speed of 373 m.p.h. and was armed with one 20-mm cannon and two 7.62-mm machine-guns, and the Ilyushin Stormovik ground-attack aircraft, which could carry a variety of weapons including armour-piercing, fragmentation and high explosive bombs, twin 20mm cannon and two 7.62-mm machine-guns, and under-wing rockets.

The Red Army had reorganised its armour into brigade-sized battlegroups, each made up of three twenty-three-tank battalions, a motor rifle battalion and an artillery element. These, it was felt, were more easily controlled than the older formations and would enable their commanders to give a better account of themselves. Even so, several senior officers were only too well aware that unit for unit, the new formations were no match for German initiative, tactical expertise and flexibility, and proposed that during 1942 the army would be best employed in gaining experience by conducting an aggressive defence along the front.

Stalin would have none of it. He was aware of the German preparations and he intended to disrupt these with a spoiling offensive; specifically, he wanted a prestige victory, and that meant the capture of Kharkov. The city would be isolated by a pincer movement carried out by Marshal Semen Timoshenko's South-West Front, which would employ fourteen armoured brigades, twenty-three infantry and eighteen cavalry divisions. The offensive opened on 12th May, breaking through the defensive crust, and for a while Russian hopes soared. Then, on 17th May, von Kleist's 1st Panzer Army and Hoth's 17th Army launched a concentrated counter-offensive against the southern flank of the salient that had been formed, penetrating no less than twenty-five miles on the first day. Timoshenko, anxious for the safety of his armoured spearheads and with no reserves in hand, requested permission to withdraw. Stalin, whose rejection of unpleasant facts could be every bit as purblind as Hitler's, bluntly refused. Within a week a substantial portion of South West Front had been surrounded and all but destroyed with the loss of 250,000 men taken prisoner, 1,200 tanks and 2,000 guns. Once more, German superiority in skill-at-arms had been manifestly demonstrated, while to add to the depression at STAVKA, the Crimea was being steadily cleared by von Manstein's 11th Army. At OKW, the planners had barely paused from their work on *Plan Blue*, the codename given to the great German offensive.

As if to emphasise the ambivalence of the whole strategic concept, Army Group South was divided into two operational halves with, on the right, Army Group A (1st Panzer Army and Ruoff's 17th Army) commanded by Field Marshal List and, on the left, Army Group B (4th Panzer Army[49] and von Paulus' 6th Army) commanded by Field Marshal Fedor von Bock, with 11th Army held in strategic reserve. Including troops from the Axis satellite armies, a total of eighty-nine divisions were available, of which nine were armoured.

Army Group B made the first move on 28th June, 4th Panzer Army driving hard for Voronezh on the Don, closely followed by 6th Army on its right. The intention was that having secured Voronezh, the Army Group would wheel south and effect a junction with Army Group A, which would advance eastwards from Kharkov, so trapping and annihilating the remains of South-West Front. At first Russian resistance was fierce but unco-ordinated and easily dealt with, for the Luftwaffe provided ample early warning of the approach of Soviet armoured formations and the T34s, after driving into carefully laid anti-tank gun-killing grounds, were destroyed by attacks on their flanks and rear by the flexible *Panzergruppen*.

Soon, however, opposition had all but disappeared and once more the German columns rolled across the empty steppe. Superficially, all was as it should be; the Russian line had been broken and the whole apparatus of *Blitzkrieg* was in top gear, the tanks of the leading battalions covering mile after mile under a glorious summer sun, followed by the half-tracks of the panzer grenadiers, the self-propelled anti-tank guns, the *Panzerartillerie* and the long divisional service convoys, while overhead roared the fighter and dive-bomber squadrons of the Luftwaffe. Hitler, delighted at the flow of good news from the Front, commented to Halder that the Russians were beaten, and even the clinical Chief of General Staff could only reply that on the basis of the evidence available, it rather looked that way. Tactical pockets were formed, but they yielded surprisingly few prisoners; this in itself might have provided food for thought, but there was general agreement that the unyielding tenacity shown by the Red Army during the previous year's battles was definitely lacking.

There was, of course, a good reason for this, and one that OKW should have suspected. On June 19th a staff officer of 40th Panzer Corps had taken off on a routine reconnaissance flight, foolishly carrying with him certain operational orders for the forthcoming offensive. He was shot down over Russian territory and his papers revealed the plan for the encirclement of South-West Front. That this was within the German capacity to achieve was beyond doubt, and STAVKA had withdrawn the Front across the Don, leaving only covering troops to the west. As to wider issues, Stalin was puzzled. The mention of Voronezh in the plans implied two possibilities; either, a wheel to the left with Moscow as its objective, or, as Fuller suggests,[50] a continued advance to the east, severing strategically vital rail communications with the Caspian and Caucasia. In any event, he retained strong forces north of Voronezh to deal with either eventuality.

It must have been with some surprise, therefore, that he noted the German armies' concerted drive to the south-east and into the great Don Bend. On the left and closest to the river was 4th Panzer Army; in the centre, 6th Army; on the right, 1st Panzer Army; and on the coast, 17th Army. And at this point, with everything apparently going well, Hitler took a number of decisions that were to destroy any chances of success that his master plan might have had.

First, and perhaps least important, von Bock was summarily dismissed for allegedly attaching too much importance to the Voronezh phase of the operation, and replaced by General

Freiherr von Weichs, the commander of 2nd Army. Then the strategic reserve, von Manstein's 11th Army, was withdrawn *in toto* and sent north to take part in the fighting around Leningrad. Next, on 17th July, Hitler decided that von Kleist's 1st Panzer Army was not strong enough to secure the Don Crossings it needed to continue its advance towards the Caucasus, and that the major part of Hoth's 4th Panzer Army should be sent south to help. This not merely had the effect of reducing Army Group B to a single army, the 6th, with which to continue its advance on Stalingrad, but also that that army's communications were thrown into confusion while Hoth moved across its rear. Moreover, Kleist was having so little difficulty in crossing the Don that many of his men found time to swim and sunbathe; in fact, at that particular moment, Hoth, with his thousands of vehicles, was just about the last person Kleist wanted to see, since his arrival meant that neither Panzer Army could be properly supplied. Having thus created a situation of unutterable chaos by his own orders, Hitler then flew into a hysterical rage, raving at the General Staff for its incompetence.

Meanwhile, short of fuel and ammunition and bereft of its armoured support, 6th Army pressed on alone towards Stalingrad, meeting stiffening opposition and finally being halted at Kalach. By now, Stalin had decided that the city should be defended, not simply as a bridgehead on the west bank of the Volga, but also because he had played some part in its defence during the Civil War,[51] and Hitler's meddling had provided just sufficient time for a strong garrison under Lieutenant-General Vasili Chuykov to move into position. The irony was that had not 4th Panzer Army been transferred to Army Group A in mid-July, it could have motored into Stalingrad without difficulty.

As if to compound his previous lunacies, Hitler announced on 30th July that Stalingrad was *the* primary objective, and that the success of the Caucasus campaign hinged on its capture. This was a far cry from the screening operation discussed in the original plans, and was described by Halder as "the rankest nonsense", his professional anger being further vented into the pages of his diary:

"This 'leadership', so called, is characterised by a pathological reacting to the impressions of the moment and a total lack of any understanding of the command machinery and its possibilities (i.e. Hitler is incapable of grasping that his constant interference is throwing everything in disorder)."

Hitler had sought to destroy his enemy by paralysing his economic nervous system, which, in terms of *Blitzkrieg*, was as acceptable as the disruption of his command structure. Now, for no clear reason, he sought a prestige objective as well, and he proposed to divide his resources between the two to the detriment of both. It was a rejection of such elementary rules that no officer cadet would have dared submit such a paper for his superiors' serious consideration.

By 1st August the tangle north of Rostov had been sorted out sufficiently for 1st Panzer and 17th Armies to have begun their journey into the Caucasus, and for 4th Panzer Army to advance north-east on Stalingrad, rejoining Army Group B. Hoth was halted by determined resistance, but his presence took some of the pressure off von Paulus, and 6th Army began to close in on the city.

After its experience at Verdun the German Army knew better than most the sterility of pursuing prestige objectives. But the German General Staff was not controlling the situation; Hitler was, and when Chuykov's men began contesting every battered yard of rubble, such a denial of his monstrous will was too much to be borne. He wanted Stalingrad because he could not have it, and his lust for possession soon obscured every other issue. Part of 4th Panzer Army was committed to the struggle, the tanks being thrown into the maelstrom of street fighting for which, by their very nature, they were unsuitable. By mid-September it was clear that Stalingrad was not going to fall save at an inordinate cost in blood, and Halder urged disengagement; the courage of his convictions cost him his appointment, and no doubt he was glad to leave.

In the meantime Army Group A was deep inside Caucasia, and on 9th August had taken the Maikop oilfields. But thereafter progress declined steadily, not because the Germans were having to fight for ground, but because the lion's share of their fuel was being diverted to Stalingrad. The original objective, Baku, had been barely attainable mechanically; now Hitler's mania ensured that it was quite unattainable logistically. Kleist later recalled that his panzer divisions were sometimes halted for weeks at a time, bereft of fuel even for their own supply lorries, and that in some cases petrol had to be brought forward by camel train.

Furious at this deceleration, Hitler sacked the innocent List, whom he had deliberately staved of supplies, and replaced him with Kleist, 1st Panzer Army being taken over by General Eberhard von Mackensen. Army Group A struggled on, its *Schwerpunkt* becoming progressively weaker, but eventually reached Mozdok on the River Terek and scaled the 18,500 feet peak of Mount Elbruz in the heart of the Caucasus Mountains. Symbolically, this proved to be the summit of its achievement, for Baku still lay more than 200 miles distant, and it lacked the ability to proceed further.

These operations had stretched the Eastern Front to a length of 2,000 miles, and by October it was obvious even to Hitler that there was a limit to the potential of Germany and her Allies. He instructed all sectors to go over to the defensive while preparations were made for the final storming of Stalingrad. That the Russians might have been working on plans of their own does not seem to have concerned him, so great was his contempt for the Slavonic *Untermensch*.

These plans had been drawn up under the codename *Uranus* by the Red Army's Deputy Commander-in-Chief, Marshal Grigori Zhukov, and his Chief of Staff, Colonel-General A.M. Vasilevsky. Zhukov, considered by many to be the ablest Russian commander of World War II, was Stalin's favourite trouble-shooter, and had already acquired sufficient stature by restoring critical situations on the Moscow and Leningrad sectors to be able to argue publicly with the dictator and get his own way.

Zhukov was quick to realise that the German fixation on Stalingrad could be turned to advantage. In 1941 it had been the Russians who had fought in static pockets and been overwhelmed after they had been isolated by fast-moving panzer thrusts; now the Germans had placed themselves in a similar position by concentrating so much of their strength against the embattled city, and von Paulus was vulnerable to moves against his flanks, which could ultimately lead to a concentric double envelopment. Such manoeuvres would be unlikely to succeed if applied directly to the tough, battle-hardened 6th Army, but this was not Zhukov's intention; instead, he would adopt the indirect approach, launching twin drives through von Paulus' neighbours and closing the jaws of the trap as rapidly as possible behind 6th Army. Operation *Uranus* would, in fact, involve no less than 250 miles of front, one million men, 900 tanks, 14,000 guns and 1,100 aircraft. In overall terms, this gave the Red Army only a slight superiority, but at the vital points of contact it was deployed in overwhelming strength.

A further factor tilted the scales in Zhukov's favour; Paulus was unlucky in his immediate neighbours. On his right was 4th Rumanian Army, and on his left 3rd Rumanian Army, whose line was continued by 8th Italian Army. Like all Axis satellite armies, these formations were under-equipped, indifferently motivated and regarded by the Wehrmacht as poor relations.

At 0730 on 19th November the 3rd Rumanian Army was subjected to the fire of 3,500 guns and suddenly overwhelmed by the concentrated onslaught of Lieutenant-General N.F. Vatutin's South-West Front. The Rumanian command structure collapsed as various headquarters were overrun, and by nightfall the T34s were running unopposed across open country.

On 20th November, before OKW had fully digested the events of the previous 24 hours, Colonel-General A.I. Yeremenko's Stalingrad Front smashed its way through 4th Rumanian Army. Three days later it effected a junction with Vatutin's troops near Kalach and the 330,000 men under Paulus' command were completely surrounded.

At this stage it is more than probable that Paulus could have fought his way out, but Hitler forbade him to do so. First, there was the all-consuming matter of prestige but, for once, there were also cogent military reasons, for by conducting a resolute defence Paulus would not only gain time for a relief effort to be mounted, but also tie down the major Russian striking force that would otherwise fall on the rear of Army Group A, which was itself beginning to come under pressure in the Caucasus.

Expressed as an equation in unpalatable military economics, the cost of Army Group A's survival was the sacrifice of 6th Army, although it did not look that way at the time. Paulus indicated that he needed 500 tons of supplies a day, and Goering promised to deliver them by air; had the Reichsmarschall consulted his own staff he would have been told that the Luftwaffe's total lift capacity was only 300 tons, without making allowance for poor weather and enemy air activity. Nonetheless, Hitler chose to accept yet another braggart affirmation from the man whose promises had been shown to be hollow in the skies over Dunkirk and southern England, and with disastrous consequences for Paulus, for the average daily total actually delivered within 6th Army's perimeter was only 100 tons, and that at a cost of 246 priceless transport aircraft.

To restore the situation on the ground, Hitler sent for the one officer whose strategic insight had never failed and in whose presence he felt at a disadvantage – Field Marshal von Manstein. Of their relationship, Guderian later wrote, "What a pity it was that Hitler could not tolerate the presence of so capable and soldierly a person as Manstein in his environment. Their characters were too opposed; on the one hand Hitler, with his great will-power and his fertile imagination: on the other Manstein, a man of most distinguished military talents, a product of the German General Staff Corps, with a sensible, cool understanding, who was our finest operational brain. Later, when I was entrusted with the duties of Chief of the Army General Staff, I frequently proposed to Hitler that Manstein be appointed chief of the OKW in place of Keitel, but always in vain. It is true that Keitel made life easy for Hitler … Manstein was not so comfortable a man to deal with; he formed his own opinions and spoke them aloud."[52]

In his book *Panzer Battles* Major-General F.W. von Mellenthin goes even further, and suggests that had Manstein held the supreme command in 1942 the Red Army could have been bled into a state of impotence, and that at worst the Eastern Front would have lapsed into strategic stalemate.

But not even a Manstein could make bricks without straw. A new formation, Army Group Don, was created for him, giving him, in theory at least, operational control over 4th Panzer Army, 6th Army and what remained of the Rumanians. His first priority was given as the relief of Paulus, and on 12th December he began to push 4th Panzer Army along the line of Kotelnikovo – Stalingrad railway. By the 21st he was within thirty miles of the trapped army and urged Paulus to break out and join him. Paulus declined, saying that he only had sufficient petrol for twenty miles, although his senior commanders' advice was that the junction could be affected by abandoning all but the fighting vehicles and cutting his way through the Russian mass with his infantry; the real reason was that he had received a specific Fuhrer Directive to stand fast, and was not prepared to act contrary to this without Hitler's personal approval.

Manstein can hardly have been surprised, for on his way to take up his new appointment he had been told by von Kluge of Army Group Centre that he would not be permitted to move so much as a single battalion on his own initiative. He was forced to fall back and concentrate all his energies on holding open a corridor through which Army Group A could be extricated from the Caucasus.

Within Army Group A few of the troops could have guessed at the scale of bungling that had ruined the campaign, or the price at which their own safety was being bought. As the tanks drove onto their railway flats for the journey north and the infantry shrugged into their marching packs the wits coined a phrase: "Kaukasus, hin und zuruck!" For all the good they had done in Caucasia, they might just as well have been given return tickets at the outset.

The details of 6th Army's agonised death struggle are too well known to require repetition. On 2nd February the newly promoted Field Marshal von Paulus capitulated; of the 200,000 Germans present with him in Stalingrad at that moment, only a tiny handful saw Germany again. Zhukov had given the Red Army its first true *Blitzkrieg* victory, and if the kill had been neither quick nor clean, at least the technique was recognisable.

Hitler did not seek to minimise the scale of the catastrophe and declared four days official mourning. Elsewhere, there had been other disasters, too; in Egypt the Afrika Korps had been virtually destroyed in the attritional Battle of Alamein, while the landings of the Anglo-America 1st Army in Morocco and Algeria spelled the end of Axis ambitions in the Mediterranean.

Even before the curtain had finally fallen on the nightmare of Stalingrad, the events of 1942 had convinced the majority of the German Army's most senior officers that they could no longer consider themselves bound by an oath given by a madman. Throughout January the Field Marshals discussed whether Hitler should be assassinated or simply deprived of his military powers, and an approach was made through neutral Sweden requesting details of the terms Great Britain and the United States would impose on a new government if Hitler was removed. The approach was made too late, for the Casablanca Conference was already in session and on 23rd January made public the principal war aim of the Allies – the unconditional surrender of Germany.

This put the whole question in an entirely different light, for ostensibly the Allies saw little difference between Germany and Nazism. The generals would fight for Germany out of patriotic duty if not out of loyalty to the Fuhrer, and the struggle would continue for a further two years with the loss of millions of lives. In the immediate vengeful post-war years the harsh accusation would be made that they fought to preserve their own privileged military caste, but to accept this is to deny that a general can also be a patriot and that a substantial group of very different individuals who had dedicated their entire lives to the service of the nation was universally devoted to the furtherance of its sole interest; an obvious contradiction in terms, since between March

1943 and the Bomb Plot of July 1944 no fewer than seven attempts on Hitler's life were planned.

A negotiated armistice in the spring of 1943 could probably have been achieved with the preservation of the major part of Germany's territorial integrity. By 1945 her generals' skill and professionalism had prolonged the conflict to such an extent that dismemberment was an inevitability.

Chapter 7: Kharkov and Kursk

The carefully planned and beautifully executed double envelopment of Stalingrad, together with the defeat of the German relief attempt, had given the Red Army a new-found confidence in its ability to wage a mechanised war in the manner of its enemies, and even before von Paulus surrendered his doomed 6th Army STAVKA was examining the possibilities of inflicting an even more shattering defeat on the Wehrmacht.

Once again, this would take the form of a double envelopment, designed to crush the German armies now scrambling out of the obvious trap of the Caucasus and streaming west through Rostov and Novocherkassk. The principal ingredient of the plan involved a huge left wheel to the Black Sea and Azov coasts by Vatutin's South-West Front, effectively isolating those German troops already engaged east of Rostov with South Front, commanded by Malinovsky. The right flank of the operation would be protected by the full commitment of Golikov's Voronezh Front.

It was a sound plan, which might have worked had it not been for several unavoidable factors. First, the mobile phase would have to be completed before the spring thaw, the arrival of which would curtail all movement for a while and so permit the Germans time to recover their balance. Secondly, Vatutin's and Golikov's troops, after several months of fighting, were already beginning to outrun their supplies and starting to suffer from the effects of mechanical attrition to such an extent that Zhukov doubted their ability to complete the task, although their replacement in the time available was out of the question and their involvement thus inevitable. And finally, Stalin, as Supreme War Lord, insisted that Kharkov, fourth largest city of the Soviet Union, should be liberated during the offensive, although such a course would indubitably open a gap between Vatutin and Golikov and so disperse the weight of the Russian effort at the very moment it should have been concentrated.

But when the offensive began on 13th January 1943 it seemed as though STAVKA's optimism was entirely justified. The blow fell once again on the poorly equipped, barely mobile and scantly motivated troops of the German satellite armies that were holding the line. Within days the 3rd Rumanian, 8th Italian and 2nd Hungarian Armies had been cut to ribbons and the Russians were pouring through a 200-mile gap in the front. Town after town was liberated, Voronezh on 26th January, Kursk on 8th February, and the great prize of Kharkov a week later. Soon Vatutin's tanks were within twenty-five miles of the great Dniepr bend, while Golikov was diverging into thin air beyond Kharkov.

Very few German units had been encountered and although droves of prisoners had been captured, the proportion of Germans taken remained consistently tiny. This in itself should have provided a warning that all was not quite as it seemed, but the by-now-jubilant Russians imagined that the Wehrmacht had accepted total defeat and was preparing to retire beyond the Dniepr, sacrificing its Allies in the process. The fact that Vatutin's tank spearheads had now been reduced by hard usage to a mere 145 vehicles, widely dispersed and for which fuel was all but unobtainable, was cause for concern but not alarm, as opposition throughout the long run had been negligible and would apparent remain so until the Dniepr was reached.

In reality both Vatutin and Golikov were chasing phantoms with armies that themselves of necessity grew progressively more skeletal the further they advanced. Their easy victories had led to a complete misunderstanding of German intentions, which involved not a withdrawal beyond the Dniepr but a concentrated counter-stroke, which would slice through the thin neck of the Russian advance, severing its head from its elongated body in the classic counter to the *Blitzkrieg* offensive. The genius behind the riposte was that of Field Marshal Erich von Manstein, author of the *Sichelschnitt* plan and Commander of Army Group South.

From the outset, Manstein had instinctively grasped that Vatutin would drive for the Dniepr Bend before swinging south to the coast, as the great river would provide immediate protection for his right. He also appreciated that by standing fast in the Rostov sector he was simply playing into STAVKA's hands, whereas a flank attack carried out by 1st and 4th Panzer Armies offered a real possibility of inflicting a sharp defeat on the Russians. However, to achieve the necessary concentration Rostov would have to be sacrificed and a new protective shoulder established some sixty miles to the west, along the line of the River Mius, behind which the panzers would move into their assembly areas. Such a move was directly contrary to Hitler's inevitable No Withdrawal order, but Manstein took the bold step of informing OKW that he intended to use his own discretion unless he received positive and precise orders to the contrary.

On 6th February the Fuhrer's personal aircraft arrived to convey him to Hitler's headquarters and the Field Marshal had every reason to suspect that he was being carpeted. To his surprise he found a thoroughly chastened Hitler who immediately accepted personal responsibility for the Stalingrad disaster, and who was for once prepared to listen to professional advice. In view of Manstein's reasoned assessment that the abandonment of Rostov could only benefit the German cause, he reluctantly sanctioned the withdrawal to the Mius although he emphasised that as a matter of principle he was totally opposed to the idea of giving up territory. Perhaps sniping at the Regular Army Establishment, he went on to say that the 2nd SS Panzer Corps was even then moving into the Kharkov area and would restore the stability of the Eastern Front.[53]

The SS Panzer Corps (1st SS Panzer Division *Leibstandarte Adolf Hitler*, 2nd SS Panzer Division *Das Reich*, 3rd SS Panzer Division *Totenkopf* and the crack Panzer Grenadier Division *Grossdeutschland*) was commanded by Obergruppenfuhrer Paul

Hausser who, like Manstein, had a mind of his own. In spite of Hitler's strict order that the defenders of Kharkov were to hold fast to the last man, Hausser had no intention of being caught in a second Stalingrad, and as Golikov's spearheads closed round the city on 15th February he gave the order to withdraw.

To Hitler this was not simply a matter of one general too many using his initiative – it was the ultimate disloyalty. On 17th February he flew with his staff to Manstein's HQ at Zaporozhe to find out what was going on in Army Group South. Manstein pointed out that as a result of the release of the SS Panzer Corps from defensive tasks it now formed a powerful addition to his own striking force, and that once his counter-offensive got under way the Russians would quickly discover that Kharkov was untenable. Slightly mollified, Hitler nonetheless demanded to know exactly how Manstein intended to use the considerable forces he had already assembled. Manstein explained that his offensive would begin when he was satisfied that Vatutin and Golikov had run themselves into the ground, and then take the following form:

Phase I. 2nd SS Panzer Corps and 48 Panzer Corps, operating under the control of 4th Panzer Army, were already assembling respectively at Krasnograd and Zaporozhe and would converge on Pavlograd, so cutting off the heads of Vatutin's columns. Further east, 40 and 57 Panzer Corps, under the command of 1st Panzer Army, would advance northwards into the Russian flank, driving South-West Front back across the River Donets.

Phase II. Both Panzer Armies would then roll up the flank of Voronezh Front, recovering Kharkov in the process.

Phase III. The offensive would continue in a northerly direction, eliminating those Russian forces remaining in the Kursk area and effecting a junction with 2nd Panzer Army, which would be sent south by Army Group Center at the appropriate moment.

Throughout the operation the German right flank would be guarded by Operational Group Hollidt, already engaged with Malinovsky's South Front along the Mius, while the left flank would be covered by Operational Group *Kempf*, which was screening Golikov's probes west of Kharkov.

The beauty of Manstein's plan, as vast in its scope as *Sichelschnitt*, was that although Army Group South could only muster a total of 350 tanks, at any point of contact they would outnumber their opponents in the ratio of 7:1. In terms of aircraft immediately available the Luftwaffe could put up three for every one that the Red Air Force could get airborne. These figures alone, discounting German tactical expertise, made a major Russian defeat inevitable.

Satisfied, Hitler and his entourage flew out on the 19th. They were unwelcome guests and Manstein would have been less than human if he had not been pleased to see them go. The same day Russian advance units were reported within twenty miles of the Army Group's Headquarters, and Manstein decided that his moment had come.

On the morning of the 20th the panzers began to roll across excellent tank country, which, although frozen hard, reminded old Afrika Korps hands of the desert. In their path they found literal sitting targets in the form of tank and artillery columns, which had stalled for want of fuel, while those Russian units that still possessed some degree of mobility were short of ammunition and obviously shaken by the weight of their allegedly routed enemy's attack. On 23rd February 4th Panzer Army's two Corps joined hands at Pavlograd, isolating Vatutin's advance guards, which rapidly disintegrated. Throughout the remainder of the month South-West Front was hounded to the Donets, losing 615 tanks, 400 guns, 23,000 men killed and 9,000 made prisoner.

Vatutin's two major formations, 6th Army and Tank Group Popov, sometimes referred to as the Front Mobile Group, were savaged out of operational existence and Golikov, his left flank hanging in the void, was compelled to halt his advance and divert his 3rd Tank Army into the gap. The army was caught redeploying onto its new axis by Luftwaffe ground-attack wings, whose Henschell Hs 129Bs and G Model Stukas dropped from the sky to engage the tanks' vulnerable rear armour and engine decks with a hail of bombs and cannon fire.[54] Those T34s that emerged from the attack were blown apart by the 88-mm guns of 2nd SS Panzer Corps' new Tiger battalions.

Manstein's Phase I had now been completed and his troops effortlessly absorbed the tactical adjustments necessary for Phase II. Golikov had constructed a defensive front south of Kharkov to hold the attack, but Manstein instructed Hausser to by-pass the city to the west and then swing south to meet 48 Panzer Corps, which was moving northwards between Kharkov and the Donets.

By 11th March Kharkov had been sealed off and 1st SS Panzer Division had begun to fight its way through the suburbs. The city contained the major part of the Soviet 69th Army, which put up a dogged resistance, and did not fall until the 15th. Three days later the *Grossdeutschland* Panzer Grenadier Division, now attached to Operational Group *Kempf* captured Belgorod, and Voronezh Front's losses could be estimated at 600 tanks, 500 guns and 40,000 men.

In Berlin the news was exploited into a propaganda triumph, much being made of the part played by the Waffen SS. In Moscow deep depression caused Stalin to despatch his favourite trouble-shooter, Zhukov, to restore some semblance of order, and reinforcements were poured into the battle zone. Whether these measures would in themselves have been sufficient to defeat Manstein's Phase III will never be known, for immediately after the fall of Belgorod the *rasputitsa*, the Great Thaw, set in and movement along the front abruptly terminated. What was clear that although STAVKA had itself contributed to the debacle it would in future be extremely cautious about letting its field commanders off the leash, but perhaps the most important single factor leading to the Russian defeat was that Manstein had been able to perfect his plans in the security of his own headquarters rather than at OKW, where any decision made was immediately transmitted to the Russians by the Lucy spy ring.

In spite of the uncompleted Phase III having left a huge bulge in the line around Kursk, 100 miles wide and seventy deep, Manstein had restored the integrity of the Eastern Front. Of his dramatic counterstroke von Mellenthin, who at the time was serving as 48 Panzer Corps' Chief of Staff, wrote in his memoirs, "It may be questioned whether any achievement of generalship in World War II can approach the successful extrication of the Caucasus armies and the subsequent riposte to Kharkov. The German military writer, Ritter von Schramm, spoke of 'a miracle on the Donets', but there was no miracle; victory was gained by masterly judgement and calculation."[55]

It was to be the Panzer Arm's last strategic victory. After the losses of the Stalingrad campaign the average strength of the panzer divisions was twenty-seven tanks; even worse, the German tank industry had lapsed into chaos and was apparently incapable of making good the deficiency. The ageing PzKw III had been withdrawn in 1942, although its chassis continued to be used for self-propelled guns; there was a very real danger that manufacture of the PzKw IV, now the mainstay of the panzer divisions, would be terminated as well so that available resources could be diverted to Panther and Tiger production; and this in spite of the fact that the Panther was still unproven and the Tiger leaving the production lines at the rate of only twenty-five vehicles per month. In contrast, Russian production of T34s alone was nearing 1,000 per month and rising steadily, while the British and American tank industries were turning out even greater numbers of fighting vehicles.

In February 1943, Hitler, still suffering from the trauma of Stalingrad, was gently persuaded to recall the disgraced Guderian to active duty. Guderian received the appointment of Inspector-General of Armoured Troops with a very wide brief that included the SS and Luftwaffe armoured formations, and his most immediate tasks were to restore order where confusion reigned and to restore the strength of the panzer divisions to acceptable levels. In these he was greatly assisted by the able Albert Speer, who had replaced Dr Todt as Minister for Armaments following the latter's death.

In Guderian's opinion, it would require the remainder of 1943 to complete the rejuvenation of the Panzer Arm and very little would be gained by committing it to a fresh offensive on the

Eastern Front after the *rasputitsa*. He was informed that such an offensive was a political necessity, and that the target would be the same as Manstein's Phase III – the Kursk salient.

A conference was held in Munich on May 3rd to discuss the offensive. It was presided over by Hitler and attended by the OKW Staff, General Zeitzler, Chief of Army General Staff, field Marshals von Manstein and von Kluge, General Model, Commander of the 9th Army, Guderian and Speer. Hitler began by introducing a plan that had been drawn up by Zeitzler, involving converging attacks against the salient's flanks by Army Groups South and Centre; such a double envelopment would trap so many Russian divisions that the Red Army would be decisively weakened; Zeitzler had told him that the new Tigers and Panthers would ensure success. Model expressed doubts, producing evidence that the Russians were constructing defences in depth along the walls of the salient, increasing the number of their anti-tank guns and moving their armour back into suitable locations for counter-attack. Manstein felt that the plan might have succeeded in April, but was now doubtful. Von Kluge liked the idea, but Guderian was entirely opposed to it, pointing out that not only were the Panther's teething troubles far from over, but also that tank losses would inevitably be heavy at a time when additional resources were needed to build up a defence against the anticipated Allied landing in France, and in this Speer supported him.

Later, in private, Guderian's long-standing feud with von Kluge erupted into angry words resulting in the latter issuing a formal challenge to a duel in which he asked the Fuhrer to act as his second. Hitler insisted that the two settle their differences in some other way, but Guderian brusquely rejected von Kluge's proposals for a form of words that would bring about a reconciliation.

Notwithstanding the unfortunate atmosphere in which the conference was conducted, Zeitzler's plan was ultimately accepted, although a week later Hitler told Guderian that whenever he thought of the implications his stomach turned over;

as well it might, since he was hazarding what remained of the Reich's offensive capacity in one gigantic gamble.

The German line-up for the battle reads like something of a Panzer *Who's Who*. On Manstein's wing the major striking force would be Hoth's 4th Panzer Army, with 2nd SS Panzer Corps on the right and 48 Panzer Corps (3rd and 11th Panzer Divisions, *Grossdeutschland* Panzer Grenadier Division and 10th Panther Brigade) on the left. Hoth's right flank would be covered by Operational Group *Kempf*, which contained 3rd Panzer Corps (6th, 7th and 19th Panzer Divisions). On the northern wing, von Kluge's assault formation was Model's 9th Army, which included 47 Panzer Corps (2nd, 9th and 20th Panzer Divisions and a weak Tiger battalion) and 51 Panzer Corps (18th Panzer Divisions, plus 653 and 654 Heavy Tank Destroyer Battalions, both equipped with Ferdinands.[56] In the air, the Luftwaffe had no less than 2,500 aircraft available to give direct support to the operation. Few offensives on such a huge scale have been so meticulously planned.

From the Russian viewpoint the Kursk salient had been an obvious target since the end of the thaw, and STAVKA's suspicions were confirmed by the Lucy spy ring almost as soon as Zeitzler's plan had been conceived. The salient was occupied by two Fronts, Central, commanded by Rokossovsky, and Voronezh, commanded now by Vatutin following Golikov's removal after the February disasters. Behind these Zhukov, in overall command of planning, placed in reserve a further army corps commanded by Koniev and later known as Steppe Front, containing most of the armoured counter-attack force.

The perimeter of the salient itself was protected by three fortified belts, totalling twenty-five miles in depth. These were covered by 20,000 guns of various types, more than one-third of which were anti-tank weapons, and corseted by minefields that were laid to a density of 2,500 antipersonnel and 2,200 anti-tank mines per mile of front. The Germans, who had almost achieved parity on the decisive sector (900,000 against 1,337,000 men and 2,700 fighting vehicles against 3,000, but outnumbered in guns two to one) would be attacking the most formidable field defences encountered since World War I; the only detail Zhukov needed to know was the precise date of the attack, and that was provided by a Hungarian deserter.

The battle, codenamed by OKW as Operation *Citadel*, began on 5th July, by which date even von Kluge had lost his earlier optimism. Its course was predictable. In the north Model's best efforts succeeded in penetrating only ten miles and then stuck fast. 9th Army's Ferdinands, used as assault tanks, lacked machine guns for their own defence, and were quickly separated from their infantry, who were pinned down by the storm of shell-fire; the slow vehicles were then hounded to death by Russian flamethrower and tank-hunting parties.

To the south, Hoth did rather better, advancing almost twenty-five miles, but at a terrible cost. The Russians fought for every yard of ground, and when they voluntarily surrendered a feature it was simply to lead the panzers onto what was a pre-planned artillery killing ground. But by the morning of 12th July, 4th Panzer Army seemed at last to have fought its way through the defended zone, and the SS Panzer Corps, 700 tanks strong, was advancing towards the village of Prokhorovka. At the same moment the 850 tanks of General P.A. Rotmistrov's 5th Guards Tank Army, recently arrived with other reinforcements from Steppe Front, were driving past the village on a precisely opposite course.

In a blaze of gunfire, the two forces simply drove into each other to fight the most concentrated and least scientific tank battle in the history of armoured warfare. Tanks rammed each other and fought at point-blank range, the Tiger's long gun equating with the shorter 76.2mm of the T34 in the brutal close-quarter melee, while overhead hundreds of aircraft from both sides snarled for mastery of the air. Control disintegrated as each crew fought for its own survival amid the ear-splitting thunder of hundreds of high-velocity tank guns, columns of smoke lifting skywards in growing numbers from the stricken victims. One Russian observer, possibly Rotmistrov, who watched the engagement from a hill outside Prokhorovka, later recalled that "the landscape seemed too small for what was taking place on it".

In the end it was the Russians who drew off to regroup, leaving behind 300 tanks they could afford to lose; 2nd SS Panzer Corps had lost about the same number, which it desperately needed. *Citadel's* cutting edge had been irrevocably blunted, but on its own this did not mean its immediate cancellation, although total German tank losses for the whole offensive had now risen to an alarming 1,500, about the same suffered by the Russians.

What did set the alarm bells ringing in headquarters all the way up to the Wolf's Lair in East Prussia was the opening of a Soviet offensive to the north of the salient, where Army Group Centre's line curved eastwards round Orel. On the same day that the Battle of Prokhorovka was fought, Sokolovsky's West Front and Popov's Bryansk Front launched converging attacks against Orel, badly mauling 2nd Panzer Army and threatening to slice across Model's rear. Dwindling German resources were insufficient to maintain the operations against Kursk and deal with this fresh crisis simultaneously. *Citadel* was cancelled forthwith and all the gains so dearly bought on both flanks were abandoned under relentless Russian pressure.

The Wehrmacht did not know it, but it had been dancing to Zhukov's tune. It would have been surprising indeed if a man of his strategic genius had simply contented himself with writing down the German armour in the defensive battles of the salient. Stalingrad had shown the scale on which he thought, and Kursk offered the same opportunities for breaking through the flanks of an embattled German mass. The counter-stroke would only be activated when the panzer formations had wasted their strength in heavy attritional fighting, and then be launched simultaneously at Orel in the north and Belgorod in the south; in the event the southern thrust was delayed because Manstein's forces were thicker on the ground, or the results might have been even more rewarding than they were.

Neither Manstein's nor von Kluge's commands gave way to panic, although the former was compelled to send several of his already attenuated panzer divisions to other sectors of the front where the Red Army was also beginning to exert pressure. But however skilfully the German commanders might manoeuvre, the only timetable that counted now was Zhukov's. Steppe Front moved into the line on the left of Voronezh Front, and by 19th July both were attacking; four days later Hoth and Kempf had been pushed back across their original start lines.

The advance on both flanks gathered momentum, Orel and Belgorod being captured on 5th August. Kharkov, threatened with encirclement, was abandoned on 22nd August and suddenly the whole of Army Group South was menaced as the entire Russian southern wing swung forward. By the end of September, Manstein had retired to the Dniepr line but was allowed little respite. Soon the Russians were across the river everywhere save in the extreme south, and on 6th November they took Kiev. When deep winter finally brought movement to an end the German Army had been all but ejected from the Ukraine.

In contrast to their advance in February, the Soviet formations moved forward by clearly recognisable bounds. For however brilliant their senior officers might be, the command apparatus was rigidly controlled from the top and the use of personal initiative was not encouraged since it might interfere with the working of an overall design. At the tactical level, great reliance was placed on detailed planning and thorough rehearsals, so that everyone knew exactly what to do and where to go on the day; to some extent this was unavoidable, as the issue of tank radios had only just reached company commander level in a few elite units. However, the result of this was an inflexible approach to any one tactical problem, coupled with command failures at regimental and company levels if commanders became casualties.

An operation would begin with a heavy bombardment by conventional artillery and Katyusha multiple rocket launchers, while self-propelled guns took up position as near as possible to the start line to shoot in the attack and destroy opportunity targets. The attack itself would be led by a wave of KVs, which relied on their heavy armour to protect them during the run in and which had the task of neutralising specific targets in the enemy's forward defended localities, such as anti-tank guns, strong-points and bunkers. The heavy tanks would be followed by a wave of T34s accompanied by infantry, and this had the job of completing the breach through the enemy's defended zone. A third wave, again of T34s, accompanied by motor-rifle troops, would then press through the gap and exploit to the predetermined objective, which ideally would include a communications centre or senior headquarters. Once taken, the objective would be consolidated and the troops involved would either prepare carefully for the next phase of the advance or, more likely, be relieved by troops who had been trained specifically for it. An advance beyond an allotted objective, even in ostensibly favourable circumstances, would not be kindly looked upon by senior commanders.

This represented the basic working of the Red Steamroller for the remainder of the war. Relying as it did for success on a combination of mass and momentum, it lacked the essential speed, flexibility and technique of the German, British and American methods, but taking into account the nature of Soviet equipment, training and rigidity of command, it was a viable, if extremely expensive, system of attack and penetration. What worked against it was its very predictability, which enabled the more tactically expert German defence to exact terrible losses, particularly when Russian local commanders insisted on launching a series of such attacks over the same ground on which earlier efforts had foundered.

Kursk was the battle that finally tilted the scales against Germany on the Eastern Front. The once-proud panzer divisions had been bled until they were white, and they were never again strong enough to become the weapon of decision they had formerly been. Sent where they were needed most, they achieved transient success, but never again victory. Dispersed too was the Luftwaffe's finely honed ground attack apparatus, distributed along the front as an aid to the defence. For Germany, the high days of *Blitzkrieg* had long passed by the winter of 1943.

Chapter 8: Antidotes to Blitzkrieg

Ostensibly, the Kursk operations showed that defence in depth represented an answer to the *Blitzkrieg* threat, albeit one based on mutual attrition. But Operation *Zitadelle* had been unique in that the Germans had indicated very clearly from the outset exactly which sector of the Front they intended to attack, and the Red Army had planned and disposed accordingly. Had there been any doubt as to where the blow was to fall, such a defence would not have been possible, since not even the Russians' vast resources in men and material would permit them to be as strong everywhere along the Front. If the apparently unstoppable force had been defeated by the genuinely immovable object it was because of the peculiar circumstances controlling the battle rather than as a result of the Red Army's having found a strategic solution to the problem.

Such a solution did exist and it had been conceived by the United States Army, which alone of all the major combatants had had the opportunity and above all the time to consider in neutral isolation the lessons of Poland, France and the early desert battles.

During the first years of the war there had been much debate as to whether the best defence against a tank was another tank or an anti-tank gun. Those who favoured the latter could claim that the anti-tank gun did not suffer the mounting and ammunition handling limitations imposed by the tank turret, and that therefore it was possible to produce anti-tank guns which were more powerful than the guns carried by the tanks themselves; the anti-tank gun, it was argued, would invariably outrange the tank. In reply, their opponents were quick to point out that cordon defence by anti-tank guns had failed repeatedly to hold the massed tank attack, particularly if the latter was supported by aircraft and infantry; moreover, once the front had been broken, the tanks moved too quickly for further cordons to be placed across their path, and for armies equipped with conventional towed guns the containment of such penetrations presented all but insuperable difficulties.

On the basis of the facts, therefore, the protagonists of tank-defence seemed to have won the day in the US Army, until they were sharply reminded by the Chief of Armor that his arm of service was specifically trained for offensive operations and that he was not prepared to see it squandered in defensive tasks.

The answer lay in the combination of fire-power with mobility, rather than in a choice between the two. If the anti-tank guns could be given the mobility of tanks, yet still retain their essential weapon superiority, they could be deployed rapidly and *en masse* to counter any developing penetration by the enemy's armour. This was clearly in the mind of General George C. Marshall, Chief of Staff United States Army, when he wrote on 14th May 1941 that the "problem was beyond the capabilities of any one arm and probably required the organisation and use of a special force of combined arms, capable of rapid movement, interception, and active rather than passive defence".

Marshall's special force was established the following day under the administrative command of Lieutenant-Colonel Andrew D. Bruce, and was known as the Tank Destroyer Force, its men being drawn from the cavalry, artillery and infantry. Its formation constituted what amounted in effect to a new arm of service with an entirely specialist role that was emphasised repeatedly in training circulars: "The primary mission of tank destroyer units is the destruction of hostile tanks by the fire of a superior mass of guns."

To achieve this aim, it would be necessary to deploy mobile tank destroyers in large numbers in the path and on the flanks of an enemy massed tank attack. Here, their superior weapons would write down the attackers' strength, while their mobility would enable them to keep pace with any continued advance. Great emphasis was placed on the value of reconnaissance in relation to the choice of suitable fire positions *prior* to the start of operations, so that once alerted, tank destroyer units could be moved at speed into the threatened area. As a badge for the new arm, Bruce chose the head of a panther crunching a tank between its jaws, together with the motto Seek, Strike and Destroy, and with one eye on potential misuse by senior commanders, he defined the symbolism: "Panther like, we *seek* information of enemy tanks and of suitable firing positions; panther like, we *strike* and *destroy* by gunfire from favourable positions. This does NOT mean that we seek out tanks with guns, NOR chase them, NOR pursue them, NOR charge them."

As regards equipment, Bruce sought "a cruiser, not a battleship", and favoured the Christie suspension because it performed so well at high speed across country. "What we are after is a fast moving vehicle, armed with a weapon with a powerful punch which can be easily and quickly fired, and in the last analysis we would like to get armoured protection against small arms fire so that this weapon cannot be put out of action by a machine gun."

However, while the Tank Destroyer Board began work on the specification, tank destroyer units had to be equipped with whatever was to hand. A number of interim designs were suggested, but of these only the 75-mm Gun Motor Carriage M3 offered an immediately available weapon system. This consisted of an old French 75-mm gun, of which the US Army had several hundred in stock, mounted on an M3 half-track so as to fire over the cab. The equipment contained a number of vices, notably the limited traverse available and a 43-inch recoil, which could knock an unwary loader flat, but it did offer mobility and a high rate of fire. It saw service during the Japanese invasion of the Philippines and with tank destroyer battalions in North Africa.[57] A light tank destroyer, the 37-mm Gun Motor Carriage M6, also served in North Africa, but was essentially an expedient, mass production weapon and was withdrawn shortly afterwards. In layout it resembled the British 2-pounder *Portee*, a 37-mm anti-tank gun being mounted on the back of a three-quarter ton truck.

The M4A2 medium tank chassis formed the basis of the TDF's first standard tank destroyer, the 3-inch Gun Motor Carriage M10. This vehicle was produced by General Motors in conjunction with the Ford Motor Company to a Tank Destroyer Board specification and consisted of an angled hull and an open-topped turret, capable of all-round traverse, fitted with a 3-inch high-velocity gun. Although the M10 did not conform to Bruce's ideal, being both heavier and slower than he thought desirable, it became the best known of all US tank destroyers and some 6,700 were built, many of which also saw active service with the British, French and Russian armies.

By early 1943 it was appreciated that the 3-inch gun was inadequate to deal with the new generation of heavily armoured German tanks such as the Tiger, and TDF stressed the need for a proportion of its vehicles to be equipped with a more powerful weapon. The choice fell upon a 90-mm high-velocity anti-aircraft gun, which could penetrate six inches of armour at 1,000 yards, but space limitations prevented this from being installed in the basic M10 turret. A larger turret was therefore designed and fitted to the M10 chassis, the combined equipment being known as the 90-mm Gun Motor Carriage M36. This vehicle, the most powerful tank destroyer in American service, was issued to battalions from June 1944 onwards, a total of 1,722 being built, of which 500 were converted M10A1s.[58]

Meanwhile, the Tank Destroyer Board had also produced its own vehicle, a purpose-built tank destroyer rather than a modification of existing equipment. This was the 76-mm Gun Motor Carriage M18, which was similar in overall design to the M10 and M36, but weighed only nineteen tons fully stowed. The preference for a Christie suspension had given way to a torsion bar system, but the 400-h.p. engine could produce a road-speed of 60 m.p.h., making the M18 the fastest tracked fighting vehicle of World War II. It began entering service in the autumn of 1943 under the title of Hellcat, a subsequent report from the European theatre of operations describing it as an "ideal *light* tank destroyer, highly praised by the using troops".

The Tank Destroyer Centre moved from its temporary home at Fort George G. Meade, Maryland, to its permanent base at Camp Hood, Texas, early in 1942. Here it trained not merely individuals but whole battalions and higher formation headquarters in tank destroyer tactics, producing 100 battalions, two brigade and twenty-four group headquarters. In addition, it established its own Officer Candidate School from which 5,299 second lieutenants graduated, and a Replacement Training Center, which processed 42,000 men.

Bruce's achievement had been truly remarkable, and his rank rose with his soaring responsibilities. He was promoted to Brigadier-General in February 1942 and to Major-General in September of that year, eventually handing over command of the Center on 25th May 1943 to Major-General Orlando C. Ward, who had commanded 1st Armored Division in North Africa.

The TDF's basic tactical unit was the battalion, which consisted of a Headquarters Company, three gun companies each of twelve guns, a Reconnaissance Company with half-tracks or M8 armoured cars, and eighteen anti-aircraft half-tracks mounting dual .50-calibre machine-guns. Light battalions similarly organised but with the GMC M6 as their primary weapon were brought up to this standard as soon as the 37-mm's performance was seen to fall below battlefield requirements. The TDF also contained a proportion of towed battalions equipped with 36 3-inch anti-tank guns M1 and eighteen anti-aircraft half-tracks.

The high proportion of anti-aircraft equipment contained in this order of battle indicates how thoroughly the Americans had interpreted the lessons of 1940 and 1941. If British, French and Russian anti-tank gunners had suffered severely at the hands of the Luftwaffe's ground-attack aircraft, the Tank Destroyer Force had no intention of doing likewise.

As mentioned earlier, tank destroyers were considered to be best used *en masse*, preferably under the control of their own specialist formation headquarters. A headquarters and three battalions would form a Tank Destroyer Group, while a headquarters and two groups would form a Tank Destroyer Brigade. The scheme provided one TD, Brigade for the support of each corps and two for each army, but in fact only two such brigades were raised and of these only one saw active service.

It was ironic that by the time tank destroyer battalions reached the battlefront the days of the German massed tank attack were, with one or two notable exceptions, virtually over. In North Africa, Bruce's fears that senior commanders would misuse the weapon he had created proved to be fully justified, and battalions were dispersed and employed on a variety of operations that had little, if anything, to do with their intended role.

Rommel's extremely dangerous thrust through Kasserine Pass offered the sort of opportunity for which tank destroyer officers had been waiting, but such TD units as were immediately available in the area fought dispersed under the command of other arms. Thus, instead of having their own advance halted by concentrated gunfire from carefully reconnoitred positions, the panzers were met with a head-long counter-attack by the inexperienced US 1st Armored Division, which their expertise easily defeated with heavy loss.

Some American officers, impressed by the interlocked anti-tank gun and artillery defence offered by the British 8th Army at Medenine, actually suggested that the tank destroyer was a maverick and that a return to towed anti-tank guns should be made, a move that was quickly reversed when the limited field of fire available to the towed gun in the Normandy *bocage* became apparent. For the remainder of the war tank destroyers performed the role of assault guns, providing direct fire support for infantry and armoured operations. It was a role that, as direct gunfire specialists, they performed extremely well, but which has tended to obscure the fact that on the few occasions when concentrated battalions countered a German tank attack and were permitted to fight in accordance with their original training, the results entirely vindicated the theory that had brought them into being. The tank destroyer did, in fact, provide an antidote to the German *Blitzkrieg*, but it had appeared too late.[59]

In spite of the spectacular defence of the road block at Beda Fomm and the suicidal courage of unprotected *portee* crews at Sidi Rezegh and other desert battles in which they actually joined in the tank battle, the British attitude to tank destroyers remained distinctly cool. "In contrast to the American policy, the idea of seeking out and destroying enemy armour was discouraged. A suitable role for the self-propelled anti-tank gun, it was thought, was the engagement of tanks that stood off and neutralised our forward localities; or when employed with armoured formations, to help in the defence of pivots or localities held by the infantry."[60]

In other words, tank destroyers were from the outset to play a subordinate role within the overall tactical picture. The fact that they were accepted at all was due to the changed nature of the fighting in Tunisia, Sicily and Italy, where the terrain-favoured defence and outgunned British tanks advanced under the muzzles of well-sited and more powerful German tanks and self-propelled guns.

"What was needed was a weapon that could move across country by a covered route to a position from which enemy tanks could be engaged by surprise. For lack of it, anti-tank protection had become perhaps the most important role for tanks in support of infantry."[61]

This had always been true of British Infantry Tank formations; what had suddenly become even more apparent was that the "I" tanks themselves required protection against the enemy armour, and that the big-gun tank destroyer could provide it. An order for 1,500 M10s was placed and by June 1943 these were beginning to replace the obsolete Deacon 6-pounder *portees* in anti-tank regiments, being known in British service as Wolverines. As quantities of the powerful 17-pounder anti-tank gun became available, Wolverines were up-gunned with this weapon, the combined equipment being known as the Achilles. A British tank destroyer, the Archer, began entering service in October 1944, and also employed the 17-pounder, mounted to fire over the tail of a Valentine tank chassis; major disadvantages of this arrangement were the limited traverse obtainable and the fact that the vehicle had to be reversed into action.

The Royal Artillery, under whose control British tank destroyer units operated, remained largely unimpressed by the weapon's versatility, but agreed that in certain circumstances tank destroyers did provide a useful alternative to conventional anti-tank guns. It was anticipated that the most probable German reaction to the Normandy landings would be a massive armoured counter-attack, and since difficulties could be expected in getting the heavy and awkward towed 17-pounder off the beaches and into the gun-line, it was agreed that the anti-tank regiments of the assault landing divisions would contain a proportion of tank destroyers that could be driven straight from their LCTs and into position.

That this was considered to be no more than a temporary expedient is clear from the following, written after the *bocage*, with its small fields, enclosed by hedge-topped banks and close cover, had imposed much the same tactics as were being practised in Italy:

> "It was as important as ever to get anti-tank guns forward quickly to a captured objective; all the more so because of the inadequate killing power of the Churchill tank. The towed 17-pdr was not easy to manoeuvre and it was often twelve to fifteen hours before it could be dug in ready for action in the new position. Hence it was decided to perpetuate the SP element introduced into anti-tank units for the initial landings. In future, infantry divisional anti-tank batteries were to consist of one troop 17-pdr towed, one troop 17-pdr SP or M10, and one troop 6-pdr towed."[62]

On 8th July 1944, just over a month after the assault landings, the Achilles battery of 62 Anti-Tank Regiment RA, fought a classic tank destroyer battle against an enemy counter-attack near

Buron. All but three of the battery's vehicles were badly damaged, but two of its guns alone knocked out thirteen Panthers and PzKw IVs before the remainder of the enemy force withdrew. It was, perhaps, typical of the Cinderella attitude towards British TD units that the victor's laurels were promptly awarded to a neighbouring armoured regiment that had taken no part in the action.

The subsequent history of British tank destroyers followed closely that of their American counterparts, and included the formation of supplementary artillery groups for such operations as the Reichswald battle.

It was, in fact, the German Army that benefited most from the tank destroyer idea. The German experience was exactly the reverse of the American, for while the latter had seen their tank destroyers used ultimately in the assault gun role, the Germans had been compelled to employ their own assault gun units for mobile anti-tank defence.

The German Assault Gun, or *Sturmgeschutz*, had its roots in the inter-war analysis of the reasons for the defeat of Ludendorff's 1918 offensives. It was argued that had the Storm Troopers had immediately available the direct gunfire support provided for the British and French by their tanks, their objectives would have been seized more quickly and at a fraction of the ultimate cost. This could not be denied, but while such direct fire support could be supplied by the expanding panzer arm, the diversion of tanks for infantry operations was considered to be a waste of valuable resources.

However, in 1935 General Erich von Manstein submitted a memorandum to the Chief of General Staff advocating the need for a fully protected self-propelled gun to be employed directly under infantry command, suggesting that eventually each infantry division should possess its own assault gun battalion of three six-gun batteries.

Having received approval, the idea was passed to the artillery to translate into fact under the supervision of the then Colonel Walter Model, Head of the General Staff Technical Section 8.

A prototype was produced in 1937, consisting of a low, fixed forward superstructure with head cover, mounting a 75-mm L/24 howitzer, the whole being carried on the chassis of a PzKw III Model B. Because of its role the vehicle was equipped with 50-mm frontal armour, sufficient to withstand the anti-tank guns of the day and far thicker than that carried by contemporary German tanks. The design was approved, although the production models employed the more familiar six-wheeled chassis used by the PzKw III from Model E onwards.

The next step was to decide which arm of service would man the new vehicle, and a conference was held to determine future policy. The infantry said that they lacked the technical establishment necessary to maintain and supply the guns in the field. The panzer officers wanted the whole project scrapped, alleging that it interfered with their tank production programme, one officer over-reacting to such an extent as to shout that if it went ahead, the decision would be tantamount to passing sentence of death on the panzer arm. The conference was brought to an interesting climax by the artillery's Inspector-General, who seems to have been imperfectly briefed as to the precise nature of the equipment; he suggested, to the consternation of his personal staff and the delight of everyone else, that any decision should be deferred until the new gun had completed its trials, and that pending the results it should be horse-drawn! Not surprisingly, the term stuck to such an extent that horse-drawn became the synonym for assault gun among senior ranks, but in all fairness to the poor man, once he had grasped the principles involved, he accepted that the weapon was primarily an artillery responsibility and immediately set up an experimental battery at the Artillery School at Juterbog, which was also briefed to establish basic training facilities and a tactical school for Assault Artillery crews.

While the Assault Artillery's infantry support role is of no direct relevance to the history of *Blitzkrieg*, it is worth mentioning in passing that its *modus operandi* was very similar to that of the British Army's Infantry Tank formations. The assault guns were manned by volunteers who were considered to be the cream of their service and who wore a distinctive field-grey uniform of panzer cut with artillery facings. In due course their branch expanded to such an extent that it established its own Assault Artillery School at Burg, near Magdeburg.

Field and troop trials took longer than had been expected, and no assault gun units took part in the 1939 Polish campaign, although four batteries did serve in France. By 1941 the tactical unit had become the three-battery battalion, of which three were employed against Greece and Yugoslavia. The opening phases of Operation *Barbarossa* saw two battalions each serving with Army Groups South, Centre and North, and thereafter the number increased steadily. Later the internal organisation of the battery was supplemented by increasing the strength of troops from two to three guns and providing the battery commander with his own gun, bringing the total battalion strength to thirty-one guns, inclusive of the commanding officer's vehicle. In 1944 the unit title was changed to brigade, and some battalions were designated Army Assault Artillery Brigades with a much larger establishment of forty-five guns and the provision of a specialist Grenadier Escort Battery. Assault gun units did not, as von Manstein had originally intended, form an organic part of infantry divisions. Instead, they were allocated by senior commanders as and where required, being released by the infantry on conclusion of the operation for which they had been detailed.

The impact of T34 and KV1 on the panzer arm has already been described. Because of their thicker armour the assault gun crews suffered less than their comrades manning the PzKw IIIs and IVs, and further protection was easily obtainable by bolting extra plates to the front of the vehicle. In addition, the roomy interior permitted the rapid installation of a more powerful weapon with an anti-tank capability, so that by early 1942 the short howitzer was being replaced by a 75mm L/43 gun, an interim weapon that was in turn superseded by the 75-mm L/48. Thus, by virtue of their adaptable design, assault guns found themselves being widely employed in the tank destroyer role to combat the Red Army's mass attacks.

In fact, at the conference attended by Guderian following his appointment as Inspector-General of Armoured Troops, he commented that: "Anti-tank defence will devolve more and more on the assault guns, since all our other anti-tank weapons are becoming increasing ineffective against the new enemy equipment ... All divisions on the main battle fronts, therefore, need to be supplied with a certain complement of these weapons; the secondary fronts will have to make do with a higher command reserve of assault guns."[63]

If the panzer divisions were the sword of the German Army, the Assault Artillery was its shield. Using the same methods that were being advocated for the TDF, it had destroyed no less than 13,000 enemy tanks by December 1943, a figure that rose to 20,000 during the next quarter, the vast majority on the Eastern Front; by the end of the war the total cannot have been less than 30,000, a bloody tribute to German skill and a fearful indictment of Russian methods. This takes no account of tanks destroyed by the panzer divisions or by specialist TD units.

The tank destroyer role did not detract from the Assault Artillery's primary function of infantry support, and a 105-mm assault howitzer began to join battalions in 1943. A useful combination within a troop was one assault howitzer and three 75-mm L/48 assault guns, it being the practice during Russian mass attacks for the former to separate the enemy infantry from their tanks, which would simultaneously be tackled by the latter.

Altogether, some 10,500 assault guns were built, plus a few hundred on the PzKw IV chassis, many being used to equip understrength panzer divisions. Guderian would dearly have liked to have the Assault Artillery placed under the control of his inspectorate, but he was fiercely opposed not only by the artillery, but also by a majority of the military hierarchy and by Hitler as well.

In the meantime, a second class of vehicle, the *Panzerjager* or Tank Hunter, had been developed out of dire necessity. Guderian had always held the view that each panzer division should have its organic unit of self-propelled anti-tank guns, but there seemed little enthusiasm for the idea and only a handful of such vehicles, equipped with an innocuous 47-mm gun had been built by the end of 1940.

However, experience of the thick-skinned British Matilda, both at Arras and in North Africa, coupled with the trauma engendered by the T34 and KV, revealed frightening inadequacies in the German Army's armour-defeating capabilities. Manufacture of expedient tank destroyers was commenced at once, utilising the chassis of obsolete tanks such as the PzKw II or 38T, while designs for purpose-built machines were put in hand.

The first generation of *Panzerjager* mounted various Marks of the German 75-mm PAK 40 anti-tank gun or a captured 76.2-mm Russian weapon, which had been rechambered to take German ammunition, and were protected by a fixed, open-topped superstructure of armour plate. As a class they were known as Marders (Martens), although they differed widely in appearance; they were imperfect instruments but handled correctly they produced excellent results. A larger variation on the same theme was introduced in 1943. This was the Nashorn (Rhinoceros), which was armed with the 88-mm L/71 PAK 43 anti-tank gun, carried on a composite PzKw III/IV chassis.

Guderian's prediction that the roles of assault artillery and *Panzerjager* would eventually merge was reflected in the design of the second generation of tank destroyers, which began entering service at the end of 1943. These followed the assault gun layout with a well-armoured fixed forward superstructure with overhead cover.

The *Panzerjager* IV, sometimes called Guderian's Duck, was based on the PzKw IV chassis and armed with a 75-mm L/70 gun, replacing the Marders serving with the panzer divisions' tank destroyer battalions. The slightly less powerful 75-mm Hetzer (Troublemaker) employed the 38T chassis and was posted to the infantry divisions' anti-tank battalions; although admired for its looks, the vehicle suffered from an awkward internal layout, both loader and gunner being located on the left of a gun designed to be served from the right.

The *Jagdpanther* (Hunting Panther) was introduced in 1944 and, as its name implied, utilised the chassis of the PzKw V. It was protected by 80-mm frontal armour set back at 35 degrees, and was equipped with an 88-mm L/71 gun, being considered by many to be the most efficient tank destroyer of World War II. The *Jagdpanther* replaced the Rhinoceros in the Heavy Tank Destroyer Battalions, which operated under the direct control of army commanders. The last German tank destroyer to be produced, albeit in small numbers, was the unwieldy *Jagdtiger*, remarkable only for its 128-mm gun, which made it the most powerful fighting vehicle in service, and for its mechanical inefficiency; it served in the Heavy battalions and was also issued to SS panzer divisions.

More than 6,000 *Panzerjager* of various types were constructed, and it was undoubtedly due to their efforts, combined with those of the assault artillery and the panzer divisions, that the Eastern Front did not collapse sooner than it did. Of all the armies of the world possibly only the Russian, and maybe the Japanese, could have sustained such truly appalling losses and still continued to attack.

True, the Russians had an apparently inexhaustible supply of manpower to draw upon, and their production of tanks outstripped that of the Germans by tens of thousands, but the Russian soldier was, and always has been, something quite unique. He was tough, because his environment made him so; he was a stoic, because history decreed that he must be; he was unimaginative, because he was discouraged from thinking for himself; he believed in his cause, because the atrocities of the SS *Einsatzgruppe* had shown him it was just; he was disciplined, because the discipline of a totalitarian state is itself total; and above all, he had a powerful and deep-rooted feeling for an abstract Mother Russia, whose soil he would fight ferociously to liberate, although abroad his motivation might be less apparent.[64]

Deeply impressed by the assault gun concept, the Red Army began producing its own versions, closely following the German layout and taking full advantage of the roomy interior to install large guns from the outset. These were known as SUs from the Russian *Samochodnya Ustanovka*, meaning simply self-propelled artillery. The T34 chassis was used as the basis for two tank destroyers, the SU85 and SU100, armed respectively as their title suggests with 85-mm and 100-mm guns, and also for an assault howitzer, the SU122. These vehicles were formed into special support regiments, which were allocated to armoured formations as circumstances dictated. The Joseph Stalin tank chassis was used for the JSU122 tank destroyer and the JSU152 assault howitzer, which fought in support of the Heavy or Breakthrough Tank Regiments; they were extremely powerful weapons, which, because of their success against the German Tigers and Panthers, became known as the Animal Killers.

Notwithstanding their great potential, the SUs were used with less flexibility than their German opposite number. In the attack, they tended to be used as a forward fire base from which to shoot in their tanks and infantry, with a special responsibility for dealing with the German armour, while in defence their mobility was often sacrificed by being dug in as part of some overall scheme of in-depth fortification.

Such a proliferation of self-propelled anti-tank artillery in all major theatres of war clearly indicated that from 1943 onwards battles would be fought on very different principles from those of the preceding years. There were other factors at work as well, notably the introduction of hollow or shaped charge ammunition, which relied on chemical rather than kinetic energy to blast a hole through the thickest armour. Against this, tanks could offer little defence save the addition of side skirts, which provided a primary detonation surface, thus permitting the effect of the explosion to disperse before it reached the hull itself, the arrangement being known as spaced armour.

Hollow charge ammunition could be fired from short-range projectors such as the PIAT, the *Panzerfaust* and the bazooka, which had, incidentally, been evaluated for the US Army by the TDF. The issue of such weapons to the infantry meant that even if their own anti-tank artillery had been put out of action, they still had a close and extremely effective defence against tanks; it also meant that in suitable circumstances, such as wooded country or built-up areas, tanks could be stalked or ambushed with a greatly enhanced chance of success.

The tank's era of total domination was at an end. From now on, the story would be one of interdependence between arms.

Chapter 9: Battle to the Death

When the Allies landed in Normandy on 6th June 1944 their overall strategy was simple and bore some comparison with Allenby's at Gaza. On the left of the line the British Second and Canadian First Armies would mount a series of operations designed to attract the bulk of the German armour and tie it down in defensive action, while on the right the American 1st and 3rd Armies would build up their strength and prepare for a break-out, which would smash through the enemy's southern flank and sweep out into the country beyond.

Some of the British formations, notably 7th Armoured, 50th (Northumbrian) and 51st (Highland) Divisions had seen extensive service in North Africa, but the majority had spent the war training in the United Kingdom. The old desert hands were battle-hardened, canny fighters, but the home service divisions were equally formidable in that they were trained to a high pitch and were more readily able to adapt their techniques to the continental battlefield.

Five armoured divisions were available on the British or 21st Army Group sector, which was commanded by General Sir Bernard Montgomery. They were the Guards, 7th, 11th and 4th Canadian, joined later by the 1st Polish Armoured Division. Several independent armoured brigades were also present, and three tank brigades, equipped with Churchills, provided direct support for infantry operations. A specialist formation, the 79th Armoured Division, commanded by Major-General P.C.S. Hobart, supplied mine-clearing, assault engineer and flame-throwing tanks in accordance with the requirements of each major operation.

The British armoured division contained an armoured brigade of three regiments and a motorised infantry battalion; a three-battalion infantry brigade; an armoured reconnaissance regiment; two 25-pounder artillery regiments, one of which was self-propelled; an anti-tank regiment with at least one battery equipped with tank destroyers; an anti-aircraft regiment; a signal regiment; a medium machine-gun company; and engineer, supply and divisional troops.

The principal weapon of the armoured brigade was the American Sherman or the British Cromwell cruiser tank, both of which carried a 75-mm gun, which was out-ranged by the majority of German tanks and tank destroyers. In an effort to counteract this deficiency, the British fitted a proportion of their Shermans with a 17-pounder gun, the composite vehicle being known as a Firefly. This achieved parity with the Panther (but not the Tiger), although the long gun instantly identified Fireflies working with standard Shermans and could result in their being picked off first; the answer to this was to group a regiment's Fireflies in a single squadron rather than issue them on the basis of one troop per squadron or one tank per troop.[65]

On the American or 12th Army Group sector, commanded by Lieutenant-General Omar N. Bradley, a total of seven armoured divisions was eventually concentrated – the US 2nd, 3rd, 4th, 5th, 6th and 7th, and the French 2nd. The American armoured division consisted of three tank battalions equipped with Shermans, a proportion of which were fitted with a 76-mm gun; three armoured infantry battalions riding in M3 half-tracks; three artillery battalions, armed with a total of thirty-six M7 105-mm self-propelled howitzers; a reconnaissance battalion; an engineer battalion; and divisional services.[66] It possessed the most flexible organisation of any armoured formation of World War II containing, in addition to its main headquarters separate Combat Commands to which the divisional commander would allot armour, infantry and artillery as required for the task in hand, a logical extension of the German panzer battlegroup concept. Each armoured division had two such Combat Commands, usually referred to as CCA and CCB, and sometimes a third was added, being known as CCC or CCR (Reserve).

A number of independent tank battalions were also available for infantry support and other tasks, as were numerous tank destroyer units. Specialist armour too was present, but to a lesser degree than on the British sector.

In the air the Allies possessed overwhelming strength, their ground troops receiving direct support from the RAF's 2nd Tactical Air Force, commanded by Air Marshal Sir Arthur Coningham, and the United States' 9th Air Force under Lieutenant-General Lewis H. Brereton. The British employed Spitfires, Mustangs and Typhoons in the ground-attack role, while the Americans used Mustangs, Lightnings and Thunderbolts; for interdiction beyond the battlefield the RAF had available Boston and Mitchell medium bombers and Mosquito intruders, the USAAF Marauder medium bombers and Havoc intruders.

Despite its neglect of ground-attack tactics between the wars, the RAF had brought its techniques to an extremely high level of efficiency in the intervening period, perfecting the system throughout the North African campaign. The Forward Air Controller, an experienced flyer who was able to visualise the situation through the eyes of the pilots above, travelled in his own armoured car with the leading elements of the advance, in direct radio contact with a squadron of aircraft overhead. A three-squadron "cab-rank" system was operated, one squadron patrolling its sector of the front, one standing by on its airfield ready to join in the attack, and one refuelling and rearming, thus ensuring air cover for the spearhead at all times.

Targets were given to the patrolling squadron by the Forward Air Controller, and these would be engaged as soon as they had been identified. The second squadron would take off and continue the attack, if necessary, while the third came to stand-by readiness; having expended its bombs, ammunition and rockets, the attack squadron would immediately return to its base to re-arm. The system eliminated the unnecessary administrative phase practised by the Luftwaffe, was easy to operate and produced impressive results. It was adopted, with minor variations, by the USAAF, with the added advantage that an excellent communications net enabled each air force to control the other's aircraft when required.

Interdiction attacks, aided by the French Resistance, had begun even before the Allied landings took place and were maintained at a high level throughout the campaign. Railway junctions and bridges were destroyed and within a short space of time three-quarters of the available stock of locomotives had been put out of action. Movement of military traffic along the road system by day became virtually impossible without attracting the immediate attention of prowling aircraft. The combined effect was to place a stranglehold around the German logistic windpipe, which the frantic efforts of the Luftwaffe were unable to release.

A further type of ground-support operation was carried out by the Lancasters, Stirlings and Halifaxes of the RAF's Bomber Command and the Fortresses and Liberators of the US 8th Air Force, temporarily diverted from their primary task of the strategic bombing of Germany itself. This was known as carpet bombing and was designed to blast a corridor through the enemy's line. Hundreds of tons of high explosive would be dropped from high altitude into the corridor, exploding minefields and pulverising the defences; few survived such an onslaught and those that did were in no condition to fight. The technique was fallible on two counts; first, too heavy a concentration would churn up the ground so badly that the corridor was impassable to vehicles; and secondly, the tail of the carpet sometimes fell short, causing casualties among the Allied troops formed up and waiting to advance.

For much of the campaign the fighting lay within range of the guns of the Allied warships cruising offshore. Controlled by observers in the front line, these could be employed on a variety of tasks from bringing down an unbearably heavy concentration of fire on German positions to engaging interdiction targets beyond the lines.

If the Allies, under their Supreme Commander General Dwight D. Eisenhower, were clear as to their aims and how to achieve them, exactly the reverse was true of the Wehrmacht. The position of Commander-in-Chief West was held by the sixty-nine-year-old Field Marshal Gerd von Rundstedt. Nominally subordinate to him but in tactical command was Field Marshal Erwin Rommel, whose Army Group B was responsible for the invasion coast, although a parallel organisation, Panzer Group West, commanded by General Geyr von Schweppenberg, controlled the armour.

The complications that arose as a result of this awkward command structure were aggravated by fundamental differences of opinion on how the panzer divisions should best be employed. Rommel, who had personal experience of the frightening speed with which the Allies could build up their forces once they were ashore, wanted the tanks to meet them on the beaches and drive them back into the sea; Schweppenberg, on the other hand, wished to hold the panzer inland and fight a decisive armoured battle out of range of naval gunfire. Rundstedt was unable to adjudicate, since not a single panzer division could be moved from the strategic reserve without Hitler's personal approval, which could only be obtained through OKW; he later commented that his real authority did not extend beyond changing the guard at his own gate.

In the event, neither course was adopted, for Hitler was asleep when the landings took place and none had the courage to wake him. By the time the armoured reserve had been released the Allies had consolidated their beach-head and as the panzer completed their difficult journey into the battle zone, they were committed piecemeal to the fighting.

Predictably, Hitler insisted that not a metre of ground should be given up. Once the line had been stabilised the panzers would be used to separate the British and American sectors; the British would then be systematically destroyed and in consequence the disheartened Americans would sue for terms. Such a strategy, it will be noted, suited the combined Allied plan perfectly.

Throughout mid-June the intelligence staff at Montgomery's headquarters pieced together sufficient information to suggest that Rommel was planning a major thrust at the coast through Bayeux, or along the Anglo-American army group boundary. Montgomery at once decided to forestall this with an attack of his own, designed to lever the Germans out of Caen, which should have been taken on the first day of the invasion.

Codenamed *Epsom*, this was mounted by Lieutenant-General Sir Richard O'Connor's VIII Corps, with 11th Armoured, 15th (Scottish) and 43rd (Wessex) Divisions under command, on 26th June.[67] Leaving Caen on its left flank VIII Corps would cross the little River Odon and proceed to the wider Orne beyond which lay the good tank country of the Falaise Plain. Most of its route lay through traditional Norman *bocage*, a landscape of deep lanes and small fields bounded by hedge-topped earth banks and trees, country that offered ideal cover for the defence and difficult going for tanks.

On the first day poor flying weather inhibited air support and the advance was bitterly contested. The situation improved slightly on the 27th and two bridges across the Odon were seized intact. 11th Armoured Division's tanks climbed the shallow slopes of a feature marked Hill 112 on their maps, and captured the summit after some fighting. It was immediately apparent that Hill 112, gentle and unimpressive in itself, commanded a panoramic view of the whole area and was thus a linchpin of the German defence. A sharp counterattack forced the British armour back beyond the crest, where it was mortared incessantly but otherwise permitted to maintain its position. The reason for this was soon to become apparent.

O'Connor's corps had pushed a long slim finger into the German lines and around this aerial reconnaissance revealed a strong concentration of enemy armour moving into position, some of it only recently arrived in Normandy. Rommel's intention was obviously to slice into the flanks of the salient, and the commander of the British Second Army, General Sir Miles Dempsey, ordered O'Connor to discontinue his advance to the

Orne but to retain his bridgehead over the Odon. To meet the attack, 11th Armoured Division pulled its tanks off Hill 112 during the night of 29th/30th June; the mere threat of the panzers' indirect approach had forced the British to abandon the feature.

For the next two days the German concentrations were bombed and strafed from the air, shelled by the massed British artillery and broken up by the terrible naval gunfire. When the counter-attack eventually took place, it was disorganised and unco-ordinated, was met by the combined fire of artillery, tanks and anti-tank guns, and stopped in its tracks with substantial casualties.

The troops involved included I and II SS Panzer Corps, in whose abilities Hitler had great faith. The implications of their failure were perfectly clear to Rundstedt – the Germans were physically unable to drive the Allies into the sea; nor could they remain within range of the naval gunfire without being bled white; nor could they withdraw to fight a war of manoeuvre without being swamped by the Anglo-American ground and air forces. The situation was painfully reminiscent of Rommel's previous dilemma at Alamein. During a telephone conversation with Keitel at OKW the Commander-in-Chief West was asked what could be done about the situation. Rundstedt's answer was straight and to the point: "Make peace, you fools! What else can you do?" He then proposed that the line should be pulled back beyond the range of naval interference, a suggestion that was rejected out of hand. On 3rd July he was relieved of his command and replaced by von Kluge.

No sooner had the last shots of the *Epsom* offensive been fired than Montgomery launched I Corps (3rd Canadian, 3rd and 59th British Divisions) in a frontal assault on Caen. The stubborn defence of Carpiquet airfield by the teenage 12th SS Panzer Division *Hitler Jugend* led to Bomber Command being requested to lay a bomb carpet through the defences. The RAF agreed but insisted on a 6,000-yard gap between the British lines and the tail of the carpet, as a safety precaution; a gap that also included the fortified villages on which the defence was based.

The carpet was to have been laid immediately before I Corps' attack at dawn on 8th July, but because of a poor weather forecast it was dropped on the evening of the 7th. More than 2,500 tons of bombs rained down on Caen, killing hundreds of French civilians, but doing little damage to the Germans who were ready and waiting when the British and Canadians rose to cross their start lines six hours later. Sustaining heavy loss, I Corps drove the 12th SS and a Luftwaffe division out of their villages, and seized the city centre, the streets of which were so blocked with rubble as to be quite impassable.

Throughout the Normandy campaign Montgomery employed the same "crumbling" technique that he had used at Alamein. Once Caen had fallen the bail was passed back to O'Connor with orders that VIII Corps should exploit the enemy's evident sensitivity concerning Hill 112 and the Odon valley generally, making use of the bridgehead gained during *Epsom*. Operation *Jupiter* began on 10th July and by evening the 43rd Division, supported by 31 Tank Brigade, had taken Hill 112 at its second attempt. Although counter-attacked continuously throughout the night the hill was held, but for the next three weeks both it and the hamlets of the Odon valley witnessed some of the bitterest attritional fighting of the war. To the Germans, whose heavy Tiger battalions were the soul of the defence, the hill came to be known as Kalvarienberg; to the British, whose infantry reserves were being sucked into the battle at a frightening rate, the whole area was known simply as Death Valley.

Once *Jupiter* had achieved its objective, control of the Odon sector passed to Lieutenant-General N.M. Ritchie's XII Corps while O'Connor and his VIII Corps headquarters moved east of Caen for the next major British effort, *Goodwood*, which was to commence on 18th July. Montgomery's directive summed up the significance of the operations as follows:

"*Object of this operation.*

To engage the German armour in battle and 'write it down' to such an extent that it is of no further value to the Germans as a basis of the battle. To gain a good bridgehead over the Orne through Caen and thus to improve our positions on the eastern flank.

Generally to destroy German equipment and personnel, *as a preliminary to a possible wide exploitation of success.*[68]

"*Effect of this operation on the Allied policy.*

We require the whole of the Cherbourg and Brittany peninsulas.

A victory on the eastern flank will help us gain what we want on the western flank.

But the eastern flank is a bastion on which the whole future of the campaign in N.W. Europe depends; it must remain a firm bastion; if it became unstable the operations on the western flank would cease. Therefore, while taking advantage of every opportunity to destroy the enemy, we must be very careful to maintain our own balance and ensure a firm base.

"*Initial operations of VIII Corps (on the 18th)*

The three armoured divisions will be required to dominate the area Bourgebus – Vimont – Bretteville, and to fight and destroy the enemy, but armoured cars should push far to the south towards Falaise, spread alarm and despondency, and discover 'the form'.

"*II* Canadian Corps

> While (the above) is going on, the Canadians must
> capture Vaucelles (the industrial suburb south of
> Caen), get through communications and establish
> themselves in a very firm bridgehead on the general
> line Fleury – Cormelles – Mondeville."

The directive ended by stressing the importance of the Canadian part in the operation and stated that when this had been completed VIII Corps would "crack about" as the situation demanded. There was, therefore, more than a hint that *Goodwood* was not simply designed as a holding action.

Once again, a corridor was to be blown through the enemy's outer defences by carpet bombing; 500-lb high explosive bombs were to be used on the fortified villages lying on the flanks of the corridor, but to prevent cratering that might delay the advance only 260-lb fragmentation bombs were to be dropped in the intervening areas. The attack itself would receive heavy artillery support and be made in column along the corridor as far as Cagny, 11th Armoured leading, followed by the Guards Armoured, with 7th Armoured bringing up the rear. At Cagny 11th Armoured would swing right to Bourgebus; the Guards would swing left to Vimont; and 7th Armoured would maintain the Corps centre-line to Garcelles-Secqueville.

The air support programme for *Goodwood* was the heaviest so far provided for a single ground operation, involving 1,600 heavy and 400 medium bombers as well as 2,500 fighters and ground-attack aircraft. For three hours following dawn on the 18th July the corridor heaved and shuddered under the incessant rain of explosives while a maelstrom of dust and smoke billowed over the tortured landscape. Then, as the last of the bombers turned for home, the 11th Armoured began moving down the corridor.

Yet, however impressive the air preparation had been it was only partly effective in that while the centres of the villages lining the corridor had been reduced to brick-dust, their perimeters and more often their forward edges were left untouched. Consequently, clearing these areas took time and in Cagny in particular the defenders were still present in strength and full of fight. As 11th Armoured began to wheel right on leaving the corridor it began to suffer from fire from Cagny, but nonetheless managed to cross the Caen – Vimont railway and advance some way up the slopes of the so-called Bourgebus Ridge, which is more accurately described as a rising plateau, where it came under fire from numerous well-prepared German positions. A troop leader serving with the division's 29th Armoured Brigade has left a vivid account of the ensuing action.

"The fateful decision was made. C Squadron would advance over the brow of a slight rise to the left in the direction of the village of Four. Bill, my squadron leader, gave his orders over the wireless in an excited voice, but they were perfectly clear. They were to be his last. The whole squadron, with the exception of my troop, which was to move forward as his right and flank protection, were to advance towards the village. By this time an incendiary shell had set alight the grass in the field we were in and a haze of smoke made it difficult to see the other tanks of the squadron.

"As soon as Bill had completed his orders, we started to move forward slowly. Within a few seconds Peter Robson's tank was hit by an 88 and went up in smoke. All the crew baled out safely. The rest of the squadron moved on and I could hear Jock Addison reporting a Panther on the outskirts of the village, which he was trying to engage. This was almost the last coherent message to be heard from the rest of the squadron. They were all brought under heavy and accurate fire and within a matter of minutes about five tanks were on fire and another three out of action.

"The Medical Officer had fixed up a temporary dressing station in a little white signal box on the railway line and casualties started streaming back from the burnt-out tanks. The chaps were all blackened, their clothes burnt, and most of them had lost their berets. A tank which had survived came roaring back with a lot of wounded lying on it.

"Repeated calls going out from the Colonel brought no replies and eventually I came up on the air and told him that I appeared to be the only surviving officer. I was then told, quite curtly, that what remained of the squadron was under my command and the line of the railway would be held to the last man and the last round.

"Just at that moment one of my sergeants' tanks was hit and although it did not brew up, the crew baled out. Everything was now in a state of chaos and the squadron on the right was also being heavily engaged by the enemy and losing tanks rapidly. A general withdrawal in the direction of the railway line took place, but it seemed to be only a matter of time before the rest of the regiment was written off.

"It was now between four and five in the afternoon and it was obvious that there was no hope of our gaining our objective that day."

By evening the 11th had lost 126 tanks, of which all but forty were repairable; personnel casualties, fortunately, were not as heavy as might have been expected.

Wheeling left from the corridor, the Guards had also been harassed by fire from Cagny and were finally halted at Frenouville, just south of the railway, having lost a total of sixty tanks. During the evening the division's infantry dealt with the last pockets of resistance in Cagny, whose defenders had put up a remarkable performance throughout the long day.

The 7th Armoured Division sustained very few casualties and in fact never really got moving. Its commander had expressed the opinion that the armour as a whole was being grossly mishandled and had temporised for much of the day, complaining that he had insufficient room to take his place in the line between the 11th and the Guards, not altogether unreasonably in view of the situation at Cagny, which lay directly on his axis of advance. However, during the evening his leading armoured regiment had reached the railway.

The three British armoured divisions had been forced to perform under the noses of invisible tanks, *Panzerjager* and emplaced anti-tank guns that outranged them. When the German armour did move to counter an aggressive British manoeuvre, it was at once assailed by ground-attack aircraft, but those occasions were few and far between. The essence of the British difficulty was that the depth of the enemy's defended zone had been underestimated; it was thought to extend only as far as the Caen – Vimont railway, when in fact it went several miles deeper and included the high ground of the Bourgebus plateau.

The fact that the area chosen for *Goodwood* was one of the few suitable for the manoeuvre of armour *en masse* had not been lost on Rommel, who had personally laid out the scheme of defence in depth. He had expected the attack to begin on the 17th and on that day was returning from a tour of the sector when his staff car was strafed by a fighter-bomber close to a village named, with curious irony, Ste Foy de Montgomery; both he and his driver were hit and the car overturned. The gravely wounded Field Marshal had fought his last battle. He was not replaced, his function as commander of Army Group B being absorbed by von Kluge.

Elsewhere on the 18th July, II Canadian Corps had succeeded in capturing Vaucelles and for the next few days pushed up onto the Bourgebus plateau, taking several fortified villages. On the VIII Corps front 11th Armoured was withdrawn into reserve and the Guards ordered to maintain their position, but 7th Armoured, covering the Canadian left flank, also advanced onto the plateau, capturing Four, Soliers and Bourgebus.

However, by nightfall on the 20th *Goodwood* was over. Ostensibly it had been a major German defensive success that had cost the British 200 tanks. It caused a temporary coolness between Eisenhower and Montgomery, the former having been under the impression that a British break-out in the east had been planned to match the projected American operation in the west, an idea that Montgomery strenuously denied.

Conversely, *Goodwood* served to reinforce the already successful Allied strategy of drawing the German armour away from the Americans. In the fourth week of July the British were faced by the 2nd, 21st, 116th, 1st SS, 9th SS, 10th SS and 12th SS Panzer Divisions and four heavy Tiger battalions; the Americans by the Panzer Lehr and 2nd SS Panzer Divisions and 17th SS Panzer Grenadier Division. Further, the German army in Normandy was slowly dying on its feet. Since D-Day it had sustained 117,000 personnel casualties but received only 12,000 replacements, a net loss of 105,000.[69] And although it was on occasion capable of inflicting a loss ratio of 4:1 on the Allied armour, British and American vehicle casualties were quickly made good whereas only seventeen machines succeeded in reaching the front to replace the German tank loss of 250. In the elite divisions morale remained high, but elsewhere strain and fatigue were now accompanied by a sense of hopelessness.

Meanwhile, on the American sector the US VII, VIII and XIX Corps had not only cleared the Contentin peninsula, taking Cherbourg on 29th June, but also pushed their general line steadily south until the capture of St Lo on 19th July enabled Bradley to state that he was able to mount Operation *Cobra*, the codename for 12th Army Group's break-out.

The Americans possessed a total of nineteen divisions, all amply equipped, and were faced by the equivalent of nine divisions, all but one of which had been in continuous action for more than a month, belonging to the German 7th Army. For a while, the *bocage* had inhibited the American armour as much as the British, but thanks to an ingenious device invented by Sergeant Curtis Culin, it now possessed the ability to move at speed through the earthen banks. The device, known as the Rhino hedgecutter, consisted of a row of spikes welded to the bow of a tank; as the tank drove into a hedge the spikes embedded themselves in the earth, so preventing the nose rising to offer the vulnerable belly-plates as a target, and the vehicle simply ground its way through the obstacle by main force.

Bradley had wanted *Cobra* to begin on 20th July, but bad flying weather had led to its postponement until the 25th. Once again, the carpet-bombing technique was used to blast a way through the German defences, this time between Marigny and St Gilles, slightly to the west of St Lo, 5,000 tons of high explosive, white phosphorous and napalm obliterating the target areas. The horrifying spectacle was witnessed by Lieutenant-General Fritz Bayerlain, commander of the Panzer Lehr Division, who later related his experience.

"My flak had hardly opened its mouth when the batteries received direct hits which knocked out half the guns and silenced the rest. After an hour I had no communication with anybody, even by radio. By noon nothing was visible but dust and smoke. My front lines looked like the face of the moon and at least 70 per cent of my troops were out of action – dead, wounded, crazed or numbed. All my forward tanks were knocked out and the roads were practically impassable."

Tragically, the bomb-carpet was a two-edged weapon. A sufficient margin for error had been allowed in the planning, but the prevailing wind drifted the cloud of dust and smoke across the American lines and it was into this that several aircraft released their loads, killing and wounding several hundred men; among the dead was Lieutenant-General Lesley J. McNair, the Chief of US Army Ground Forces.

Slightly shaken, the men of Major-General J. Lawton Collins' US VII Corps moved forward into the devastated area, three infantry divisions, the 9th, 4th and 30th fighting to secure the flanks of the corridor. By nightfall it seemed likely that the back of the German defence had been broken and Collins decided to release his exploitation force, consisting of the 2nd and 3rd Armored Divisions and the fully mechanised 1st Infantry Division the following day. Initially progress was delayed by the last stubborn defenders and the need to fight off local counter-attacks, but the day ended with 3rd Armored having reached Marigny and 2nd Armored moving on Canisy, having taken St Gilles.

On the 27th the offensive became general along the American front, VII Corps being joined by Major-General Charles H. Corlett's XIX Corps on its left and by Major-General Troy H. Middleton's VIII Corps on the coastal sector, the latter unleashing two further armoured divisions, the 4th and the 6th. On the VII Corps Front itself CCA 2nd Armored continued its advance south, taking Le Mesnil-Herman, while CCB 3rd Armored swung west towards Coutances, hoping to trap the troops facing VIII Corps in a pocket against the coast. As the tempo of the battle accelerated the enthusiasm of the moment was captured by the comment of the delighted commander of the 30th Infantry Division: "This thing has busted wide open. We may be the spearhead that broke the camel's back!" However suspect the metaphor, it spoke the truth – von Kluge's line had been smashed beyond hope of repair.

The following day the advance of CCB 3rd Armored and 1st Infantry was halted by elements of 2nd SS Panzer and 17th SS Panzer Grenadier Divisions two miles from Coutances in a desperate attempt to keep open a corridor that would enable their comrades to escape from the trap. However, the approach of 4th and 6th Armored from the north levered the SS out of their position and during the afternoon Coutances was taken, together with 4,500 prisoners.

On the 29th, 3rd Armored and 1st Infantry returned to the VII Corps axis while 4th and 6th Armored continued to batter their way through the wreck of retreating enemy divisions. Southeast of Coutances a German column of tanks, guns and lorries was pounced on by fighter-bombers and pounded into scrap. 4th Armored's commander, the hard-thrusting Major-General John S. Wood, then ordered his CCB to get to Avranches by any route it chose, and to get there quickly. In a dashing advance that was the epitome of *Blitzkrieg*, CCB covered twenty-five miles in thirty-six hours, driving into the town at dusk on the 30th. The next day CCA passed through and took Pontaubault, securing a bridgehead over the Selune; the 4th Armored was in Brittany.

Von Kluge had been slow to react to the implications of VII Corps' break-in operations. He did not take any effective counter-measures until the 28th, when he ordered 2nd and 116th Panzer Divisions to move from the British to the American sector. On the 30th, with his left flank all but turned, he assumed personal direction of the Seventh Army, horrified at the situation he found. "The infantry have completely disintegrated and the troops are no longer fighting properly," he advised his own Chief of Staff by telephone. "They are putting up a wretched show."

For his part, Montgomery was not going to permit von Kluge to transfer any more armour to the west than he could possibly help, and Dempsey was ordered to launch a further British offensive on the hitherto quiet Caumont sector. Two corps were to be involved, O'Connor's VIIIth (Guards Armoured, 11th Armoured, 15th (Scottish) Divisions and 6th Guards (Tank Brigade) and Lieutenant-General G.C. Bucknall's XXXth (7th Armoured, 43rd and 50th Divisions and 8th Armoured Brigade), the object being to capture Hills 361 and 309 and exploit southwards towards Vire.

The operation, named *Bluecoat*, began at first light on 30th July following localised air attacks. On the left XXX Corps' divisions were held up by extensive minefields and made little progress, but in VIII Corps' area the 6th Guards Tank Brigade achieved a spectacular success while supporting 15th Division. It was rare for the regiments of a tank brigade to fight in such close proximity to each other, but in this case 174 Churchills smashed through the front held by the tired German 326th Infantry Division in the most concentrated Infantry Tank attack of the war. Soon the tanks had left their infantry far behind, the slow but powerful Churchills clawing their way through *bocage* that would have been impassable to other vehicles. Hill 309 was captured during the evening after a six-mile advance, O'Connor commenting that "no tank unit has ever been handled with greater dash and determination". It was, in fact, 6th Tank Brigade's maiden action.

On the right 11th Armoured also made good progress on the 30th but this was eclipsed by the events of the following day. At 1035 a faint message was received from an armoured car troop of the Household Cavalry, which had worked its way through the enemy lines and was now five miles beyond: "I say again, the bridge at 637436 is clear of the enemy and still intact, over." The bridge crossed the little River Souleuvre and its significance was immediately apparent to the divisional commander, Major-General G.P.B. Roberts, who at once rushed reinforcements up to the troop. During the night 11th Armoured pushed across the river and established itself on the hills west of Le Beny Bocage.

On learning of the coup, O'Connor immediately brought the Guards Armoured into the line between 11th Armoured and 15th Division at St Martin des Besaces. Here elements of 21st Panzer Division and at least one Tiger battalion were encountered, having been despatched with all haste and in daylight by von Kluge to plug this new and totally unexpected gap. It had taken the German tanks five hours to cover twenty miles and they had been harried all the way by the Allied air forces.

However, on the XXX Corps front the situation remained disappointing, for although 43rd Division had maintained level progress with 15th Division, the 50th Division was pinned down and the experience of 7th Armoured had been anything but happy; it had been slow to get into action, at one stage becoming entangled with VIII Corps traffic across the inter-corps boundary in Caumont, and its attack on Aunay-sur-Odon had been repulsed.

Dempsey was in no mood to be tolerant; he could not afford to be in a climate of incessant pressure from London for a speedy end to the Normandy battle and the capture of the V1 Flying Bomb sites in the Pas de Calais. XXX Corps' commander was dismissed and replaced by Lieutenant-General B.G. Horrocks, and 7th Armoured was ruthlessly purged, losing its commander, his chief of staff, the commander of its armoured brigade and its senior artillery officer. The appointment of Brigadier G.L. Verney of 6th Guards Tank Brigade as the new divisional commander reflected the harsh but necessary philosophy that in the final analysis results were all that counted.

During the next week hard fighting carried the British line an average of six miles further south and von Kluge was compelled to commit II SS Panzer Corps (9th SS and 10th SS Panzer Divisions), which could otherwise have been used against the Americans, to contain the advance. It was not immediately apparent to either side that a product of *Bluecoat's* success was the establishment of a hard shoulder against which the German field army in France was to be crushed to destruction.

On the America Front events had begun to move with bewildering speed. On 1st August Lieutenant-General George S. Patton's Third Army,[70] which had been secretly building up strength inside the beachhead, was officially declared operational, with the specific brief of exploiting the break-through gained by *Cobra*.

Patton, aged fifty-eight, was the ideal choice for the task. A cavalryman by training, he was one of the very few American senior commanders to have actually served in armour during World War I. He had commanded 2nd Armored Division in 1941, risen to prominence during the Tunisian campaign and had achieved dramatic success while commanding the US Seventh Army in Sicily. Careless of speech and action, he was frequently a controversial figure, but he had the gift of asking, and receiving, more effort than his men thought they could give. His decisions were rapid and had to be implemented at a moment's notice; speed was something he insisted had to exist at every level in the collective minds of Third Army's staffs, and not simply on the battlefield itself. Once he had given a formation a mission to execute he did not care how it was done, provided the required results were produced.

In Bradley's estimation Brittany was a side issue that Patton, on the right of the American line, could deal with using Middleton's VIII Corps alone, aided by some 50,000 loosely organised but armed resistance fighters. The real business lay in the east and, as Montgomery put it, "Once a gap appears in the enemy front we must press into it and through it and beyond it into the enemy's rear areas. Everyone must go all out all day and every day. The broad strategy of the Allied Armies is to swing the right flank towards Paris and force the enemy back to the Seine."

Patton responded with a will. The gap already existed at Avranches and through it passed Major-General Wade E. Haislip's XV Corps on 5th August, racing south-east through country bare of organised opposition, covering the seventy-five miles to Le Mans in three days. No sooner was Haislip clear of the gap than Major-General Walton H. Walker's XX Corps was through, heading south to the Loire and then swinging east, with Major-General Gilbert R. Cook's XII Corps in hot pursuit. Third Army was now in full cry with nothing to stop it while on its left First Army's VII Corps formed a pivot for the great wheel that was being executed, capturing Mortain.

Von Kluge's position was now impossible. He proposed that the exposed southern flank should be protected from the American incursion by a screen of mobile divisions while the rest of the army withdrew behind the Seine, a logical solution that Hitler found unattractive. Instead, the Fuhrer decided that a counter-attack with *eight* panzer divisions, launched through Mortain to Avranches, would not only close the gap but also isolate Patton's corps in their head-long drive, close their supply routes and ensure their disintegration. It all looked frighteningly simple on the map table, but, in reality, von Kluge was being told to make bricks without straw.

With considerable effort four weak panzer divisions, possessing between them only 185 tanks and self-propelled guns, were assembled and began their attack on the morning of 7th August. It had been impossible for the Germans to conceal their preparations and on the right 116th Panzer was forced onto the defensive almost immediately by an American spoiling attack. Aided by darkness and poor flying weather 2nd Panzer affected a penetration and advanced seven miles before being halted by CCB 3rd Armored. In the centre 1st SS Panzer made very little progress. On the left 2nd SS Panzer recaptured Mortain but not the commanding Hill 317 overlooking the town from which the encircled defenders continued to direct artillery fire onto the German columns.

By noon the cloud and ground mist had dispersed and the Allied fighter-bombers swept across the battlefield, bringing the German advance to a standstill and shooting up the stalled convoys with deadly effect. Collins' VII Corps had weathered the storm and returned to the offensive the same day.

Even as the implications of the failure were being digested that night at von Kluge's headquarters, word was received of yet a further hammer blow, this time at the northern end of the line. 1st Canadian Army's II Corps, under Lieutenant-General G.G. Simonds, had launched a heavy night attack and the crack 12th SS Panzer Division had only been saved from complete rout by the personal intervention of its commander.

The Canadian offensive, Operation *Totalize*, was made astride the Caen – Falaise road with 2nd Canadian Division on the right and 51st (Highland) Division on the left, the infantry riding in improvised armoured carriers known as Unfrocked Priests.[71] Once they had seized their objectives two armoured divisions, 4th Canadian and 1st Polish, would pass through and exploit to the south. During the opening phase coloured marker shells fired by the artillery would guide the Allied bomber force onto its targets in spite of the darkness.

The attack was predictably confused, but did not break down. The movement of the mass of armour through their front and on into the night caused a panic among units of the 89th and 12th SS Panzer Divisions, which was only arrested with difficulty. By 11th August, when the battle ended, the German front had been pushed back ten miles.

Up to the first week of August the Allies had been fighting to reach the Seine. After Patton's break-out it was inevitable that they would obtain that objective, but now an even more glittering prize was offered. Logic dictated that von Kluge should have withdrawn, but instead he was clinging desperately to ground with evidently dwindling resources. Sensing victory, Montgomery and Bradley both saw that the small salient gained during the abortive Mortain counter-attack could be used as a fulcrum around which the German line could be bent, since von Kluge would have to respond to any threat from the south by deploying his depleted reserves in forming a prolonged defensive shoulder. This in itself would form a pocket which would be encircled and destroyed.

The end was as swift and it was dramatic. Haislip's XV Corps was ordered north from Le Mans on the 10th, and by the 13th was facing stiff opposition at Argentan. Collins' VII Corps continued to advance east and then north, coming in on Haislip's left, while the British Second Army maintained a steady pressure all along its front. On 14th August the Canadians returned to the attack, reaching the outskirts of Falaise two days later. By the 16th the pocket, some twenty-five miles long and fifteen wide, was a fact. Inside were the German Seventh Army, most of Fifth Panzer Army (as Panzer Group West was now called) and Panzer Group Eberbach, which consisted mainly of the divisions employed at Mortain, a total of 100,000 men. At last Hitler sanctioned a withdrawal, but it was too late.

Under continuous attack from all sides the walls of the pocket crumbled steadily while a flood of men and vehicles strove frantically to escape through the contracting corridor to the east. Those who remained were subjected to incessant artillery fire and strafed by fighter-bombers from dawn to dusk. Much of the German transport and artillery was horse-drawn and fearful jams ensued when the animals were killed in their traces. The slaughter continued without pause until 21st August, when the last exit was closed by 1st Polish Armoured Division.

The interior of the Falaise pocket stank of death and destruction. As one Canadian put it: "The road, as were all the roads in the area, was lined and in places practically blocked by destroyed German vehicles of every description. Horses and men lay rotting in every ditch. Most of the destruction must have been caused by the air force, but the Poles had done their share." Ten thousand

Germans were dead and 50,000 surrendered; among the wreckage were 344 tanks and other fighting vehicles, 252 towed guns and 2,447 items of motor transport.

Field Marshal von Kluge did not witness the death of his army. Throughout 15th August, he was out of touch with his headquarters, pinned in a ditch by an air attack; Hitler groundlessly believed that his absence had been used to negotiate a local armistice with the Allies, and replaced him with Field Marshal Walter Model. Von Kluge set out for Germany by car, without the slightest intention of completing the journey; he was too deeply implicated in the 20th July bomb plot for the Gestapo not to have been aware of his part in the affair. Near Metz, he ate a short meal by the roadside, then calmly took his own life.

Model could salvage little from the wreck; the Allied victory had been too complete and the overall situation was complicated by further French and American landings in the south. He had no alternative other than to abandon France altogether, harried across the Seine and beyond by Patton's armour, which had covered 400 miles in twenty-six days, while to the north Dempsey raced through the Pas de Calais to enter Brussels on 3rd September and Antwerp the following day, an advance of 230 miles in seven days.

The sudden German collapse took the Allied Supreme Command by surprise. There was optimistic speculation that the war in Europe could be ended in 1944; the question was how to achieve this. Several American commanders were for an advance on a broad front, but Montgomery favoured one powerful narrow thrust into the heart of Germany. There was insufficient fuel for both, and what there was had to make the long journey from Normandy until more convenient harbour facilities were acquired. With the American armies about to outnumber the British in Europe, Eisenhower felt obliged to support his countrymen, but conceded that Montgomery's drive to secure a bridgehead across the Rhine should be reinforced by the strategic drop of 1st Allied Airborne Army ahead of the advancing British XXX Corps in an operation to be known as *Market Garden*.

On 17th September the main drops took place: the US 101st Airborne Division north of Eindhoven to secure crossings of the Wilhelmina and Zuit Willemsvaart Canals, the US 82nd Airborne Division at Grave to capture the bridge over the Maas, and the British 1st Airborne Division west of Arnhem to advance into the town and take the great bridge over the Lower Rhine.

The 101st were relieved by XXX Corps on the 18th and the 82nd the following morning. The bridge at Nijmegen was captured by a joint attack on the 20th, but further progress along the only road available was barred by strong enemy counter-attacks.

At Arnhem 1st Airborne had been tragically unlucky. It had landed in the area where II SS Panzer Corps was refitting after its ordeal in Normandy, and although one battalion reached the bridge and held it for several days against all comers, the German reaction was so swift that the rest of the division was forced back to the suburb of Oosterbeek, where it was besieged. On 22nd September the 1st Polish Parachute Brigade was dropped on the opposite bank and established contact with Oosterbeek and XXX Corps. During the night of the 25th remnants of 1st Airborne, some 2,000 of the original 10,000, slipped across the river into the Poles' perimeter. The long advance that had begun at Falaise was over.

The war would not end in 1944. It would continue as a response to Hitler's demonic will, but more immediately because of Model's energetic reaction to *Market Garden* and above all because of the Wehrmacht's startling resilience in the face of losses on the Eastern Front, which made the Normandy debacle pale into relative insignificance.

Chapter 10: Death of an Army Group

Throughout the winter of 1943/44 the Red Army maintained its inexorable pressure against Army Group South, pushing it steadily across the Ukraine until by spring the whole province had been liberated and the Russians stood on Rumanian soil.

There was nothing inevitable about this, for in terms of numbers the Germans were only at a slight disadvantage and had, in fact, rather more tanks in hand than their immediate opponents. However, because of the vast distances involved, the Front was not a continuous entity as in the west, but a series of defended zones and successive river lines running broadly from north to south. From these positions, Hitler had absolutely forbidden the slightest withdrawal, and Manstein was thus effectively prevented from assembling any effective reserve to deal with an almost continuous state of crisis, being forced to commit everything simultaneously and send reinforcements into action as they arrived, whereas the Russians held a permanent initiative and were always present in overwhelming strength at the point of contact.

The Red Army of 1944 was, moreover, a very different being from that which had existed a year earlier. Its commanders were more confident in their own ability to execute mobile operations, and its tank crews were combat hardened, better trained and better equipped than ever before. The T34/76 had been countered by the long 75-mm gun fitted to the later models of the PzKw IV, but now this had in turn been overtaken by the appearance of the T34/85, which mounted an 85-mm gun in a three-man turret. In the heavy tank field the break-through battalions had been provided with an answer to the Tiger in the form of the IS (Iosef Stalin), which possessed a 122-mm gun and 140-mm frontal armour, while SUs of all types were in quantity production. The overall flexibility of armoured formations had also been improved by the arrival of thousands of British and American supply lorries shipped painfully to Russia by the long Arctic route, as well as large numbers of western tank radios, which permitted an allocation down to company level in many units, a factor rarely mentioned by Soviet historians.[72]

The size of these formations, too, was increasing as commanders gained confidence in handling large masses of vehicles, a process begun during the Stalingrad campaign. Generally, three tank brigades formed a tank corps with a nominal strength of about 180 tanks, supported by a motor rifle brigade, and sub-machine-gun battalion and a heavy artillery element. Two or more such corps would form a tank army. During offensive operations one corps of the tank army would, with an attached heavy tank battalion, affect the break-through, while the second, possibly supported by a cavalry formation, would exploit to the predetermined objective.

A second type of formation was the mechanised corps, in which the proportion of tanks to infantry was reversed. The principal weakness of both formations was the lack of personnel carriers for their motor rifle battalions, the men of which went into action either riding in open trucks or on the backs of the tanks themselves.

Again, although the set-piece attack, thoroughly planned and rehearsed down to the last sub-unit detail, still formed a major part of the Russian command philosophy, senior commanders were learning to apply their doctrine of mass a little more scientifically in that objectives were isolated rather than attacked frontally.

Facing Army Group South at the end of 1943 were 1st – 4th Ukrainian Fronts, roughly echeloned back from the right between Kiev and Zaporezhe. In the north 1st Ukrainian Front, commanded by Vatutin, opened the offensive on 24th December, forcing 4th Panzer Army to withdraw and thus ensuring the dismissal of its commander, Hoth. Hardly had this blow been absorbed when Marshal Ivan Koniev's 2nd Ukrainian Front, with Rotmistrov's crack 5th Guards Tank Army as its cutting edge, launched a fresh attack on 5th January. Five days later 3rd Ukrainian Front (Malinovsky) joined in, and on 31st January 4th Ukrainian Front (Tolbukhin) also went over to the offensive.

For Manstein the next few weeks became a nightmare. With the whole front now ablaze it was difficult to identify the enemy's principal thrust lines and in any case he lacked the means to manoeuvre against them, even if he had been permitted to do so. Many German formations, obedient to the Fuhrer's directive, were surrounded in their static defences and destroyed in detail.

First Panzer Army, cut off at Kamenets-Podolsk, fought its way out in a brilliant series of mobile actions, but others were not so lucky. On the night of 17th February, a group of more than eight divisions attempted to break out of a pocket that had been formed near the village of Shanderovka on the lower Dniepr,[73] Shortly after dawn they were overtaken by a Russian tank corps, which cut to pieces the escorting 5th SS Panzer Division *Wiking* and then ploughed on into the marching columns of men and horse-drawn transport, the T34s crushing man and beast alike beneath their tracks. The survivors, including a Belgian volunteer SS brigade, broke and fled across country, only to die in their thousands under the sabres of the vengeful Red cavalry. Afterwards, viewing the trampled, blood-stained snow with its carpet of corpses, a veteran of Stalingrad commented that he had never seen such concentrated slaughter.

At the lower tactical levels, the Russians were elsewhere forced to pay a heavy price in men and vehicles for their success, but it was a price that they could afford and were prepared to pay with T34 chassis production alone now reaching the figure of 20,000 per year. Even the *rasputitsa* was only of limited value to the Germans, for the wide Russian tank tracks provided traction in mud where those of the panzers did not, and although it did eventually bring fighting to an end there was, as Manstein put it, "every reason for viewing the future with anxiety".

By the end of March, Army Group South had withdrawn some 200 miles and was fighting with its back to the Carpathians. It was not a situation Hitler was prepared to tolerate, and after presenting Manstein and Kleist with the Swords to their Knights' Crosses, he dismissed them both. Thus, in addition to their material gains, the Russians had rid themselves of three of Germany's most experienced commanders; the loss of Manstein in particular was deeply regretted by all save Hitler's toadies at OKW, as many considered that he was the only man who could have pulled the Eastern Front together, had he been given a free hand. This loss was only fractionally balanced by the death of Vatutin, ambushed and shot dead in February, allegedly by anti-communist partisans, but Zhukov had stepped personally into the breach and assumed temporary command of 1st Ukrainian Front.

It was the collective opinion of OKW that following the thaw the Red Army would resume operations against Army Group South, and for this reason most of the available panzer strength was grouped opposite the huge Ukrainian salient. However, OKW had guessed badly wrong, for STAVKA's eyes were now turned on the overextended Army Group Centre, commanded by Field Marshal Busch since Kluge's departure for France.

Here the two sides were evenly matched in manpower, but the Russians had managed to concentrate 4,000 tanks against 900 German, 28,600 guns against 10,000, and 5,300 aircraft against the 1,300 that the Luftwaffe could put up, the majority of the latter's strength having been diverted to the air defence of the homeland. Once again, the Red Army's plans had been drawn up by the formidable team of Zhukov and Vasilevsky.

Busch's problems were similar to Manstein's in that he had everything in the shop window and very little in reserve. However, Russian preparations had not been carried out with the total secrecy claimed for them by several Soviet historians, and Busch's appreciation of the situation was that he was going to be attacked in strength very shortly. He requested permission to withdraw behind the Beresina, a move that would have meant that the Russian blow would initially strike a tactical vacuum, so disrupting their minutely planned timetable. Hitler was of course outraged by the suggestion, but he had no alternative to offer other than his usual no-retreat-at-any-cost syndrome.

Facing Busch were, from north to south, 1st Baltic Front (Bagramyan); 3rd Belorussian Front (Chernyakovsky), which included 5th Guards Tank Army, brought up from the south; 2nd Belorussian Front (Zhakharov); and 1st Belorussian Front (Rokossovsky). The date chosen for the offensive was 22nd June, symbolically the third anniversary of *Barbarossa*, and as if in recreation of a mirror image, fleets of Soviet bombers crossed the lines to pound the Luftwaffe's airfields and remove it almost completely from the order of battle.

Zhukov's tanks moved with unprecedented speed, riding through their not inconsiderable losses and leaving behind isolated pockets of resistance for later reduction. Repeatedly, major objectives were cut off by double envelopment while the advance flowed on, Vitebsk on 27th June, Mogilev on the 28th, Bobruysk the following day, Minsk on 3rd July, Wilno ten days later, Lublin on 23rd July and Brest-Litovsk on the 28th. A 250-mile gap had been blown in the line and forty tank brigades were rolling across what had been the plains of eastern Poland with nothing to stop them. A thrust to the coast west of Riger succeeded for a while in completely isolating Field Marshal Lindemann's Army Group North in the Baltic States, but after desperate fighting the Germans were able to re-open a narrow corridor.

Army Group Centre had effectively been destroyed with the loss of twenty-five divisions when the Russian advance at last ran down on the banks of the Vistula, having covered 450 miles in four weeks. This was an astonishing feat for an army that thirty-six months earlier had entered hostilities with crews barely able to man their tanks. It was true, of course, that the Russians were present in overwhelming strength, but the fact remains that in spite of their stiff command system, momentum was maintained throughout, indicating how much had been learned in the intervening period.

In the west, little mention has been made of this most celebrated of Russian *Blitzkriegs*, partly because Anglo-American interest tends to become focused on contemporary events in Normandy, and partly because of a distinct cooling in relationships between the Allies brought about by the tragedy of Warsaw.

As the Red Army closed in on the Vistula the pro-western Polish Home Army rose in the capital, anticipating early relief by the Russians. That relief never came, for although they were within striking distance, the Russians sent only a token force to the assistance of the insurgents, and this was easily held by a German counter-attack. The world was forced to watch impotently as the rising was crushed without mercy and the city deliberately devastated.

The fact was that the affair suited the Soviet Government admirably, since it concluded the destruction of the anti-Bolshevik pre-war Polish Establishment that had begun with the massacre at Katyn Wood. The official Party Line is that "The aim of the rising, as the Polish reactionaries who organised it openly stated at the time, was not to help the Red Army to liberate Poland, but to obstruct it. They considered that by seizing the capital they could establish themselves in power and prevent the people's democratic order from coming into being in Poland."[74] Actually, as part of STAVKA's overall planning for the offensive, radio contact had been made with every partisan and resistance group in the path of the *Blitzkrieg* asking them to commence operations against German communications, and the Polish Home Army received several such appeals. However, the Party finds an unusual ally in Guderian, who comments that: "We Germans had the impression that it was our defence which halted the enemy rather than a Russian desire to sabotage the Warsaw uprising."[75] Soviet authors might, therefore, have been better advised to state frankly that after their tremendous effort the Belorussian Fronts had simply shot their bolt; which would have been infinitely less convoluted than their patently obvious attempts at self-justification. In any event, the Vistula sector remained static for the next six months while communications were re-established and supplies built up for the next leap forward.

Elsewhere, the Ukrainian Fronts had returned to the attack in July and had made considerable advances against Army Group South, which had been forced to send part of its armour to aid its stricken neighbour. Malinovsky's 2nd Ukrainian Front, led by 6th Guards Tank Army, made a dashing 250-mile advance into Rumania in twelve days; the result was that on 25th August Rumania changed sides and declared war on Germany, followed on 8th September by Bulgaria. The German Army Groups E and F, stationed respectively in Yugoslavia and Greece, were now in danger of being isolated from Central Europe and conducted a hasty withdrawal into Hungary, Germany's sole remaining Balkan ally. In the three months June – August 1944 the Wehrmacht had sustained one million casualties.

In the north the three Baltic Fronts, assisted by Leningrad Front, mounted their own offensive against Army Group North during the autumn. 1st Baltic Front reached the coast near Memel on 10th October, while simultaneously 2nd and 3rd Baltic Fronts closed in on the defensive perimeter of Riga, which fell five days later. The remnants of Army Group North, some thirty-three divisions, retired into the Courland peninsula, where they remained blockaded for the rest of the war. Finland had long recognised the meaning of the writing on the wall and had negotiated her own peace treaty with Russia in September.

The end of the war in Eastern Europe was in sight, brought about largely by the dramatic destruction of Army Group Centre, but the Red Army's advances in 1945 lacked the same depth and pace as those of the previous year, and were bought at a comparatively higher cost in blood and machinery, for the Germans fought with every ounce of skill at their disposal to keep the hated enemy and his creed out of their homeland. Men now realised that the defeat of Germany was inevitable, but looked anxiously over their shoulders, hoping that it would be the British, Americans and French who would be their eventual occupiers, if only the crumbling eastern rampart could be held for long enough. The emaciated panzer divisions and assault gun brigades would give of their best, but what was needed was a substantial armoured reserve with which to manoeuvre against the Russian thrusts. By the end of 1944 such a reserve had been painstakingly brought together, but in his paranoia, Hitler decided that it should be used on the Western Front; the Red Army rolled on, and the boundaries of Europe were adjusted irrevocably.

Chapter 11: Panzerlied for Ghosts

The last shells were being fired into the Falaise pocket and Operation *Market Garden* still lay one month ahead when Adolf Hitler announced that the German Army in the west would go over to the offensive in November 1944. With the multiple disasters of Normandy and on the Eastern Front still vivid in their minds, his senior officers protested that such a course of action was impossible, but Hitler was adamant; he had decreed it, therefore it would be done.

By reducing the call-up age to sixteen and by taking men from reserved occupations, by conscripting the sick into special "stomach" or "ear" battalions and by scraping the manpower barrel as far down as convicted criminals, eighteen new divisions were raised and given the title of *Volksgrenadier.* In addition, the lion's share of tank production was used to flesh out the skeletons of those panzer divisions that had limped back from the Normandy debacle.

It was Hitler's custom to hold daily conferences to review the overall war situation, and at the conference held on 16th September he finally decided how he would use his rebuilt strategic reserve. Jodl, the Chief of Operations, passed a comment that the Ardennes sector remained totally inactive. The effect on Hitler was electric. The strategic situation in the west bore some similarity to that of 1940 in that 1st Canadian, 2nd British, 1st and 9th American Armies were all operating in the Low Countries. The Ardennes represented a gateway through which the brilliant *Sichelschnitt* plan could be re-enacted. Once more the German Army, led by its panzers, would burst out of these hills and secure crossing of the Meuse; then it would carry out a lightning advance to seize Antwerp, thus isolating those Allied armies in the north. Enclosed in an iron ring, those armies would be faced with an alternative of destruction or an evacuation by sea. Once this had been achieved, Hitler reasoned, the Western Allies would recognise that Germany could never be defeated and conclude a negotiated peace, leaving him free to get on with the war in the east.

Leaving his staff to grapple with the virtually insuperable logistic problems posed by such an undertaking, Hitler personally supervised Jodl's operational planning. The final draft, code-named *Wacht am Rhein*, went into the minutest detail of how the operation was to be conducted and was superscribed in the Fuhrer's own hand: NOT TO BE ALTERED. Copies were sent to Field Marshal von Rundstedt, who had been persuaded to return to active duty as Commander-in-Chief West, and to Field Marshal Walter Model, whose Army Group B would carry out the operation. After reading the document, Rundstedt passed the contemptuous comment: "Antwerp? If we reach the Meuse we should go down on our knees and thank God!" Model, a particular favourite of Hitler's, was even more direct in his appraisal: "This damn thing hasn't got a leg to stand on!"

Both field marshals prepared plans for more limited offensives that were designed to strengthen the overall position of the Western Front. These were duly presented to Hitler, who waved them aside. The Fuhrer was filled with confidence. The trouble with his generals, he said, was that they lacked the imagination to see the Grand Solution, and they refused to learn from history. When Frederick the Great's fortunes were at their lowest ebb had he not gone over to the offensive, winning the great victories of Rossbach and Leuthen? And, as a result of these, had not the alliance of his enemies suddenly collapsed? History, Hitler announced, was about to repeat itself; *Wacht am Rhein* would be *his* Rossbach and Leuthen.

Following this interview, Rundstedt took very little active interest in the subsequent execution of the plan. There was no point in advising the Fuhrer that an important difference between *Sichelschnitt* and *Wacht am Rhein* was that in the former the scanty Ardennes road system had favoured the general south-west thrust line, whereas there were few good roads running west and north-west, the direction required by the latter; in other words, this time the Germans would be advancing across the grain of the country rather than with it. *Wacht am Rhein* was an expression of Hitler's Indomitable Will, and that was that.

The sector chosen for the break-through lay between Monschau in the north and Echternach in the south, a front of eighty-five miles. On the right was 6th SS Panzer Army under Obergruppenfuhrer Sepp Dietrich, an old crony of Hitler's from his street-brawling days and a former commander of 1st SS Panzer Division; in the centre was 5th Panzer Army, commanded by General Baron Hasso von Manteuffel, sometime gentleman-jockey and veteran of the Eastern Front who was at that time enjoying the Fuhrer's particular favour; and on the left was General Brandenberger's 7th Army, whose principal responsibility lay in protecting the southern shoulder of the salient once it had been formed.

To demonstrate to the world the superiority of the Nazi ethic, Hitler had decided that the decisive thrust would be made by 6th SS Panzer Army, and had arranged for its passage to be eased by the dropping of Germany's sole remaining parachute unit, named *Kampfgruppe* von der Heydte after its commander, behind the American lines opposite. However, when von der Heydte reported to Dietrich for briefing he received only vague general instruction. In response to a request for details of the American troops in the area, Dietrich, who was drunk and disliked aristo-cratic paratroop colonels, snarled that he wasn't a prophet, but that "behind their lines there are only Jewish hoodlums and bank managers". At length his embarrassed Chief of Staff was able to tell von der Heydte that he was to drop on a heath near Baraque Michel.

"You're to go there and cause confusion," said Dietrich, rejoining the conversation.

"Von der Heydte's role is *not* specifically to cause confusion," explained the Chief of Staff coldly. "You have confused his operation with Skorzeny's Operation Grief."

The newly promoted Colonel Otto "Scarface" Skorzeny was one of the Reich's more piratical characters who is best remembered for his rescue of Mussolini from the dictator's mountain prison. Leading a specially trained unit of English-speaking Germans, dressed in American uniforms and riding in captured American vehicles, Skorzeny was to take advantage of the disorganisation caused by the opening attacks to cross the lines and disrupt the enemy's lines of communication, re-directing reinforcement convoys and generally spreading alarm and despondency, thus providing an echo of the Trojan Horse parties of the 1940 *Blitzkrieg*.

German preparations continued apace and in the greatest secrecy. Large fuel and ammunition dumps were established close to the Rhine and bridges were strengthened to take the weight of the invincible Royal Tigers that were to smash their way through all opposition. Even so, it quickly became obvious that all would not be ready by November and Hitler agreed to a postponement of one month, encouraged by the thought that in the depths of winter the Ardennes weather would prevent the Allies from exercising their almost total superiority in the air.

Throughout the first half of December the panzer divisions began to assemble slowly under cover of the snow-laden forests behind the front, while artillery batteries began dumping shells and inconspicuously registering the targets that they would engage during the initial bombardment. Without any doubt, German morale and motivation was at the highest level it had been for many months, men recording in their letters their eager anticipation of taking part in the offensive that would rid their homeland of the enemy.

By coincidence the Ardennes was, as it had been in 1940, the weakest sector of the entire Allied line. This was not because the Allies were under any old-fashioned illusions that the area was tank-proof, but because they did not understand the way things were run in Germany. Rundstedt was known to have returned as Commander-in-Chief West, a respected figure with a first-class military brain to whom the prospect of committing his last reserves to a major offensive would, in the opinion of Allied Intelligence, seem completely illogical. What the Allies failed to appreciate was that Rundstedt did not give orders; Hitler did, and Hitler was not a slave to logic.

Because nothing ever happened there, the Ardennes was known to the men of Lieutenant-General Courtney Hodges' US 1st Army as the Ghost Front. It was, in fact, just the sort of sector on which tired divisions could be rested and green divisions given their first, small-scale, introductions to battle. In the line and almost totally unprepared for the explosion that was to follow were four divisions, two of which had been bled white in the fighting for Aachen and which had been made up to strength with replacements, and two recently arrived divisions.

From Echternach to the Losheim Gap, more than sixty miles, the Ghost Front was held by the 28th and 106th Divisions of Major-General Troy Middleton's VIII Corps, with Combat Command A of 9th Armored Division in support. From the Losheim Gap to Monschau the front became the responsibility of Major-General Leonard Gerow's V Corps, two of whose divisions, the 2nd and 99th, lay directly in the path of the offensive together with CCB of 9th Armored Division, although they were in much closer proximity to each other than Middleton's thinly stretched formations; the remainder of Gerow's Corps was fighting offensively towards the Roer dams. The boundary between the two corps, and indeed the Losheim Gap itself, was protected by a weak regimental group provided by the armoured cars of 14th Cavalry.

Of course there were indications that the Germans were up to something; it would have been almost impossible to keep such an undertaking a total secret. However, the suspicions of regimental officers were evaluated by higher formations as having little substance, so that when at 0530 on 16th December 2,000 German guns opened fire along the Ghost Front senior commanders were not even psychologically prepared. Even if they had been it would have been difficult to exercise control over such a wide area, since the bombardment quickly severed the telephone links connecting the various headquarters.

At 0730 the guns passed to local control and white-sheeted *Volksgrenadiers* began moving forward to the attack, flitting across the snowy landscape like phantoms in the heavy morning mist, which in itself seemed to augur well, for on 6th December the codename *Wacht am Rhein* had been changed to *Autumn Fog*.

In fact, all was far from well. In the north the US 99th Division resisted stoutly throughout the day, piling up *Volksgrenadier* casualties along their front. On this, the vital sector, this was a most unfortunate check to the German plans, which involved the tanks passing through only *after* the infantry had punched a gap in the American line, and the result was that the 12th SS Panzer Division was unable to advance, its stalled columns clogging all roads leading into their forward zone.

Further south, in the Losheim Gap, 14th Cavalry had also inflicted severe loss, but were too few in numbers and too lightly equipped to prevent a break-through by Kampfgruppe Peiper, the spearhead of 1st SS Panzer Division. Notwithstanding, by the end of the day SS Panzer Army's progress was well behind schedule.

On von Manteuffel's sector the Germans could feel more cause for satisfaction. Two regiments of the US 106th Division were outflanked and isolated on the Schnee Eifel and eventually forced to surrender. At 1600, in the gathering winter dusk, the panzer divisions were called forward and began to move out into the country beyond to continue their advance by the light of search-lights reflected from the clouds.

Skorzeny's men also did their work well. Some were caught and shot but the majority returned safely having caused such chaos that for days even senior officers were held at gunpoint and closely questioned concerning some aspect of American life.

Out of contact with their divisional, regimental or even battalion headquarters, the Americans fought a junior leaders' battle. Unlike 1940, these defenders of the Ardennes were not elderly reservists whose nerve had been broken by dive bombing; they were young, fit, disciplined, well trained, and above all they were angry. Here and there a lost village would be retaken, lost again and retaken a second time; *ad hoc* battlegroups congealed around a few Shermans, tank destroyers or anti-tank guns to shoot it out with a panzer spearhead; a German tank column, racing to secure an important bridge, would see it blown in their faces and be forced to find an alternative route. There were hundreds of such minor incidents, which, in themselves, could not halt the enemy's advance but which collectively cost him precious time when he could afford it least.

Senior American officers differed widely in their interpretations of the day's events. Middleton at VIII Corps, out of touch with most of his units, lacked detailed information on which to base conclusions, but was committing the last of his reserves. Gerow, V Corps commander, realised that the attack his troops were holding off was "something big". At 1st Army Headquarters Hodges was not, at first, inclined to agree; nor was the Army Group commander, General Omar Bradley, who happened to be visiting Eisenhower that evening and who thought that the German offensive was designed to divert troops from Patton's drive in the Saar. Eisenhower, observing the length of front involved, supported Gerow and ordered the immediate despatch of two armoured divisions, the 10th from Patton's 3rd Army in the south and the 7th from Simpson's 9th Army in the north, into the Ardennes.

During the night, von der Heydte was scheduled to drop behind the lines of the embattled US 99th Division but his transports were utterly dispersed by anti-aircraft fire while crossing the lines and only a few score paratroopers actually joined their commander in the drop zone on the lonely heath near Baraque Michel. These were too few to accomplish anything and spent the next few days trying to evade capture and reach their own lines. 2nd Division, covering the withdrawal of the 99th to better defensive positions along the Elsenborn ridge, knew of the drop but remained unaffected by it.

The next morning 12th SS Panzer Division tried again to break through Gerow's position, and failed. The 7th Armored Division, commanded by Brigadier-General R.W. Hasbrouck, began entering the combat zone after an epic road march and by afternoon was arriving in St Vith, which had become a rallying point for troops pouring back from the broken front. Ultimately Hasbrouck was able to muster, in addition to his own division, CCB of 9th Armored and two infantry regiments that had been badly mauled. These he deployed in a twenty-five-mile arc east of the town, which remained a thorn in the enemy's side for several days.

Kampfgruppe Peiper actually motored across 7th Armored's tracks during the day, taking Stavelot and threatening 1st Army's main fuel dumps. At a crossroads near Malmedy a small artillery observation battery was captured and without the slightest justification its men were shot down in cold blood. Nor were these the only murders committed by 1st SS Panzer Division that day, but sufficient witnesses escaped for the crimes to be reported almost at once and in consequence newly arrived American units went into battle with vengeance in the forefront of their minds.

At Supreme Headquarters the overall picture had begun to clarify and it was sufficiently menacing for Eisenhower to commit his strategic reserve, the 82nd and 101st Airborne Divisions, to the fighting. However, these formations were at Rheims and would not reach the Ardennes before the following afternoon.

The morning of the 18th found Peiper, now critically short of fuel, probing his way along the tortuous valley of the Ambleve towards the American dumps, one of which was reached after several diversions made necessary by blown bridges or the resistance of scratch units. He found his way blocked by a small covering force commanded by Major Paul J. Sollis, which had stacked petrol drums across the road at the top of a hill. As the panzers ground up the slope the drums were ignited and a roaring wall of flame leapt skywards in front of them. As Sollis' men rolled fresh drums into the inferno the tanks backed off, unable to by-pass the obstacle because of a steep hill on one side and a sharp drop on the other. Balked, they turned tail leaving behind enough fuel to take 1st SS Panzer Division well beyond the Meuse.

Peiper tried an alternative line of advance through Trois Ponts. Here a single 57-mm anti-tank gun stalled his column long enough for the American engineers to blow the bridge over the Ambleve. The SS men's angry frustrations were released by the murder of twenty-two Belgian civilians.

In fact, Kampfgruppe Peiper had gone about as far as it was going. That afternoon Gerow's redeployed 30th Division recaptured Stavelot, cutting the road to the rear, and the 82nd Airborne Division came into the line at Werbomont to the west. Peiper had driven into a blind alley.

Meanwhile, south of St Vith, von Manteuffel was continuing his drive to the west. An independent panzer division, the 116th, was advancing on Houffalize, while the three divisions of von Luttwitz's XLVII Panzer Corps, 2nd Panzer, Panzer Lehr and 26th *Volks grenadier*, stormed their way through Clervaux and headed for Bastogne.

Five major roads met at Bastogne, which was also an important railway junction, and possession of the town was vital not only for the continued German advance to the north-west, but also because any American counter-stroke into the Ardennes would have to pass through it to succeed. Middleton had his VIII Corps headquarters there, but on 18th December he had only a handful of administrative troops available as a garrison and was forced to watch impotently as his few outposts to the east were driven in one after the other by the tide of German armour.

However, during the evening, Colonel William Roberts' CCB of 10th Armored Division drove in and was quickly deployed in three teams on the roads leading into Bastogne from the north, east and south. This in itself might not have been enough to save the town, for the crack Panzer Lehr Division, under the energetic leadership of the veteran Bayerlein, succeeded in working its way between two of the teams and headed directly for Bastogne along a minor road. It was Panzer Lehr's ill luck that the road ended in a mud-wallow two miles from the objective and dawn found the division still shaking itself free of the morass.

By then the golden opportunity had gone, for during the night the 101st Airborne Division had arrived and was already setting up a defensive perimeter. Middleton was ordered by Hodges to leave Bastogne, and this left the 101st's acting commander, Brigadier-General Anthony McAuliffe, the senior ranking officer.

Although it was not immediately apparent to either side, the fate of *Autumn Fog* was sealed on 19th December. Eisenhower had already cancelled 3rd Army's offensive in the Saar and ordered Patton to advance northwards into the German flank. Asked how soon he would be ready to move, Patton replied that three of his divisions would be on the road within twenty-four hours, commenting cheerfully on the enemy's deep penetration: "Let the bastards go all the way to Paris; then we can cut 'em off and chew 'em up!" Eisenhower's response was that as far as he was concerned, they were not even going to be allowed across the Meuse.

On the 21st Army Group sector of the Allied line Field Marshal Montgomery had been following the German progress with interest and had already deduced that Model's first objective was the Meuse at Liege and, after that, Antwerp. Acting on his own initiative he began moving the four divisions of the British XXX Corps into blocking positions along the west bank of the river so that, if and when the time came, Model would have to fight extremely hard for a bridgehead, let alone continue his drive to the sea.

During the day Montgomery received a call from Eisenhower who explained that as the great bulge in the line had physically separated direct communication between the headquarters of Bradley at 12th Army Group and Hodges at 1st Army, the only logical step was to place Montgomery in command of all troops north of the bulge while Bradley continued to control operations in the south. Montgomery, who had been kept up to date by his team of liaison officers, agreed, although the involvement of a British officer in the solution of an American problem was by no means universally popular.

On 20th December, Montgomery swept into Hodges' headquarters "like Christ come to cleanse the Temple", as one American officer put it. The effect was unfortunate, even if the intention was to inspire confidence, and many officers received a distinct impression that the Field Marshal was less than pleased by their efforts. Even so, Montgomery was in agreement with Hodges that the line should be straightened. Under the control of Major-General Matthew Ridgway's XVIII Airborne Corps, the 82nd Airborne, supported by a combat command of 3rd Armored Division, attacked the same day and established a link with the St Vith defence line. One effect of this was to further isolate Kampfgruppe Peiper, now trapped in the Ambleve valley; after trying unsuccessfully for several days to fight his way out, Peiper abandoned his equipment, including thirty-nine tanks and seventy halftracks, and worked his way through the American lines with only 800 of the 2,000 men with whom he had begun the offensive a week earlier.

Another was the creation of an American salient within the great German bulge. Concerning this Ridgway became increasingly anxious throughout the morning of the 21st as 116 Panzer Division began to advance northwards from Houffalize along the Ourthe valley, effectively outflanking him to the west. Simultaneously, Hasbrouck reported that an attack of unprecedented violence was being launched against St Vith itself. It seemed as though the Germans had more reserves than anyone had bargained for.

St Vith lay directly in the path of the second major German assault wave. As the pattern of the battle emerged, Model had made representations to Hitler that since Dietrich was still making no progress at Elsenborn ridge, the logical step would be to reinforce von Manteuffel's success on 5th Panzer Army's sector by committing the reserves there. As the most important element of these reserves consisted of II SS Panzer Corps (2nd and 9th SS Panzer Divisions) plus the elite Fuhrer Escort Brigade, Hitler insisted that it was not politically acceptable for SS formations to be seen to be playing a secondary role to those of the Wehrmacht. He was disappointed in Dietrich, but he was going to give him another chance; the reserves would be employed to secure a break-through on his southern flank.

By the evening of the 21st the last tired defenders of St Vith had been forced out of the town and the curved shoulders of Hasbrouck's line were crumpling inwards under sustained pressure. Ridgway, to whom denying ground to the enemy had become a matter of principle, ordered Hasbrouck not to retreat beyond the River Salm and, if necessary, to form a pocket that could be supplied by air. Hasbrouck agreed to do this under protest, commenting that such a course of action would mean the end of 7th Armored Division.

He found an ally in Montgomery, who took a more clinical view of the situation and felt that 7th Armored would be better employed on the northern shoulder of the bulge. Ridgway was overruled and the remains of the St Vith garrison was withdrawn across the Salm to safety.

On 23rd December it was the turn of 82nd Airborne to come under heavy pressure from II SS Panzer Corps. A penetration was made by 2nd SS Panzer Division, which was contained only with difficulty by Ridgway's last reserves at Grandmenil. Further west 116 Panzer Division was attacking Hotton, but was fortunately unable to co-ordinate its activities with those of 2nd SS Panzer since the two formations belonged to different armies. Once more Montgomery intervened, instructing Ridgway to evacuate his seven-mile salient and return 82nd Airborne to its position at Werbomont.

It seemed as though a crisis was approaching on the northern front. However, by moving Lieutenant-General J. Lawton Collins' VII Corps headquarters down from the US 9th Army and providing it with divisions culled from quieter areas of the Allied line, Montgomery was able to extend his shoulder of the bulge westwards from the Ourthe towards Dinant.

To a degree he agreed with Patton. The Germans should be allowed to go wherever they liked, provided it was not in the one direction they really wanted to go, which was north-west to the Meuse between Liege and Namur. At Alam Haifa he had seen the enemy exhaust his potential against prepared defences, and in Normandy the panzer divisions had been destroyed by sheer attrition. He was well aware that German reserves of fighting vehicle and fuel were strictly limited and that these could best be absorbed by fighting defensively, which he proceeded to do for the next week, resisting pressure from Hodges and other American commanders to mount a counter-offensive.

In the south von Manteuffel had decided to leave Luttwitz to reduce Bastogne with the infantry divisions while he by-passed the town with 2nd Panzer and Panzer Lehr and continued with his advance to the Meuse, which, according to the Fuhrer's timetable, should have been reached by the second evening of the offensive.

Bastogne was completely encircled by the morning of 21st December, but Luttwitz was unable to make any impression on the defences. The following day he sent two officers under a flag of truce to see McAuliffe, offering an honourable surrender; if this proposal was rejected, his note continued, "One German artillery corps and six AA battalions are ready to annihilate the USA troops in and near Bastogne."

McAuliffe, a former artillery officer, knew exactly what guns were capable of and what they were not, read briefly through the note and muttered "Nuts", a simple expression of professional disdain. He then left the command post to talk to some men who had distinguished themselves in a recent action. When he returned the two Germans were still waiting and demanded a written reply to Luttwitz's note. McAuliffe, wondering what to say, consulted his staff. His operations officer remarked that his initial reaction would be hard to beat, and reminded him of it. McAuliffe sat down and scribbled three lines.

To the German Commander:

Nuts!

– The American Commander.

The reply was handed to Colonel Joseph Harper, who passed it on to the two intermediaries. Understandably they asked what it meant.

"It means 'Go to Hell,'" said Harper. "And I'll tell you something else. If you continue to attack we'll kill every goddam German that tries to break into this city!"

"We will kill many Americans!" replied one of the officers as they saluted and turned smartly on their heels.

McAuliffe's inadvertent response may have lacked the traditional military courtesies reserved for such occasions, but the Army and the American public loved it; it possessed the terse, confident qualities required of a determined commander in a tight corner.

And for the next four days Bastogne became a very tight corner indeed. The 101st Airborne and CCB 10th Armored were bombed, shelled and assaulted daily, the attacks reaching their climax on Christmas Day, when the defences were breached in two places. However, McAuliffe had deployed his reserves skilfully and those Germans who broke through were wiped out or forced to surrender, as Harper had promised.

On 26th December the attacks were resumed but no penetrations were made. Towards evening the men manning the southern edge of the perimeter heard the sound of tanks approaching and, imagining that they were to be assailed yet again, tucked in their heads. But, to their surprise, the tanks halted a little distance away and a voice called, "Come here! This is the 4th Armored!"

Cautiously they looked up at the platoon of Shermans. An officer was standing in the cupola of the leading vehicle and one of their own lieutenants was reaching up to shake hands with him.

"I'm Webster, 326th Engineers, 101st Airborne Division. Glad to see you."

"Charles Boggess, 37th Tank Battalion, CCR 4th Armored."

Bastogne had been relieved. True to his word, Patton had swung his 3rd Army's axis of advance left through ninety degrees in a remarkably short space of time and since 20th December the

228

IIIrd and XIIth Corps had been moving north against stiff opposition from Brandenberger's 7th Army. Absolute priority had been given to III Corps' thrust towards Bastogne, spearheaded by Major-General Hugh Gaffey's redoubtable 4th Armored Divisions, which had had to fight almost every step of the way. On 26th December the Fourth's CCR was in the lead with the 37th Tank Battalion out in front under Lieutenant-Colonel Creighton W. Abrams, a future Commander-in-Chief of the anti-communist forces in Vietnam.

At 1330 Abrams asked Gaffey to sanction an all-or-nothing dash through the last few miles separating him from the Bastogne perimeter. Gaffey put the request to Patton, who readily agreed. Shortly after 1500 the 37th moved off with Lieutenant Boggess' nine Shermans in the lead. By 1445 Boggess had fought his way through the village of Assenois and cut a narrow corridor through to the 101st Airborne; his 75-mm was almost glowing with heat from incessant firing.

During the last few days, a dramatic change had come over the Ardennes battlefield. The low cloud and fog that had assisted the Germans' early advances had been replaced by good flying weather and the Allies' air superiority immediately made itself felt. The Luftwaffe did what it could to assist the ground troops, but was steadily driven out of the skies. Bastogne was supplied by parachute drop while ground-attack Lightnings circled the perimeter in support of the garrison or pounced on knots of resistance that were holding up 3rd Army's advance.

Far to the west of Bastogne, von Manteuffel's twin spearhead, 2nd Panzer and Panzer Lehr, were also suffering from the attentions of the Allied air forces. A further handicap was that fuel was in critically short supply and because of this progress had been painfully slow. However, during 24th December 2nd Panzer Division reached Celles and crossed the last ridge separating it from the Meuse at Dinant. Its columns immediately came under destructive fire from the Shermans of 3rd Royal Tank Regiment, part of the 11th Armoured Divisions, which had been deployed to cover the crossing sites. From beyond the river the British field and medium artillery joined in, bringing the Germans to a standstill.

This was the chance the impatient Collins, commanding VII Corps on the extreme right of Montgomery's hard shoulder, had been waiting for. On Christmas Day, he launched the fresh 2nd Armored Division with its 390 tanks in a sweeping attack on the German flank. In two days' hard fighting, 2nd Panzer Division was effectively destroyed and Panzer Lehr's relief attempt beaten off. 2nd Armored destroyed or captured 82 panzers, some of which had not a drop of fuel left in their tanks.

Manteuffel had no alternative but to order the survivors to withdraw. The Battle of the Bulge would continue well into the New Year, and German attempts to capture Bastogne would reach a new peak of intensity, but *Autumn Fog*, Hitler's last *Blitzkrieg*, had failed.

When the Fuhrer met Rundstedt on the 28th there was no talk of Rossbach and Leuthen but he remained wildly optimistic, speaking of the "tremendous easing of the situation which has come about … a transformation such as nobody would have believed possible a fortnight ago". Such transformation as there was, was short-lived and had been bought at the price of Germany's last reserve of armour. When the Red Army resumed its offensive in January the sorely depleted panzer divisions were pulled out of the Ardennes to meet the threat, leaving only a handful of tanks and assault guns in the west. Soon afterwards the British, Americans and French themselves returned to the attack, and four months later Adolf Hitler was dead.[76]

There were many technical reasons why *Autumn Fog* could never have succeeded, but perhaps the most important was that the British and American armies were fully conversant with the *Blitzkrieg* technique and, in spite of their initial surprise, soon identified the main thrust line and took decisive steps to contain it. For his part, Hitler had sought to conjure the ghosts of 1940, but his will alone was not sufficient to give them substance.

Chapter 12: The Far East 1941-45

Of all the soldiers who fought in World War II, the Japanese was perhaps the most individually formidable, and even those who loathed, detested and ultimately conquered him will freely admit that he was the bravest man they ever met.

It was his motivation that made him such a dangerous opponent, a motivation not merely sustained by animal courage, but implanted deeply within his subconscious from birth, a sincere belief that Japan was first among the nations of the world and that her very spirit was enshrined in the divine status of her Emperor, the Son of Heaven. To sacrifice oneself in the Emperor's cause was the noblest of ideals, possessing a profound religious significance barely intelligible to the occidental, so that while many armies might speak of fighting to the last man, only the Japanese did so as a matter of course. In such an army the pain of a wound had to be borne until a man could fight no longer and illness was barely tolerated; to surrender or to be captured alive was the ultimate disgrace, which would place a soldier outside the pale of Japanese society and bring unutterable shame on his family. To this was added an iron discipline in which superiors employed ritual violence against their inferiors as a matter of course and to a degree that would not be tolerated for one minute in a western army. In the light of this the Japanese Army's contempt for its prisoners is understandable if not excusable.

The Japanese Army was essentially an infantry army in which tanks played a secondary and supportive role. It was modelled on the German pattern and the tactics it favoured were those of Ludendorff's Storm Troops; its senior commanders were ruthless and capable professionals who were adept at exploiting an enemy's weakness. It was, moreover, an army that had been hardened by years of active service in China and which enjoyed the backing of a powerful Navy and Air Force.

The reasons for Japan's entry into the war were simple. Without such raw materials as tin, rubber and oil she could not conclude her war with China. In Malaya, Burma and the Dutch East Indies these commodities were readily available, but were denied her by pro-Chinese western embargoes. Therefore, since she could not trade for such goods, she would have to take them by force. To the Japanese there was nothing dishonourable in this; all they sought was a short victorious war that would bring the west to its senses.

Malaya was, of course, a prime target, although the Japanese were worried by their lack of experience in jungle warfare. In January 1941 they set up a special unit on Formosa to study all aspects of the problem, while details of the Malayan topography, road and track systems were gathered on the spot by "businessmen" working under the control of the Military Attache's office.

By September 1941 it had been agreed that neither the jungle nor the topography presented insuperable difficulties, and General Yamashita's XXV Army, consisting of the Imperial Guard, 5th and 18th Divisions, supported by the 3rd Tank Brigade, was detailed for the invasion, which would take place on 8th December, one day after the American Pacific Fleet had been sent to the bottom of Pearl Harbour.

For many years the British in Malaya had been living in a sort of cloud-cuckoo Edwardian afterglow, far removed from the realities of the total war being fought in Europe and North Africa. Service chiefs were relaxed and departmental in their approach, as were the senior officials of the civil administration, upon whom would fall the burden of establishing emergency services in the event of war. People felt secure because they had been told that the mainland jungles presented an impenetrable barrier to an invader, and that the huge guns on Singapore Island would effectively defeat any seaward approach to the Gibraltar of the East. In the light of such assurances, it is hardly surprising that vested interests objected to the Army's apparently pointless manoeuvres among the rubber plantations, or that the secretary of a golf club should regard as an absolute outrage the suggestion that trenches should be dug on his fairways.

British defensive strategy was, therefore, based on the road system, and such jungle training as was carried out was done so on the initiative of individual battalion commanders. Malaya was not considered to be tank country, although in fairness to the GOC, Lieutenant-General A.E. Percival, two armoured regiments were requested in August 1941, together with reinforcements of anti-tank and anti-aircraft guns; the RAF also asked for more modern fighters to replace the obsolete Brewster Buffaloes with which it was equipped. However, Malaya held a low priority and the War Cabinet was not inclined to grant such requests, believing that the Japanese intention was to attack Russia.

The Malayan garrison consisted of some 80,000 British, Australian and Indian troops, the equivalent of six divisions, the vast majority of whom lacked any combat experience. In the newly raised Indian divisions the situation was aggravated by many British officers not having attained the necessary fluency in Urdu, so that even elementary orders could only be carried out with difficulty.

Notwithstanding these difficulties, both Percival and the Commander-in-Chief Far East, Air Marshal Sir Robert Brooke-Popham, correctly appreciated not only the true Japanese intention, but also the strength of the attack and the actual landing place, which was Singora on the Kra Isthmus, just across the border in Thailand. An operation, codenamed *Matador*, was planned to seize the port before the Japanese arrived, but permission to carry this out was refused by the Cabinet on the grounds that it was provocative.

Yamashita's landing took place exactly as planned on 8th December, accompanied by a diversionary landing on the north-east coast of Malaya at Kota Bharu.

The Japanese 5th Division immediately headed south across the frontier to Jitra, where on 11th December it encountered the 11th Indian Division, which had been detailed for *Matador* and which was consequently deployed for advance rather than defence.

The 5th Division's attack was led by a medium tank company, which immediately overran an unmanned 2-pounder anti-tank battery, broke through and caught a brigade withdrawing in column to a new position, virtually destroying it as a fighting formation. The British excuse for this disgraceful episode is that the guns were limbered up and ready to move, but a Japanese officer with no axe to grind thought differently: "Ten guns with their muzzles turned towards us were lined up on the road, but beside them we could not find even one man of their crews. The enemy appeared to be sheltering from the heavy rain under the rubber trees and through this slight negligence they suffered a crushing defeat."[77]

There can be little doubt that this "slight negligence" was the first rolling pebble of what was to become a giant landslide. During the next few days 11th Indian Division was harried mercilessly as it was driven south, each position being penetrated by tanks or outflanked by infantry. British morale began to slump while that of their opponents reached new heights of optimism.

The irony of the situation was that the Japanese tanks were unquestionably the worst in the world, having been designed for use against the Chinese, who had no tanks of their own and very little anti-tank capability. For example, the three-man Type 95 Light, armed with a 37-mm gun, was protected by 12-mm armour plate; the elderly Type 89 Medium by only 17-mm armour; and the most modern tank in the Japanese armoury, the Type 97 Medium, equipped with a short 57-mm gun, by only 25-mm. None of these vehicles was a match for their British equivalents, and all were easy victims for the 2-pounder. Their crews had never encountered a determined anti-tank defence and subsequent operations in Burma revealed that once they had sustained sharp losses they were not inclined to press their attack when faced with tanks or anti-tank guns. However, for the moment they had the field to themselves.

The fate of the 11th Indian Division and of other formations sent against him soon convinced Yamashita that he was not opposed by a first-class enemy, and he decided to take risks that he would not have done in other circumstances. It was clear that the British were mentally road-bound and relied heavily on their mechanical transport, attempting to form successive lines along the various rivers that flowed down to the west coast. By maintaining the momentum of his advance, Yamashita reasoned correctly that each defence line could be turned or broken before it was properly established; it was not enough that 5th and 18th Divisions' advance down the peninsula should be assisted by the Guard Division's series of amphibious operations that outflanked the river lines – what was needed was speed, correct use of which would deny the enemy priceless time to reorganise.

The means to this end were provided by the humble bicycle, which was commandeered in its thousands. Whole regiments pedalled or pushed their machines along any sort of road or track that offered reasonable going, and carried them when it did not. Thus, the British rearguard never gained sufficient space to permit time for rest and reorganisation, so that men soon began to drop from exhaustion.

Nor was logistics the problem it might have been for the Japanese. They fed from captured British supplies and barely needed to touch their meagre marching rations; so was born the legend of the man who could survive the jungle for days on a handful of rice. Ammunition had top priority on the supply trains, which consisted of pack animals, bicycles and impressed local labour. Again, it had been foreseen that the British would destroy the numerous bridges as they withdrew, which might have prevented the artillery from keeping up with the advance had not each division been provided with an enlarged field engineering element for this very purpose.

When the Japanese encountered a defensive position, they usually committed about one-third of their strength to a direct attack designed to pin the enemy down. The remainder carried out a wide loop through the jungle and emerged back on the road some miles in the defenders' rear, where they would establish roadblocks. These were usually sited near a bend and were covered by mortar, machine-gun and small-arms fire. An ambushed vehicle generally formed the basis of the block, to which a local cart or a felled tree might be added; attempts by unarmoured vehicles to batter their way through were welcomed since they were rarely successful and simply contributed to the jam. If time permitted, several such blocks might be constructed in the space of a few miles.

It would not take the British commander long to learn that he had been cut off. Already engaged with a frontal attack that might include tanks, he was faced with the dilemma of either asking friendly troops beyond the block to clear the road, or fighting his own way out. More often than not, the latter was the only alternative available, and in practical terms this meant that if the block could not be broken his men might escape by filtering through the jungle, but his artillery, anti-tank guns, vehicles and heavy equipment would have to be abandoned along with his stores.

Whatever he decided to do, his troops would be strafed and bombed as a matter of routine by the Japanese Air Force, which had established its control of the sky very early in the campaign, destroying almost half of the available British aircraft in North Malaya on the first day of the war. Too late, reinforcement Hurricanes were flown into Singapore, but the new arrivals were too few in number to make much difference, and the further the Japanese advanced the more airfields became available to them for the close support of their ground troops.

In this manner, by exploiting their superior mobility to torment the British Army's very nerve system, its communication and supply routes, the Japanese induced disorganisation, disintegration and despair. The sickening smell of defeat pervaded all levels of the British command system, for whatever was planned the Japanese always seemed to be one move ahead. By 28th

December they were in Ipoh; on 11th January they took Kuala Lumpur; a week later they stormed Malacca; and by the end of the month the British had been forced to evacuate the mainland and retire to Singapore Island.

Here they were allowed little respite, for on the night of 8th/9th February 5th and 18th Divisions swarmed across the straits and quickly penetrated the defences to secure the vital water reservoirs. Sir Archibald Wavell had specifically instructed Percival that "no question of surrender (was) to be entertained until after protracted fighting among the ruins of Singapore City", but on 15th February the British commander asked Yamashita for terms. He felt that if the Japanese were forced to storm the city, they would unhesitatingly massacre the civilian population as they had done following the fall of Shanghai, and he wished to avoid this at all costs. He could not possibly have guessed that Yamashita had dangerously overreached himself, that his stretched supply system was unequal to the strain, or that only three days' ammunition remained to the Japanese, and that when this had gone they faced either a withdrawal to the mainland or defeat on the island. At their meeting, Yamashita gave nothing away, bluffed angrily, and insisted on immediate and unconditional surrender. Percival agreed, so setting the seal on the greatest disaster in British military history.

The campaign had lasted seventy-three days and cost the British 9,000 casualties, 130,000 prisoners of war and an immense amount of equipment. Japanese casualties also amounted to 9,000, of whom 3,000 were killed, plus a handful of tanks and aircraft lost. The victory was that of an outnumbered but thoroughly organised and well-led army over one that subscribed to a flawed tactical doctrine. Yamashita had carried out a brilliant infantry *Blitzkrieg*, which had covered 350 miles in the fifty-four days between the initial landings and his troops' arrival at the Johore Straits; as a recruiting poster for an earlier war had put it, there had been a walking tour with a little shooting thrown in, and no amount of heroism or self-sacrifice by the British had been able to halt it. True, Yamashita's methods contained a major flaw of their own, and the ease with which the Japanese gained their victory led to their drawing a number of false conclusions, but none of this would become apparent for another two years.[78]

Meanwhile, Lieutenant-General Shojiro Iida's XV Army, consisting of the 33rd and 55th Divisions, had invaded Burma on 12th January 1942, being opposed by the inexperienced 17th Indian Division and the newly raised 1st Burma Division, both under strength and badly equipped. Using the same techniques as Yamashita, Iida quickly prised his opponents out of Lower Burma and then defeated their attempt to hold the line of the Sittang River in mid-February.

On 5th March, General Sir Harold Alexander arrived in Rangoon to take command, and quickly realised that neither Burma nor the port itself could be held with the forces available. It was also clear that the army could not be evacuated by sea, and it was decided that the only alternative lay in a long overland withdrawal to India, during which assistance would be provided by Lieutenant-General Joseph Stilwell's Chinese divisions, which had moved into Burma to protect their country's lifeline, the famous Burma Road.

The retreat, the longest ever carried out by a British army, began at once and continued until the Chindwin was crossed in May.[79] Returns showed that of the original 42,000 effectives, only 12,000 reached India with their units, although stragglers continued to arrive for some weeks afterwards. Of the remainder, a substantial proportion consisted of Burmese troops who had simply given up and gone home. Japanese casualties amounted to 7,000. It was unquestionably a major defeat, but it had not been a rout.

Superficially, the First Burma Campaign was very similar to the Malayan experience. However, there were two important differences.

First, the RAF and Colonel Claire Chennault's American Volunteer Group of the Chinese Air Force more than held their own against the Japanese, destroying not less than 150 of their aircraft and materially assisting in the ground fighting.[80]

Not until 21st March, when they mounted a massive series of raids against the Allied base at Magwe, did the Japanese succeed in achieving complete air superiority.

Secondly, 7th Armoured Brigade had arrived in Rangoon on 22nd February. The brigade, consisting of 7th Hussars and 2nd Royal Tank Regiment, had actually been in transit to Singapore when the city fell, and was immediately diverted to Burma. It was the most experienced armoured formation in the British Army, both regiments, it will be recalled, having been present at Beda Fomm and more recently at the great tank battles that had raged around Sidi Rezegh.

In their first encounters with Japanese tanks the latter stood no chance at all. The Japanese crews could perform their short-haul infantry support role well enough, but were utterly inept when it came to a tank battle; indeed, they seem to have received no training for such an event. They had little idea of how to combine fire and movement, and none at all on how to use ground for cover. After several of their machines had been picked off like sitting ducks, they were rarely encountered in the forefront of the Japanese advance.

However, even without tank support, Iida's men moved with astonishing speed, and several times during the retreat managed to establish strong roadblocks across the British rear. These were usually smashed by the Stuarts, which also broke up infantry attacks, ferried their own rearguards out of danger, and carried out a number of counter-attacks, which caused the Japanese severe loss and delay. But for the presence of 7th Armoured Brigade, very few men would have completed the long journey from Rangoon to the Chindwin.[81]

Sad to relate, only one tank succeeded in reaching India, as space on the Chindwin ferries was at a premium and men held a higher priority than vehicles; the remainder were so thoroughly destroyed by their crews that not one could be salvaged by the enemy.

In January 1943 the British attempted a limited conventional offensive along the Arakan coast of Burma, using a single division, the 14th Indian. The Japanese succeeded in halting the advance several miles north of Foul Point, and then initiated a wide turning movement through the jungle. 14th Division, in danger of being cut off, was forced into a hasty and difficult withdrawal. Once more, it seemed as though the Japanese could not be beaten at their own game, but in fact the lessons of the short campaign were thoroughly learned and digested.[82]

A year later the British returned to the Arakan, and this time they came in force, employing the 5th, 7th and 26th Indian and 81st West African Divisions, plus a complete regiment of Lee tanks, the 25th Dragoons. Further, the arrival of the Spitfire in the war zone had ended the reign of the fast, manoeuvrable, but highly vulnerable Zero, and air superiority now belonged to the Allies.

The campaign opened as before, with an advance along the coast, and the Japanese countered as they had the previous year, the flanking move being expertly executed by their crack 55th Division. The headquarters of 7th Indian Division was overrun, although the divisional commander, Major-General F.W. Messervy, managed to escape with most of his staff to the defended locality known as the Admin Box.

The Japanese closed in for the kill, only to find that the Box contained most of 25th Dragoons' tanks. The Lee was equipped with a 75-mm gun mounted in a sponson for direct fire ahead, a 37-mm gun in a turret with all-round traverse, and a number of machine-guns; whatever its limitations had been in the Western Desert, it was the ideal fighting vehicle for northern Burma and the Arakan, where the close country often dictated an advance on a one-tank frontage. In such circumstances the limited traverse available to the main armament was not a disadvantage, and the 37-mm's canister round enabled the tank commander to sweep the trees on either side of a track while his 75mm was engaging targets to the front.

In the face of such firepower, early Japanese attempts to storm the Box in daylight withered and died. Night attacks succeeded in penetrating the perimeter, but at first light tanks and infantry invariably arrived to pitch the attackers out of their hard-won gains.

Incidents such as the massacre of the patients and staff of the main dressing station merely hardened the garrison's determination to resist to the bitter end, and were entirely counter-productive in that they provoked a deep personal hatred of the Japanese throughout the army; if formerly they had been regarded as a cunning, ruthless and efficient enemy, they were now looked upon as a species of sadistic animal to be hunted down and destroyed whenever possible.

Suddenly the major flaw in the Japanese system of *Blitzkrieg* became apparent – it depended entirely on its own success to maintain momentum. If the enemy's supplies could not be captured men would starve and wounded would die; and if the tenuous supply lines were cut ammunition shortage would soon compel withdrawal.

This was exactly the position in which the 55th Division found itself as it watched the Allied air-supply parachutes drifting down into the Admin Box. Its flanking thrust at the coast had been blunted and turned back; its ammunition trains were being ambushed by British and Indian troops who had learned to use the jungle to their own advantage; it had taken totally unexpected casualties; and it was now faced with a relief column, headed by armour, steadily fighting its way through the Ngakyedauk Pass towards the beleaguered garrison. By the end of February, the division was beginning to withdraw, starving, tattered, a mere skeleton of its former proud self, its losses in killed alone falling only slightly short of the total Japanese fatalities for the entire Malayan Campaign.

The Japanese were planning a major offensive on the Central Front, and by their counter-attack in the Arakan had hoped that British divisions would be diverted away from Manipur, where the fighting would take place. In fact, following their defeat, the reverse happened, and it was they who were forced to rush reinforcements into the Arakan while the British were able to air-lift the 5th and 7th Indian Divisions to the Imphal and Kohima sectors.

Although sometimes referred to as the March on Delhi, the Japanese offensive, codenamed *U-go*, was simply designed to secure a defence line along the Naga Hills, possession of which would prevent the British from invading Burma from India. A major obstacle was the presence of Lieutenant-General G.A.P. Scoones' 4 Corps on the Imphal Plain, but it was felt that this formation could be outflanked, surrounded and eventually starved into surrender. Entrusted with the task was the 15th Army (15th, 31st and 33rd Divisions) under Lieutenant-General Renya Mutaguchi, who had commanded a division in Malaya.

Subsequently the Japanese admitted that they would not have undertaken this venture so lightly if it had not been for their early victories in Malaya and during the First Burma Campaign. They failed to appreciate that Indian troops, properly trained and led, were among the best in the world, and a very different proposition from the recruits they had met earlier; they all but discounted the ability of the Allies to keep 4 Corps' three divisions (17th, 20th and 23rd Indian) supplied by air; and they did not fully understand the true potential of 4 Corps' armoured formation, 254 Tank Brigade, which had been trained hard for hill fighting under the corps commander's brother, Brigadier Reginald Scoones.[83]

The battle began late in March and lasted until the middle of June 1944. It raged around the edges of the Imphal Plain and along the approaches to the town itself, while a second and strategically interlinked struggle took place further north on the road to India, at Kohima. The course of the action is best seen as a large-scale reconstruction of the Admin Box battle, with 4 Corps besieged but supplied by air, while 33 Corps fought its way through Kohima to affect a relief. It contained some of the bitterest fighting of the entire war, with neither side asking or receiving quarter.

It was soon apparent that when deprived of the tactical initiative the Japanese were poor battle practitioners whose lack of flexibility was aggravated by a meagre communications network and a command system that failed to co-ordinate the activities of its units. Like the Russians, once the Japanese had made a plan they stuck to it needlessly, being slaughtered in their bunkers and trenches by the more sophisticated and fully developed British infantry/tank tactics. They had arrived carrying only their marching rations and driving a herd of cattle, and when this had been eaten, they starved on a diet of grass and slugs. In the end, amid a tirade of mutual recrimination, those of them that were left crawled back to the Chindwin leaving 55,000 of their comrades behind them – killed in battle, or dead because of wounds untreated, tropical disease or starvation. In the true spirit of *bushido* those hospital patients unable to walk were awarded a bullet through the brain, so saving them from the dishonour of being taken alive by the enemy. Very possibly the death toll would have been even higher and the battle brought to a conclusion earlier had not a considerable force of Chindits, landed behind the Japanese lines to harry their communications and rear areas, been diverted to the assistance of Stilwell's Chinese-American troops, stalled by the obstinate defenders of Myitkyina on the Northern Front.

Be this as it may, never had the Imperial Japanese Army sustained such a shattering defeat. Not only were Mutaguchi and his divisional commanders removed from office, so too was General Kawabe, commander of the Burma Area Army. In other circumstances court martials would have been held as a matter of course, but this further ordeal was avoided on the grounds that full disclosures by the officers concerned would have a disastrous effect on public opinion in Japan itself.

If on the Japanese side *U-go* had been characterised by mutual antipathy at the highest levels, for the British the reverse was true. General William Slim, 14th Army Commander, Lieutenant-General Scoones, Major-General D.T. Cowan (17th Indian Division) and Major-General D.D. Gracey (20th Indian Division), had all served together in 1st/6th Gurkha Rifles, understood each other and got on extremely well. 14th Army was, therefore, something of a family from the outset, and its commander was one of very few general officers to have been both genuinely liked and respected by their men. He shared their hardships, he spoke to them as individuals in plain soldier's language, he was honest in his appraisals, and above all he understood their problems, not least of which for the British troops was a feeling that their war was of no interest to the Establishment at home. He was a soldiers' soldier and he looked it, but he also had a gift of instinctively recognising the strategic potential of a situation while it was actually developing, and this places him in the foremost rank of *Blitzkrieg* commanders.

The Japanese retreat continued beyond the Chindwin to the Irrawaddy, where the new commander of the Burma Area Army, Lieutenant-General Hayotoro Kimura, was able to affect some form of reorganisation. Kimura, an optimist sadly lacking in imagination, did not consider the campaign lost by any means, and hoped to tempt 14th Army into crossing the river, so stretching its lines of communication to the limit, and fight a decisive battle in the Mandalay area.

Slim read his opponent's mind almost as soon as 33 Corps (2nd British, 19th and 20th Indian Divisions, supported by 254 Tank Brigade) began reporting that the Japanese were simply fighting rearguard actions on the Shwebo Plain. He guessed correctly that Kimura would deploy 15th Army along the Irrawaddy on either side of Mandalay, and saw that the enemy's reinforcements and supplies would have to come north through the vital communications centre of Meiktila. He likened the Japanese dispositions to a closed fist of which Meiktila was the wrist; slash that wrist and blood would cease to flow into the fingers, nerves would be unable to perform their proper function, and the lifeless fist would soon open of its own accord.

He planned, therefore, to seize Meiktila by *coup de main*, aided by the fact that central Burma is semi-desert and therefore ideal tank country. 4 Corps (7th and 17th Divisions, supported by 255 Tank Brigade[84]) would move in secret down the Kabaw and Gangaw valleys, cross the Irrawaddy below its confluence with the Chindwin, where the enemy was not expected to be strong, and then take and hold the town against all comers. The approach march would be made under strict wireless silence, while phantom units on the Shwebo Plain simulated the presence of the corps with a flow of simulated radio traffic.

But Slim was aiming at the complete destruction of the Japanese Army, and not simply its disruption. To achieve this, he would have to rivet Kimura's attention on the Mandalay sector and be seen, apparently, to be falling into the latter's trap. This would have the effect of concentrating most of 15th Army's strength along the river line, and provide an opportunity to write down its strength even before the main blow was struck.

On 9th January 1945 19th Indian Division, commanded by Major-General T.W. Rees, seized a bridgehead some sixty miles north of Mandalay; on 12th February 20th Indian Division established a second bridgehead forty miles west of the city, at the other end of the Japanese line; and a week later Major-General Cameron Nicholson's 2nd British Division landed several miles to the east of 20th Division. Each crossing had been carefully timed to keep the Japanese off-balance and to coincide with specific phases of 4 Corps' operations.

The bridgeheads were immediately subjected to frenzied counterattacks, which simply piled up bodies around the perimeters under the combined fire of infantry, artillery and 254 Brigade's tanks, a proportion of which had been allocated to each of 33 Corps' divisions. It never seems to have occurred to Lieutenant-General Katamura, commanding 15th Army, that he was playing the enemy's game. Literal obedience to orders is a vice if unaccompanied by a realistic appreciation of the situation, and it was a vice to which the Japanese Army was particularly prone and which was now used against them.

Assailed by tanks and infantry, the garrison of a village would fight until exterminated. After dusk the British would deliberately withdraw and permit fresh Japanese troops to re-enter the village in the knowledge that they would almost certainly occupy the identical positions held by their late comrades. In the morning the British would return and systematically slaughter the new arrivals throughout the day, before retiring again. In places, this type of action was repeated for days at a time, until 15th Army's divisions had been bled white.

Meanwhile, 4 Corps had reached the Irrawaddy south of Pakkoku and eliminated the few local garrisons in the area selected for their crossing. Imagining that most of 14th Army was committed to the bridgeheads around Mandalay, the Japanese rashly evaluated the new arrivals as a Chindit operation, and beyond deploying troops to protect the oil installations at Chauk and Yenaungyaung, took virtually no counter-measures.

Consequently, when 7th Indian Division slid across the river during the early hours of 14th February, it experienced little difficulty in securing a bridgehead, the perimeter of which was constantly expanded during the next few days. Into this bridgehead crossed the two brigades of 17th Indian Division, while the Shermans of 255 Tank Brigade and the Corps' armoured cars were rafted over onto the east bank.

By 21st February preparations for the break-out were complete and 17th Division suddenly burst through the flimsy Japanese screen, heading for Meiktila on two parallel axes. On the right, Probyn's Horse led the advance of 63 Brigade, while to the left the Royal Deccan Horse formed the spearhead of 48 Brigade. Ahead probed the fast-moving Humber armoured cars of 16th Light Cavalry, commanded by Lieutenant-Colonel J.N. Chaudhuri, later to become the Indian Army's Chief of Staff, and the Daimlers of B Squadron 11th Prince Albert Victor's Own Cavalry. With the cars travelled the RAF's ground liaison officers, in constant communication with the cab ranks of Thunderbolts circling overhead, ready to bring them roaring down at the slightest sign of resistance – "very effective gentlemen", as one armoured car commander put it, "sometimes almost *too* effective for the leading cars!" But leading the field in the best *Blitzkrieg* tradition was the Corps Commander himself, Messervy, flying forward in his light Auster to spy out the land and returning to alight beside a startled troop leader with a shout of, "Press on! There's nothing in front of you!"

By coincidence, a senior officers' conference was taking place that very day in Meiktila, attended by Kimura's Chief of Staff, Lieutenant-General Sumichi Tanaka, Lieutenant-General Katamura of 15th Army, and Lieutenant-General Masaki Honda, commander of 33rd Army on the Northern Front. During the conference a signal was received to the effect that a column of 200 vehicles had broken out of 7th Division's bridgehead and was heading towards the town. Tanaka and Katamura, still under the impression that 4 Corps was a diversionary Chindit operation, were inclined to dismiss the column as a hit-and-run raid; Honda, who had always regarded Meiktila as a sensitive target, was less sanguine. However, the majority view prevailed, and nothing was done. In fact, in its original form the signal had put the Allied vehicle strength at the more accurate figure of 2,000, but this had been corrupted in transmission and was not repeated, producing one of the most significant communications blunders of World War II.

Nonetheless, 17th Division did not have a clear run all the way. On 22nd February, Probyn's and 63 Brigade fought a bloody but successful battle for possession of the village of Oyin, encountering for the first time the enemy's anti-tank equivalent of the Kamikaze pilot, the Nikuhaku Kogeki, or Human Combat Tank Destruction Squads, when several men carrying heavy satchel charges suddenly broke from cover to run the gauntlet of fire and throw themselves under or onto tanks before blowing themselves to eternity; their suicidal bravery produced little return for their bravery.[85]

On 24th February, Probyn's succeeded in crossing a potential tank obstacle, the Sinzewa Chaung, while the Deccan captured Taungtha, and that evening both columns joined forces to continue the advance together. The vital airfield of Thabukton was taken on the 27th and as soon as sappers had rendered it operational, transports began to land with additional fuel and supplies. The next day 17th Division's third brigade, the 99th, was flown in from Palel.

There could now be no further doubt about 14th Army's intentions concerning Meiktila. The garrison commander, Major-General Kasuya, halted the 168th Infantry Regiment, marching through the town *en route* to the Mandalay Front, issued weapons to every man he could round up, including patients in the military hospital, and gave instructions for every building to be turned into a fortress.

Time was not on Kasuya's side. On 28th February 255 Tank Brigade swept round Meiktila's northern approaches and then turned south to roar across the landing-field before swinging west towards the South Lake, this indirect approach effectively isolating the town while 48 and 63 Brigades probed their way into the suburbs.

During the next three days tank and infantry teams fought their way steadily through the blazing ruins. Amid hand-to-hand fighting, burning buildings were brought crashing down on their defenders, burying gun positions carefully concealed in their foundations. House by house, street by street it went on with the Nikuhaku Kogeki providing a bizarre variation on their theme by concealing themselves in craters in the road, a 250-lb bomb between their knees and a stone in one hand ready to strike the exposed primer the minute a tank passed overhead; the majority were found and shot dead by the tanks' escorting infantry. Kasuya and his garrison of 3,500, only half of whom were professional infantry, died to a man, giving 14th Army's most experienced division the hardest fight of its career. They fought on in the vain hope that Burma Area Army would send help before it was too late to save the town, and when the last handful waded out into the lake to avoid capture, they drowned or were shot down in the shallows by British and Indian troops who might have felt something like admiration, but never pity; the Japanese had committed too many deliberate barbarities to be forgotten or forgiven.

The news that Meiktila had fallen struck Kimura like a thunderbolt. At a stroke Slim had placed his Northern and Central Fronts in dire jeopardy. The town must be recaptured immediately, but from where could the necessary troops be drawn? Preferably not from Katamura's 15th Army, already fully committed and stretched to its limits; nor from the Arakan, where Sakurai's 28th Army was trying to halt a renewed offensive by Lieutenant-General Sir Philip Christison's 15 Corps, accompanied by a series of amphibious landings designed to intercept the Japanese withdrawal. The only solution lay in the virtual abandonment of the Northern Front and the appointment of Honda to control the Meiktila operations. Every unit that could be theoretically spared, including the 14th Tank Regiment, the only Japanese armoured formation in Burma, was rushed into the area.

As already mentioned, the Japanese tank crews were less experienced in every way than their western counterparts. The difficulty of movement *en masse* under enemy controlled skies was dramatically demonstrated when the RAF caught 14th Regiment on the road in full daylight and pounded it to scrap; only seven Type 97 Mediums succeeded in reaching the Meiktila siege lines, where they were employed as mobile pill-boxes.

Siege is perhaps not quite the right word to describe the fighting centred on Meiktila during the first three weeks of March. True, links between the town and 7th Indian Division's bridgehead were cut, and Honda did succeed in moving the 18th and 49th Divisions into the area, but all this had been allowed for in Slim's overall planning. True to form, both Japanese divisional commanders ran their formations as private armies, making virtually no attempt to co-operate with each other, so that the best Honda could achieve was a distant blockade.

Even discounting the enemy's difficulties, Cowan's garrison was in little danger. Daily, aircraft landed with hundreds of tons of stores and took off again with the few casualties incurred; indeed, on 17th March a fourth infantry brigade, the 9th from 5th Indian Division, was actually flown in to join 17th Division. Daily, too, columns of tanks, armoured cars, guns and lorried infantry sallied forth in aggressive sweeps, which caused the Japanese severe loss and broke up their preparations for an attack.

Desperate, Honda launched a weak attack against Meiktila airfield on 20th March. It broke down under heavy defensive fire and during the next twenty-four hours the survivors were hunted down. Even if he had succeeded, his effort had been made too late, for as Slim had predicted, Katamura's Irrawaddy Line, starved of men, ammunition and food, had collapsed like a house of cards.

Taking advantage of the situation at Meiktila, 33 Corps' divisions had instinctively increased the pressure around their perimeters, and as early as 3rd March 19th Division had begun pushing south towards Mandalay, led by an armoured task force known as Stilettocol. On the day Honda launched his abortive assault, the Union Flag rose over Fort Dufferin for the first time for three years, accompanied by 19th Division's own standard, a yellow dagger on a scarlet ground. To the west, 2nd Division was also closing in on the capital and had taken Ava, while 20th Division, in addition to sending out a further armoured task force, Barcol, to disrupt the enemy's communications as far south as Wundwin, was intent on effecting a junction with 7th Division.

Their command structure in ruins, their supply line severed, the men of 15th Army strove to escape from the trap as best they could, working their way to the south-east as individuals or in small groups, having abandoned what remained of their artillery, only the elite 33rd Division maintaining any form of cohesion. In later years those that survived freely admitted that the seizure of Meiktila had been the Master Stroke of the entire Burma campaign.

Slim had destroyed his opponent as he intended; his next task was to deny him any chance of recovery, and that could only be achieved by the capture of Rangoon, 300 miles away. With the monsoon about to break, such a move was a finely calculated risk, since the torrential rains would not only make the going more difficult, they would also inhibit the all-important air supply and support when flying became impossible.

Knowing that Kimura would expect him to have the prize of Rangoon firmly within his sights, Slim decided to attack in strength down both available axes, thus keeping the Japanese commander constantly off-balance. 4 Corps, now consisting of 5th, 17th and 19th Indian Divisions, supported by 255 Tank Brigade, would advance down the railway corridor, while 33 Corps, 7th and 20th Indian Divisions with 254 Tank Brigade, would move south along the east bank of the Irrawaddy.

Kimura had instructed Honda to form a defence line based on Pyawbwe, which would also form a rallying point for survivors trickling south. On 10th April, Messervy despatched an armoured battle group under Brigadier Pert to harry Honda's left flank and rear, and when the latter became thoroughly unsettled, smashed his way through the Japanese position in a converging attack carried out by two brigades, each supported by an armoured regiment.[86]

Thereafter, there was no holding 4 Corps, which thundered south through Yamethin, Pyinmana, Toungoo and Pegu, arriving at Hlegu on 3rd May, having covered 300 miles in three weeks, brushing aside or fighting its way through isolated pockets of resistance on the way. The momentum of the advance was actually increased towards the end by placing the spearhead on half rations and giving priority to petrol and ammunition on the air drops. During this period, Honda became a fugitive, escaping capture by a hair's breadth on several occasions.

It had not been necessary to fight for Rangoon. The deserted city had been occupied the previous day following an amphibious landing by 15 Corps, which quickly effected a junction with 4 Corps at Hlegu, and then advanced up the Irrawaddy to meet 33 Corps' leading elements at Tharrawaddy on 15th May.

The Burma Area Army was finished. Between 1st January and 14th May 1945, it had lost all its armour, 430 guns, and the bodies of 28,700 of its men had been physically counted. This takes no account of bodies buried by the Japanese themselves, nor of those who crawled away to die in the jungle, nor of the heavy losses inflicted as the survivors of 28th Army tried to escape from the Arakan across Burma to Thailand several weeks later. During the same period 14th Army lost 2,800 men killed and had about thirty of its tanks destroyed or seriously damaged.

Without doubt, Slim's *Blitzkrieg* victory had been gained over a badly flawed army; an army with bad tanks, badly handled, ineffective anti-tank guns, shaky logistics, an inefficient signals system and no air cover; but its conception was none the less brilliant for that, and its execution was professional in the extreme. It was the last pure application of the technique in World War II, although *aficionados* of the Red Army will be quick to point out that Russian operations in Manchuria also have a claim to that title.

Japanese Manchuria was held by the Kwantung Army Group, commanded by General Otozo Yamada, who had under his control several Area Armies, each containing a pair of armies.[87] Yamada's strength was nominally 900,000, but a third of this number was made up by local conscripts who could be discounted by virtue of their unreliability. Again, the Army Group had been forced to send replacement drafts and heavy weapons to other theatres for so long that all its formations were under strength – for example, one division's artillery consisted of only four guns. Such armour as there was, about 1,200 vehicles of various types ranging from the useless Type 94 tankettes to a handful of tank destroyers, was spread thinly over a vast area.

The Russians had been preparing to invade Manchuria since the end of the war in Europe. Apparently, STAVKA did not rate the qualities of its Far Eastern generals or their troops very highly, and several experienced officers were sent to take command, including Malinovsky, Vasilevsky and Meretskov, while numerous battle-hardened units, of which 6th Guards Tank Army was one, were shipped along the Trans-Siberian Railway.

Yamada was fully aware of these preparations, but appreciated that as Manchuria was flanked on three sides by Russian territory, there could be no question of holding ground near the frontier; instead, he planned that his Area Armies should conduct a withdrawal and concentrate in a kind of national redoubt covering the Korean and Liaotung peninsulas. His plan *might* have worked had it not been for the deliberate disobedience of Third Area Army's commander, General Jun Ushiroku, a favourite at Court, who chose to fight his battles as close to the border as possible.

The Russians attacked on 9th August, more than 5,000 T34/85s and SUs leading the advance of some eighty divisions, covered by a swarm of Yaks, Shturmoviks and Pe2s. Japanese resistance was sufficiently fierce to cost the Red Army 8,000 killed and 22,000 wounded, but once Third Area Army had been destroyed and 6th Guards Tank Army began carving a swathe across the base of the great Manchurian salient, Yamada's grand design was doomed.

Although the Emperor broadcast the news of Japan's surrender on 15th August, the Russians continued to advance, bundling what remained of the Kwantung Army across the Yalu into Korea, dropping parachute troops ahead of their leading elements to prevent the destruction of coveted industrial plant. By 2nd September they had got what they wanted and fighting was at an end.

As an administrative achievement the Red Army's swift redeployment to the Far East was truly remarkable. Whether the short, and extremely expensive, campaign falls within the definition of *Blitzkrieg* is a point that can be argued; certainly, there were elements of the technique present, but the general impression is that the Russians simply swamped their opponents. It is, perhaps, significant that Soviet historians claim that it was this massive demonstration of armed might that brought about the Japanese decision to surrender, rather than the delivery of two atomic bombs; the Japanese themselves do not agree, and point to many other contributory factors, none of which involved Russia in any way.

Chapter 13: "If we do not win, we have nowhere to come back to"

Since the end of World War II, the science of weapon technology has advanced further and faster than at any time in recorded history. Fighting vehicles of every type and description dominate the land battle, their armour providing crews with protection not merely against conventional ammunition but also against nuclear and biological weapons. Tanks themselves have assumed the best shape for ballistic defence, improved guns and ammunition extending their capacity for mutual destruction to the limits of visibility. In the air, the piston engine has given way to the high-performance jet thrust, blurring the old distinctions between fighter and bomber, close-support aircraft and interceptor. Ground-attack weapons include multi-barrel miniguns, capable of producing up to 6,000 rounds per minute, napalm, cluster bombs, rockets and other missiles, many of which are delivered with clinical accuracy by means of radar "fire and forget" techniques.

New weapon systems include the ATGW (Anti-Tank Guided Weapon) and the helicopter. While capable of impressive performance under ideal range conditions, the ATGW suffers from a number of disadvantages. Its delivery cannot exceed a certain speed, or the operator will be unable to guide it onto its target; it therefore has a slower rate of fire than the conventional tank gun and although it has the ability to kill at longer ranges, geography is seldom so kind as to provide a direct line of sight over the distance for which its optimum performance has been designed. Its operator, too, is subject to battlefield stresses that are immediately reflected in the missile's flight. Only in the most unusual circumstances has the ATGW fulfilled the promise of its manufacturers.

The helicopter, on the other hand, has added an altogether new dimension to the battlefield. Originally developed by the US Army as a means of rapid casualty evacuation during the Korean War, it is now used in a wide variety of roles including ground-support gunship, tank destroyer, reconnaissance vehicle and personnel carrier, the larger versions also being capable of ferrying artillery and heavy stores. Its versatility permits commanders to lift an attack force deep into enemy territory to seize an objective or execute a raid, providing a flexibility that purely armoured or airborne troops do not possess.

There have been many wars since 1945, but few applications of the *Blitzkrieg* technique. In Korea the mountainous nature of the country reduced the role of armour to infantry support, thus providing a parallel with the Italian campaign. During the Indo-Pakistani Wars both sides fought with strictly limited resources in areas that lacked a critical strategic objective. The end product of their tank battles was simply knocked out vehicles. The two armies were boxers from the same stable, each fully conscious of the other's strengths and weaknesses; it will, for example, be recalled that the Deccan Horse (India) and Probyn's Horse (Pakistan) fought side by side in the same brigade at Meiktila.

Nor, save in the local context, does the long Vietnam War provide examples of armour and air power being used jointly to produce a decisive result. It was, however, remarkable in that the communists were able to destroy the American will to fight by skilfully exploiting the then fashionable wave of liberal idealism sweeping the west, manipulating a television reportage that nightly displayed the ever-present inhumanities of war to a horrified general public for the first time in history.

Two thousand years ago, the Chinese soldier-philosopher Sun Tzu wrote: "Break the will of the enemy to fight, and you accomplish the true objective of war. Cover with ridicule the enemy's tradition. Exploit and aggravate the inherent frictions within the enemy country. Agitate the young against the old. Prevail if possible without armed conflict. The supreme excellence is not to win a hundred victories in a hundred battles. The supreme excellence is to defeat the armies of your enemies without ever having to fight them."

This the communist leadership in Hanoi had learned well. In the words of General William C. Westmoreland, former Commander-in-Chief of the anti-communist forces in Vietnam, "Having achieved ridicule of their enemy's tradition, having exploited and aggravated inherent frictions within their enemy's country, and having agitated the young against the old, they had removed their primary adversary from the fight and were free to exploit their raw military power, with only minimal assistance from the southern revolutionaries, to conquer South Vietnam."[88]

Of the final South Vietnamese collapse, Westmoreland comments: "The country still faced a powerful external military force entrenched within its borders and the cut in American aid left South Vietnamese military units short of equipment, ammunition, and replacement parts and virtually devoid of air support, severely impairing morale at all levels. The enemy meanwhile was amply equipped and supplied and remained free to concentrate at the time and place of his choosing."[89]

The last act of the tragedy was not that wish-fulfilment of parlour-pink intellectuals, the soldier-peasant wheeling his bicycle to victory, but a conventional drive on Saigon by the North Vietnamese regular army, using tanks and artillery. By then, most of the soldier-peasants were dead, the majority killed during the Tet offensive, and the purely local opinions of those that survived were of small interest to the Hanoi establishment. They, like the sincere idealists of the western media, had been shamelessly used.

It is to the Arab/Israeli wars that one must look for a modern application of *Blitzkrieg*, and immediately a comparison between the problems facing the Israeli Defence Force and von Seeckt's Reichswehr in the Twenties becomes inevitable. Both possessed only limited resources with which to defend long frontiers, and both in consequence were compelled to develop their potential for mobility to the utmost in order to fulfil their aims. It is, therefore, not simply an historical accident that following its starveling birth the Israeli Armoured Corps has developed into a force that inspires as much respect in the Middle East as did the *Panzerwaffe* in Europe.

War is fought by the Israeli Defence Force with a degree of emotion seldom found in other armies. It fights, always against odds, for the survival of a small nation returned to the homeland of its ancestors, in the certain knowledge that it cannot afford to be beaten. Perpetually short of men, it seeks to minimise its casualties by every means possible. Ever since the War of Liberation a strict but unwritten code demands the rescue of a unit in trouble, a call for assistance exercising a fierce emotional pull on the recipients. Self-sacrifice is not demanded, but is often freely given. Israeli soldiers can be volatile and while success can act on him like a spur, failure can depress him deeply. Much reliance is placed on the initiative, judgement and drive of junior leaders in all branches of the service.

The Israelis are Western in outlook and are a technically minded people. Sophisticated tank designs such as the British Centurion and the US Patton M60 present no problems and are successfully modified to suit local conditions. The Armoured Corps favours a version of the flexible American combat command system, its field commanders leading from the front, taking decisions and issuing orders on the spot in the German manner, this philosophy being encapsulated in the Corps' motto, 'Follow Me'.

In contrast, the percentage of technically educated men in Arab armies is often lower. The Arab requirement, therefore, is for simple, robust tanks that recruits can be trained to use quickly, and in this connection Russian equipment has obvious advantages. However, the receipt of Russian equipment and advisors is inevitably accompanied by the adoption of the rigid Russian command and control apparatus, presenting a sharp contrast with Israeli methods. It is not without interest that the small Royal

Jordanian Army, alone among the major Arab protagonists to retain British equipment, organisation and standards of training, has given the Israeli Defence Force some of its hardest battles.

The conflict between the two has raged from the Mount Hermon massif through the Judean hills to the wastes of the Sinai Peninsula. Tanks have been employed extensively on all fronts, but only the Sinai offers the space for the deployment of armour *en masse*. The peninsula has its maximum width of 130 miles in the north and is 240 miles long from the Mediterranean to Sharm el Sheikh. It is separated from Egypt proper by the Suez Canal. From the northern coast the ground rises steadily across a sand, rock and gravel plateau to reach a height of 8,664 feet on Mount Sinai, whence it falls sharply into the Red Sea. Long ago the landscape was well-watered, but today it is hot and arid, carved by dried-up watercourses and receiving less than ten inches of seasonal rain per year.

Three main routes cross the Sinai from Israel to the Suez Canal. In the north a good road and railway follow the coast from Gaza through Khan Yunis, Rafah, El Arish and Mazar to reach El Kantara; in the centre the route lies from Kuseima through Abu Agheila to Ismailia; in the south the road begins at Kuntilla and follows the line Themed – Nakhl – to the Mitla Pass, through which the town of Suez can be reached. The principal north – south connection between these roads is a track running from El Arish on the coast through Bir Lafan to Abu Agheila and on past Jebel Libni to Nakhl, with a branch joining Abu Agheila with Bir Gifgafa and the Mitla Pass. From this it will be seen that Abu Agheila is the hub of the central Sinai communications network.

In October 1956 the Suez Crisis was approaching its climax and the armies of Egypt, Jordan and Syria were placed under a unified command. Israel responded with a secret mobilisation and prepared for a pre-emptive strike across Sinai while appearing to be on the brink of attacking Jordan. A three-pronged offensive was planned, to be accompanied by a parachute drop on the eastern end of the Mitla Pass, astride the enemy's communications, which it was hoped would draw the Egyptians into the open where they could be destroyed.

The Israeli Armoured Corps was now beginning to emerge from its lean and hungry years. Its first tanks were two British Cromwells, a Sherman rescued from scrap and a few old French H35s. Some weaponless Shermans had then been purchased and fitted with a vintage 105-mm howitzer, a combination that produced wildly erratic results. In more recent times France had provided high-velocity 75-mm tank guns, which had replaced the howitzers, the Shermans being modified with a turret counter-weight, and also a quantity of AMX 13 light tanks. Total Israeli armoured strength on the eve of the war was 100 up-gunned Shermans, 100 AMX 13s and 42 self-propelled guns. Some of the mechanised infantry rode in M3 halftracks, the remainder in commandeered civilian vehicles.

The Egyptians could muster forty 20-pounder Centurions, 150 Shermans, forty AMX 13s, 150 T34/85s, fifty IS IIIs, 200 17-pounder Archer and 100 SU 100 tank destroyers, and 200 BTR 152 wheeled armoured personnel carriers. However, only a proportion of this strength was deployed in Sinai, since the Egyptian General Staff was compelled to retain considerable forces west of the Canal to guard against the anticipated British and French landings. In immediate opposition to the Israelis were two infantry divisions, dug in on the northern sector and at Abu Agheila, plus the 1st Armoured Brigade, equipped with T34/85s and SU 100s, in reserve at Bir Gifgafa; a number of tank and tank destroyer battalions were also attached to the infantry divisions. Elsewhere, the Sinai was only lightly held.

Israel's Operation *Kadesh* began at 1700 on 29th October when a battalion of Colonel Ariel Sharon's 202nd Parachute Brigade was dropped close to the Mitla Pass. The remainder of the brigade, supported by a squadron of AMX 13s, immediately began to push along the southern axis, the civilian element of its transport floundering through soft sand and falling steadily behind. A number of abandoned BTR 152 personnel carriers were found at

Nakhl and these eased the situation, enabling the relief force to reach Mitla by midnight on the 30th.

The Egyptians still held the Pass itself, in greater strength than had been anticipated, and decisively repulsed an attempt by the paratroops to fight their way through the next day, assisted by four Meteor jets, which strafed Sharon's column. At dusk a volunteer sacrificed his life by driving into the Pass, drawing fire from concealed positions in caves. The location of these was noted and in a second attack, made from the hillsides above, the Israelis methodically wiped out the defence.

In the centre a formation known as Task Force 38, consisting of 7th Armoured, 4th and 37th Infantry Brigades, had the task of eliminating Kuseima and the Abu Agheila stronghold. The force moved off at midnight on the 29th and by dawn Kuseima had been taken. Abu Agheila, however, put up a stiff fight, which halted the advance with some loss. Colonel Uri Ben Ari, 7th Armoured's commander, immediately despatched his reconnaissance unit to find a way round the position. To his delight the difficult passage of the Wadi Daika was reported clear, giving direct access to the Ismailia road west of Abu Agheila; the troops guarding the defile had been swept away by the tide of fugitives from Kuseima.

Ben Ari at once reached the conclusion that the reduction of Abu Agheila was of secondary importance to the chance of unleashing his battalions across central Sinai and, leaving one to assist the infantry, he embarked on a whirlwind advance that brought him to the canal the following day. His decision has been described as high-handed, but having been presented with such a splendid *fait accompli* the IDF Chief of Staff, General Moshe Dayan, had little alternative but to approve it. Abu Agheila, now largely irrelevant, continued to resist courageously until 2nd November.

On the coastal sector the targets of Task Force 77, consisting of 27th Armoured, 1st and 11th Infantry Brigades, were El Airsh and the Gaza Strip. It too commenced operations on the night of the 29th, but at Rafah was held up by minefields covered by heavy

Egyptian fire, which pinned down the infantry who were leading the assault. For the sake of speed the 27th Armoured, commanded by Colonel Haim Bar Lev, passed through, losing surprisingly few vehicles on mines, and split the defence in two.

Leaving the infantry to wheel north from Rafah into the Gaza Strip, Bar Lev set off in pursuit of the Egyptians withdrawing towards El Arish. At Jiradi the coast road passes through a natural defile formed by sand dunes and the advance was halted for a while until an AMX 13 Battalion, accompanied by mechanised infantry in half-tracks and screened by an air strike, worked its way with difficulty through the soft sand and routed the defenders with a flank attack. The remainder of the brigade poured through the defile and on into El Arish, completely surprising the garrison who believed Jiradi to be impassable. The road to El Kantara and the Canal was now wide open, and Bar Lev took it with alacrity.

The Egyptian 1st Armoured Brigade at Bir Gifgafa had taken little part in the fighting. One has more than a little sympathy for its commander. Events had moved at such a break-neck pace that he suddenly found himself in a Pig in the Middle situation, required to catch not one but four balls simultaneously. Ought he to relieve Abu Agheila? Or intercept Ben Ari – or Bar Lev? Or should he try to reopen the Mitla? Paralysed by indecision as to which course held priority, he remained immobile too long. The Israeli jets pounced, destroying and demoralising. A weak thrust towards Abu Agheila was easily contained, and then 1st Armoured retired across the Canal, shedding vehicles as it went.

The 1956 Sinai campaign was over. The Israelis had lost 181 killed and twenty-five tanks. About 2,000 Egyptians were killed and 6,000 taken prisoner. Israeli booty amounted to 100 tanks and tank destroyers and a large quantity of artillery.

The military effects of the Anglo-French landings were eclipsed by the political. Israel was forced to withdraw within her boundaries and the Arab bloc was pushed even more firmly into the Soviet sphere of influence. Arab nationalism reached new heights, accompanied by a feeling that had it not been for western interference Israel would have been met by superior forces in Sinai and defeated.

In Israeli military circles there was general agreement that the Armoured Corps, hitherto regarded as little more than an adjunct of the mechanised infantry brigades, had now won its spurs as the arm of decision and should be expanded. Under the direction of the newly promoted Ben Ari, followed by Bar Lev, this policy was energetically pursued. M48 Pattons were purchased from West Germany and 20-pounder Centurions from Great Britain, both being up-gunned with the excellent British 105-mm, while the Sherman was re-armed with a French gun of the same calibre. Additionally, the Centurion's petrol engine was replaced by a more suitable diesel, the conversion being known locally as the Ben Gurion. In 1964, Brigadier Israel Tal took over the Corps and concentrated on improving its long-range gunnery techniques. This was put to good use the following year during the so-called Water War, fought for control of the upper Jordan, the Centurions picking off an assortment of elderly Syrian PzKw IVs, *Jagdpanzer* IVs and assault guns emplaced in static roles on the Golani foothills.

By 1967 it was apparent that the Arabs, now armed to the teeth by Russia, were intent on a further attempt to crush Israel. Diplomacy having failed, the Israelis decided to strike first, destroying the enemy's air forces on the ground.

The Meteors and Vampires with which the Israeli Air Force had fought in 1956 had now been replaced by French Mystere and Mirage fighter-bombers and Ouragan and Vautour light bombers. Under Major-General Motti Hod the Air Force had, through incessant practice, reduced the turn-round time for each aircraft between missions to a mere seven-and-a-half minutes, a fraction of that required by its opponents.

Hod planned that the destruction of the Arab air forces, Operation *Focus*, should begin at 0745 on 5th June 1967. The time was chosen to fall between the dispersion of the enemy's dawn patrols and the arrival of senior officers at their headquarters at 0900.

Egypt, possessor of the strongest air force in the Arab alliance, was to be hit first.

Promptly at 0745 the Israeli jets screamed over the Sinai airfields of Bir Gifgafa, Bir Tamada, Abu Suweir, Faid and Kibrith, bombing and strafing the neatly aligned MiGs, Sukhois, Ilyushins and Tupolevs; simultaneously the Egyptian Air Force headquarters at Cairo West was also raided. Next it was the turn of Beni Sueif, south of Cairo, followed by Mansura in the Delta and Helwan at 1000 and Minia fifteen minutes later. Bilbis was struck at noon and Luxor at 1230. The airfield at El Arish was left in peace, since the Israelis required it themselves to supply their ground troops.

The IAF now turned its attention to Jordan and Syria, hitting Amman International at 1245, Damascus International and Mafraq at 1300, and Seikhal, Damyr and Halhul at 1315. During the afternoon the attack was carried to bases in northern Syria and Iraq, returning to Egypt in the evening with strikes at Cairo International at 1715 and Ras Banas on the Red Sea at 1800.

The first hours of this astonishing air offensive cost Egypt 300 aircraft, three-quarters of her effective strength. The much smaller Syrian Air Force lost a similar proportion, the Iraqi Air Force was badly mauled and the Royal Jordanian Air Force all but disappeared. Nor was this all, for the Israelis, in addition to attacking aircraft on the ground had also used penetration bombs fitted with a delayed timing device on the runways, making them difficult and dangerous to repair. Radar installations, too, had been eliminated, so that when the few remaining Arab aircraft took to the air they fought blind and were swamped by Israeli fighters. During six days of fighting the IAF destroyed 456 enemy aircraft, only seventy-nine of which fell in air combat, for the loss of only forty-six of its own machines. So successful had been Operation *Focus* that by the afternoon of 5th June itself Hod was able to divert an increasing number of squadrons for ground support.

The difficulties facing the IDF in Sinai were infinitely greater than those that had existed in 1956. The Egyptians had four infantry divisions in the area, the 20th (Palestinian) in the Gaza Strip with fifty Shermans; the 7th at Rafah with 100 T34/85s and IS IIIs; the 2nd at Abu Agheila with ninety T34/85s and T54s; and the 3rd at Jebel Libni with 100 T34/85s and T54s. At Bir Hasana, south of Abu Agheila, was a special armoured group known as Task Force Shazli with 150 T55s, while covering the southern axis at Nakhl was the 6th Mechanised Division with 100 T34/85s and T54s. The 4th Armoured Division's 200 T55s were based on Bir Gifgafa, in tactical reserve. Altogether, the Egyptians had 800 fighting vehicles in the field with a further 150 in reserve (300 T34s, 400 T54/55s, 100 IS IIIS, fifty Shermans and 100 SU 100s), although of these about half were under infantry control, many being dug into static defence systems.

Despite Radio Cairo's violent declamation that Israel was about to be torn apart, the Egyptian disposition was essentially defensive, a situation that has led to the suggestion that the propaganda war was out of phase with events on the ground. This may be true in part, but the Commander-in-Chief of the Sinai Front, General Abdul Mortagy, was a keen student of Montgomery's methods and an *aficionado* of the Red Army, and his establishment of a deep Kursk-style defensive belt in the north with his armour ready to meet any mobile threat from the south is sharply reminiscent of British tactics during the 1942 Battle of Alam Haifa; once the Israelis had blunted their potential against his fixed positions, he intended to go over to the offensive, driving them across the Negev and deep into their own country.

Mortagy clearly regarded his opponents as a conventional army with adequate reserves. This the IDF was not; it could not afford to fight an attritional war of position and had no intention of doing so. Instead, it intended to use its armour in the break-in role (a decision reached with great reluctance) and then penetrate to the Canal in the manner of 1956, isolating the substantial enemy forces on the frontier; denied water, the Egyptian formations would either disintegrate or try to fight their way back to the Canal.

Three armoured divisions were available for the task. One, equipped with 250 tanks (Centurions, Pattons, Shermans and AMX 13s) and including the crack regular 7th Armoured Brigade, was commanded by the now Major-General Tal and faced the formidable defences of the Gaza Strip and Rafah. A second, smaller, division with 150 tanks (Centurions, Shermans and AMX 13s) was commanded by Major-General Sharon and was located opposite the Abu Agheila complex. The third, commanded by Major-General Avraham Yoffe and equipped with 200 Centurions, lay in reserve between the two, its initial function when hostilities began being to prevent intervention by the Egyptian 4th Armoured Division and Task Force Shazli. Two small independent armoured brigades were also present, Mendler's with fifty Shermans in the southern Negev, and Reshef's with thirty AMX 13s, near Gaza. The total number of tanks available to the IDF in Sinai was 680 with seventy in immediate reserve. It will thus be noted that although the Israelis had fewer fighting vehicles, in terms of tanks serving with armoured formation, as opposed to those tied to infantry divisions, they outnumbered the Egyptians by a wide margin, an interesting parallel with the respective deployment of German and French armour in May 1940.

Because of the air offensive against the Arabs the first, most difficult, hours of Operation *Red Sheet*, the Israeli invasion of Sinai, would be almost devoid of air support; virtually everything depended on the drive and will to win of junior leaders in what was unavoidably going to be a confused battle. As 7th Armoured's commander, Colonel Shmuel Gonen, put it to them: "If we do not win, we have nowhere to come back to."

At 0815 on 5th June a two-pronged attack, led by Tal's division and Colonel Eitun's parachute brigade, crossed the frontier and stormed their way into Khan Yunis and Rafah. The Centurions (impressively impervious to Egyptian shellfire) and Pattons ground their way through tortuous alleys and along roads criss-crossed by a chicane of anti-tank ditches, over fields bordered by difficult earth banks and stone walls, exchanging fire with the defence and executing a series of tactical hooks to by-pass the areas of fiercest resistance whenever possible.

For the Israelis there was only one criterion – to keep moving and not let the attack bog down in the defended zone. At times it was a tank commander's battle with a multiplicity of local situations, invariably difficult, inevitably dangerous, with Centurions and Pattons covering each other's movements with their own fire. Throughout, by radio and hand signal, the young troop and squadron leaders implemented the philosophy that had been drummed into them for years: Follow Me!

In part the Israeli difficulties were caused by the Egyptian anti-tank batteries, which fired in salvo, so reducing the chances of giving away their positions by continuous gunfire; and in part by the intervention of the enemy's armour in a series of local counter-attacks, which were usually met by manoeuvring to a flank in the old tradition of the Afrika Korps.

> "The Pattons surged forward to storm the objective. From his previous reconnaissance of this enemy position, Ehud (Elad) knew he was climbing straight for the anti-tank gun locality. Now able to read the battle well, he allocated the various assignments against the anti-tank guns and T34 tanks which were seen to be drawing near. At this moment, the anti-tank guns which were hidden behind the ricinus plants thundered in unison; three Pattons were hit and ground to a halt. A second later the battalion Second-in-Command, Major Haim, appeared with the bulk of the battalion's tanks at the back of the defence area. His tanks had come through the sand dunes from a direction which the Egyptians had not anticipated. Practically undisturbed they had calmly taken up firing positions behind the Egyptian tanks which were now bearing down upon Ehud and his tanks. Major Haim advanced within a range of 800 metres before ordering 'Fire!' Nine Egyptian

tanks burst into flames simultaneously. The Pattons now turned their fire onto the anti-tank guns, the ammunition trucks and the field guns.

"'Don't waste ammunition! Don't fire heavy ammunition at trucks!' Ehud's voice was calling over the battalion's radio. 'On trucks, crews and the like, use only machine-guns!' Major Haim's force advanced on the enemy defences like a hurricane. A Patton whose machine-gun had jammed rode through the positions, crushing anti-tank gunners under its tracks.""[90]

Suddenly the Israelis were through. Gaza to the north was irrelevant and could be left to the infantry and Reshef's independent armoured brigade; so too were the remnants of broken Egyptian units streaming west along the coast road, since Tal intended to reach El Arish before they did. Led by its Centurion battalion, his division smashed through the subsidiary fortified zone at Sheikh Zuweir and drove on towards Jiradi.

The Jiradi defile was even more formidable than it had been in 1956, but its defenders were taken completely by surprise as the Centurions hammered down the road towards them, steel tracks flashing in the sun and turrets swinging one by one alternately to right and left. Before the Egyptians could man their weapons the tanks' HESH rounds were exploding among them and the dunes were spurting sand from thousands of rounds of machine-gun ammunition. The Centurions motored through, unscathed.

However, by the time the Patton battalion appeared the Egyptians had recovered from their initial shock. Several tanks were knocked out and every vehicle that broke through bore a scar of some kind. The AMX/Sherman battalion, following behind, found the defences closed so tight that it required a set-piece attack with artillery support and an armoured infantry battalion before it was able to rejoin the rest of 7th Armoured Brigade in El Arish during the night.

Tal was now operating well in advance of the *Red Sheet* timetable; so much so that a parachute brigade, detailed to drop on El Arish *before* he arrived, had to be found an alternative mission. The cost in tanks had not been cheap, but was acceptable. The cost in tank commanders was tragically high; among the casualties were Major Ehud Elad, commander of the Patton battalion, killed at Jiradi, and his three company commanders, all wounded while trying to force their way through the defile.

On Tal's left, Avraham Yoffe's all–Centurion division had crossed the frontier west of Nitsana and had advanced throughout the day almost unopposed, travelling over dune country that the Egyptians considered impassable and which they had, therefore, not bothered to defend. The going was certainly difficult but by 1800 Yoffe's leading battalion was moving into position at Bir Lafhan, due south of El Arish, having covered sixty miles in ten hours.

It was not anticipated that Major-General Ghoul, commanding the Egyptian 4th Armoured Division at Bir Gifgafa, would stand idle during this critical period of the battle, as did his predecessor in 1956. Having been informed of developments on the coast he was expected to despatch substantial reinforcements to El Arish via Bir Lafhan, were Yoffe was deployed to stop him.

Ghoul did not know that most of Gonen's armoured brigade had already reached El Arish, and certainly did not suspect the presence of Yoffe's division. His reinforcements, a T55 brigade and a mechanised infantry brigade, were spotted approaching Bir Lafhan at 2300, their column a long necklace of blazing headlights in the darkness. Yoffe's Centurions opened fire at extreme AP range and destroyed fourteen tanks and several fuel and ammunition trucks. By the light of burning vehicles the column, its lights now extinguished, could be seen scattering into the outer shadows. A sporadic, long-range fire fight ensued, notable in that although the Russian-built T55s were fitted with infra-red night-fighting equipment, the only Israeli vehicle to sustain damage was the sole Centurion to use its light projector.

If Ghoul's commanders thought that dawn would enable them to regroup their scattered units, they were disappointed. Instead, the tanks of 7th Armoured, despatched south by Tal from El Arish, appeared on their left flank. The Egyptians were not only caught between two fires but also opposed by superior weapons and better gunnery techniques. By 1000 they had broken and were in full flight for Jebel Libni with the Israelis, in urgent need of a fuel replenishment, in hot pursuit. The IAF, now able to give its full attention to ground support, harried the fugitives on their way with a rain of bombs, rockets and napalm.

During the night Sharon's division had also stormed the forbidding defensive complex at Abu Agheila, situated on three ridges, which incorporated concrete trenches and bunkers and which was supported by plentiful artillery and well provided with armour. A Centurion battalion worked its way through the difficult going to the north, having to fight a series of battles on the way, and then went into a blocking position behind the defences, which were engaged by a hull-down Sherman battalion at close range. Three infantry battalions, arriving by civilian bus, marched up to their start lines during the evening and then rested until H-Hour.

At 2230 the Israeli artillery, consisting of two 25-pounder battalions, one 155-mm howitzer battalion, one 160-mm mortar battalion and two 120-mm mortar battalions, began firing the heaviest concentrations in the IDF's history to date. The Egyptian artillery replied in kind, hitting the approaches from the east.

Sharon now played his trump card. A parachute brigade under Colonel Danny was lifted by S-58 helicopter into the rear of the Egyptian defences, close to the main artillery position. The move went undetected and the gunners were swiftly overwhelmed. As their fire died away the Israeli infantry launched its attack from the east, equipped with coloured light flashers to signal their progress to the Shermans, which provided direct gunfire support with the assistance of their xenon searchlights. Egyptian resistance was fierce and Sharon was compelled to commit his reserve infantry battalion before the last ridge was captured. The

Shermans now moved into the position to tackle the enemy's armour in a confused night action, the *coup de grace* being given when the Centurion battalion broke in from the west, aided by Danny's paratroopers. The Egyptian defence suddenly collapsed, those who could clambering aboard vehicles and escaping to the south-west.

In twenty-four hours, the frontier defences had been destroyed and the 4th Armoured Division severely mauled. At a conference with his three divisional commanders on the morning of the 6th, Major-General Yeshayahn Gavish, GOC Southern Front, outlined the strategy for the next phase of the campaign. Tal and Yoffe would advance *through* the retreating enemy and secure the three passes leading from the Sinai plateau to the Canal; the Mitla in the south, and the lesser Gidi and Tassa further north. Sharon's division would act as beaters and drive the Egyptians towards them.

Replenished, partly by air and partly from their own three-day supply, the Israeli armoured divisions moved out. Tal sent one brigade along the coast road to El Kantara, and moved with his tanks against Ghoul's 4th Armoured Division at Bir Gifgafa. A converging attack by the Centurion and Patton battalions further wrote down the Egyptian armour, and when it attempted to withdraw during the night it ran into the AMX battalion in a blocking position some miles to the west; in the ensuing night action several Israeli light tanks were lost, but the arrival of the Centurions eased the pressure and led to the virtual disintegration of Ghoul's force. The next day Tal reached the Canal and closed the Gidi and Tassa passes.

Yoffe's mission was to capture the Mitla, lying on the enemy's principal withdrawal axis. An armoured infantry and two Centurion battalions were detailed for the task, heading south-west from Jebel Libni through Bir Hasana throughout the 6th. Retreating Egyptian columns were frequently encountered and ploughed through; sometimes there was resistance, and some-times men simply abandoned their vehicles, and even their boots, to escape across the sand. It was a long, gruelling march by any standards. Break-downs and fuel shortage steadily eroded the strength of the task force until all that remained when Mitla was reached that evening were nine Centurions, some of which were on tow, two armoured infantry platoons and three 120-mm mortars.

This tiny group turned to bar the path of thousands of men and hundreds of armoured vehicles heading for the Canal in a disorderly retreat. All through that night and the following day attack after attack was beaten off, one Israeli tank commander providing an echo of Beda Fomm by siting his vehicle so that he could fire into the rear of the enemy's T55s as they closed on the block. Many Egyptians, on foot, were able to work their way round, but the long columns choking the road were attacked incessantly by the IAF, which also defeated a determined attempt to reopen the pass from the western end. It was, nonetheless, a close-run thing, for when Yoffe's relief force arrived at dawn on the 8th the last four Centurions in action were down to their last few rounds of ammunition.

By then the Egyptians had had enough. Sharon's drive south from Abu Agheila and Mendler's west from Kuntilla met at Nakhl, where the discovery of a complete brigade of abandoned IS IIIs symbolised the utter rout of Mortagy's army. All over Sinai men from broken units, tormented by demon thirst, willingly surrendered in their thousands in the hope of receiving a little water.

Elsewhere, by sheer hard fighting, the Israelis had captured Jerusalem, ejected the Jordanians from the West Bank and thrown the Syrians off the Golan Heights. 15,000 Arabs had died, 50,000 had been wounded and 11,500 were prisoners. Between them, Egypt, Syria, Jordan and Iraq lost more than 1,100 tanks, 450 of which were captured intact, countless artillery pieces and lorries, and 70,000 tons of ammunition; the cost to Israel was 679 killed and 2,563 wounded.

If the results of the Six-Day War were deeply humiliating for the Arab world, for Russia they were deeply disturbing since the inadequacy of Russian equipment and methods was somewhat more than implied. In addition to quickly making good the Arabs' physical losses, the Red Army also embarked on a series of show-piece exercises in which no expense was spared to convince the doubtful among client states that the Soviet system was best. Exercise *Dniepr*, in particular, was filmed in lavish colour and exhibited around the world. Sequences included long shots of close-packed tanks and APCs racing to the attack with guns blazing, their objective blanketed by thundering artillery air-bursts, rocketed time after time by low-flying jet aircraft. As an example of good direction, the film was truly impressive; as an historical document it was curiously "in frame".

For the Israelis, too, success brought its problems. The drives of Ben Ari and Bar Lev in 1956 and Tal, Yoffe and Sharon in 1967 all suggested that it was the tank, almost unaided, that was the weapon of decision. In consequence armoured formations reduced their mechanised infantry and artillery elements and relied on drive, dash and the 'Follow Me' spirit. It was a fallacy that would become painfully apparent when Israel next found herself at war with her neighbours in 1973.

Just as the IAF had carefully timed the opening of its 1967 air offensive for the period when the enemy was at his most vulnerable, so too did the Arabs choose the one day in the year when Israel was at a complete standstill – Yom Kippur, the Day of Atonement, the holiest day in the Jewish religious calendar.

At 1350 on 6th October Syrian MiGs and Sukhois screamed across the bare hills of the Northern Front to attack Israeli headquarters while artillery opened up all along the line from Mount Hermon to the Jordanian border. By 1400 the first of 1,100 T55s and T62s, accompanied by APCs, were smashing their way through the frontier wire; in their path lay two Regular Centurion brigades, the 7th and the Barak, with only 130 tanks between them.

Simultaneously the Egyptian Army under the command of General Ismail with Major-General Saad Shazli as Chief of Staff, launched an assault along the entire length of the Suez Canal, obtaining bridgeheads everywhere and advancing on the chain of isolated outposts that would become known as the Bar Lev Line, although it was never intended to be a form of linear defence.

The Canal crossing was not a difficult operation, since the eastern bank was not defended, it being the Israeli practice to hold their forces in mobile reserve behind the outpost line. The Egyptian General Staff had considered every aspect of the operation in the minutest detail and detailed rehearsals had been going on for months. Every man knew his part, what to do and where to go. Moreover, this thorough training and the fact that he was fighting to restore the honour of his race had given the Egyptian soldier a motivation that he had previously lacked.

In Israel reservists, of necessity the major constituent of the country's armed forces, left home and synagogue to join their units, numb with shock and incomprehension that the Arabs had been able to achieve such total strategic surprise. The IAF went into action on both fronts only to run into intense fire from a radar controlled and fully integrated air defence system including large numbers of quadruple heavy-automatic mountings and Russian SAMs (Surface to Air Missiles). It took days for the Israelis to solve the technical problems, but in the meantime Phantom pilots continued to sacrifice their lives in suicidal attacks in support of their ground troops as well as fighting to maintain air superiority over the homeland.

Since the Northern Front was closest to the centres of population, it held absolute priority in the minds of Israel's Defence Staff; until the situation there was resolved the Sinai Front would have to soldier on as best it could. It was, unfortunately, in the Sinai that the next shock was to come.

Saad Shazli was an officer with a reputation for determination, hard fighting and good planning. In 1967 he, almost alone, had brought his men back from the Sinai debacle as a formed body. Now, he was well aware that the inevitable Israeli response to the Canal crossing would be an armoured counter-attack. In the normal course of events this would be met by tanks that began crossing as soon as the engineers had completed their pontoon bridges, but he had strong reservations as to whether the air-defence system could prevent the IAF from destroying those bridges. He could not, therefore, rely on tanks getting across in the required numbers, and his alternative solution was to cover his front with a dense cordon of easily carried Sagger[91] ATGWs, backed up by such tanks as were available, and by RPG–7 rocket launchers for close-quarter work.

The Israeli area commander, Major-General Albert Mendler, had three armoured brigades available with a total of approximately 300 tanks. His difficulty lay in identifying the main Egyptian thrust lines, an impossible task since at that stage there were none. He therefore dispersed his brigades to those sectors where he thought a break-out seemed likely and mounted a series of local attacks, which were complicated by frantic calls for assistance from besieged garrisons in the outpost line, calls that by tradition must be answered.

The attacks went in with their customary dash. Every account affirms the complete surprise of the Israeli tank commanders at being faced not by their opposite number but by distant lines of men crouching behind their individual missile launcher. Then the Saggers struck, destroying vehicle after vehicle at impossibly long ranges. Within two days, Mendler's force had lost two-thirds of its tanks; the commanders of those that survived often found their turrets draped with the slack but sinister wires that had trailed from near-misses.

Egyptian morale soared at the defeat of the dreaded Israeli counterattack. Some sections of the world's press and television, surprised, hinted that the Sagger was a wonder weapon which had overnight rendered the tank completely obsolete. Others, more thoughtful, reflected that the tank's demise had already been the subject of a number of premature announcements following the respective appearance of the anti-tank gun; hollow-charge ammunition; the bazooka; and, for some reason, the atomic bomb. Further reflection revealed that similar, or slightly better, ATGWs had been in service with every major army for a number of years without causing undue excitement, and that Shazli's deployment was an *ad hoc* solution to a local situation that was unlikely to occur again.[92]

In Israel the mood was one of black despair. Scarcely had the shock of the Yom Kippur attack worn off than it was discovered that the IAF no longer ruled the skies; the defeat of the Armoured Corps in Sinai was almost the last straw. It was not that the IDF was unaware of the Sagger's presence in the Egyptian armoury, it was more that Shazli's unorthodox use of the weapon had taken everyone by surprise. In these depressing circumstances the Armoured Corps reacted quickly to the changed tactical pattern by raising the proportion of APCs to tanks from 1:3 to 1:1 and increasing the amount of artillery available to armoured formations, a reversion in fact to the concept of the balanced armoured division. In future a storm of automatic fire from mechanised infantry and thorough artillery preparation would make it impossible for the enemy's Sagger teams to operate in the open.[93]

Time for these adjustments was provided by the Egyptians, who made no attempt to exploit their victory. As soon as the Syrian Front had been stabilised the Israelis' reserve armour began pouring into Sinai until four weak divisions were in the line, watching the enemy build up his resources and waiting for the next move.

But beyond improving his positions locally, General Ismail did little. He now had two armies (in fact strong corps) across the Canal, the Second under Major-General Mamoun covering the front from the Mediterranean to Deversoir, just north of the Great Bitter Lake, and the Third under Major-General Wassel stretching from Deversoir to the Gulf of Suez. By nature a cautious man, Ismail had faithfully followed the Russian rule-book for this type of operation, so far with great success. Having obtained the crossing, he had consolidated his gains within range of the SAM system; he had then defeated the Israeli counter-attack and was now, theoretically, able to embark on the third stage, a breakout into Sinai. On the other hand, he did not want to move until the SAM system had been brought forward to cover the advance, and even then was extremely reluctant to embark on a war of movement with the IDF. Shazli, his Chief of Staff, differed radically in his approach and wanted a fast-moving campaign in the Israeli manner. These fundamental differences seem to have been settled by a compromise in which the Egyptian objectives were set as the Tassa, Gidi and Mitla Passes, followed by the main administrative and supply base at Bir Gifgafa. This alone, it was hoped, would compel the IDF to retreat within its own frontiers.

Yet somehow Ismail could not bring himself to hazard all he had won. In the end, it was events elsewhere that forced his hand. On the Golan Heights the Israeli reserves had arrived in the nick of time and, together with the regular brigades, had shot repeated Syrian attacks to pieces. The Syrians had come on bravely but without imagination, attacking again and again in the same places in the Russian manner, and their tank losses were appalling. By 10th October the Israelis had gone over to the offensive and were pushing up the road to Damascus itself. Syria began to feel that she was carrying the burden of the war unaided and demanded immediate Egyptian action to relieve the pressure.

On 14th October, Ismail finally launched his offensive. Along the entire front the T55s and T62s of his armoured brigades moved forward in their hundreds. Waiting for them, hull down, were elderly but still formidable Centurions, M60 and M48 Pattons and T55s, up-gunned to 105-mm standard following their capture in the Six-Day War. The battle, a gunnery contest to which the Saggers contributed little, raged all day and ended in a significant victory for Israeli marksmanship. Nowhere did the Egyptians affect a penetration; everywhere they were flung back to their start-lines, leaving behind 300 smouldering tanks and a similar number of APCs.

It was suddenly a different kind of war with the initiative swinging back to the Israelis. The reconnaissance battalion of Ariel Sharon's armoured division had detected a gap between the Egyptian Second and Third Armies as early as 9th October. Sharon had immediately asked the GOC Sinai Front, Major-General Shmuel Gonen, for permission to cross the Canal and establish a bridgehead on the western bank. Gonen, well aware that Ismail was fighting the Russian three-stage battle, knowing that a break-out attempt could not long be delayed and needing all his resources to meet it, had refused. Now that Ismail had been decisively checked, full approval was given to Sharon's plan, which was codenamed *Gazelle*.

During the evening of 15th October, covered by a diversionary attack against the Ismailia Sector, Sharon reached the Canal and by midnight had rafted seven tanks across, accompanied by 200 paratroopers under the command of his old partner Danny. This small force established a defensive perimeter without being opposed and was only attacked after it had raided and destroyed a number of SAM sites the following morning.[94] Unfortunately, Sharon was unable to bring up his Gillois bridging train to complete the crossing that night.

Ismail was taken completely aback by this unexpected development and it was not until the 16th that he was able to organise a counterstroke. Throughout the afternoon and all through the night his two armies tried desperately to sever Sharon's narrow corridor leading down to the launching site. Third Army's 25th Armoured Brigade, equipped with T62s, was ambushed in flank by Major-General Adan's armoured division while approaching the scene of the action in column along the shores of the Great Bitter Lake, and routed with the loss of eighty tanks. At the "Chinese Farm" (actually an agricultural station built by the Japanese before the Six-Day War) and the entrance to the corridor a murderous close-quarter fight raged between Egyptian infantry and Israeli paratroops and their respective supporting armour, both sides suffering very severely. However, by the morning of the 17th the Egyptians had been pushed back and the bridging train was moving along the corridor.

Twenty-four hours later Adan had two armoured brigades across. The question now facing Ismail was that which had faced Gamelin when the panzers crossed the Meuse in 1940 – which way would they go? Towards Cairo, a dazzling political prize? Or north to sever Second Army's communications? Or south to sever those of Third Army? The strain on senior Egyptian commanders suddenly became intolerable; Shazli, exhausted, suffered a total collapse, Namoun, of Second Army, a heart attack.

Adan soon provided the answer. Cairo was not important in the immediate military context, and operations against Second Army were likely to run into bitter resistance from the Egyptian reserve army. He swung south, operating under a protective umbrella of IAF interceptors, cleared the western shores of the Bitter Lakes, and reached Suez on the 23rd. The Third Army was cut off, deprived of water and in danger of dying of thirst.

At this point Russia, dismayed at her clients' further defeat and with her own prestige at stake, brought intense pressure to bear on the United States to stop the war. Israel was forced to agree to a ceasefire or be deprived of American support. Notwithstanding, the IDF's application of the Indirect Approach had brought her to the brink of total victory only a fortnight after she had faced total defeat.

The cost of the war to both sides had been prohibitive. The Arabs had lost more than 2,500 tanks, 450 aircraft and many thousands of dead; the Israelis half their tanks, 100 aircraft and 2,500 of their men killed, enough to bring grief to every household in the land and more than in any other of their wars. From it came good in that Israel and Egypt eventually settled their differences, President Anwar Sadat even ridding his country of its Russian advisors.

There was nothing new in the technique of the Sinai *Blitzkriegs*, except possibly the Israelis' development to the full of their potential for night fighting; rather, they tended to repeat lessons already learned, and even the use of thirst as a weapon had its precedent in Wavell's 1940 Operation *Compass*. Latterly, new and dangerous weapon systems had been met, but these had been countered and in the end mobility and air power had won.

The story continues, and will do so until science produces conditions in which the powers of the defence exceed those of the attack.

Chapter 14: Thrust Line to Armageddon: How the Soviets planned to attack Europe

In 1914 Grigori Efimovich Rasputin, the so-called Holy Devil of Imperial Russia, prophesied that the Tsar's declaration of war on Germany would ultimately lead to the downfall of the monarchy and the established Church, and that following these events no nobles would be seen in the land for fifty years.

The present Russian aristocracy is even more repressive than its slightly dim forebears. It avoids open use of the knout and its methods are subtle, coldly efficient and quiet, but even so its troops have ruthlessly opened fire on East German, Hungarian and Czech civilians when the latter have dared to voice their discontent with the Party Line. Its members avow profound faith in the teaching of Karl Marx as interpreted by the saintly Lenin, whose icon appears on almost every vacant wall, although such teachings are concerned with nineteenth-century economics and have little relevance today. Being intelligent men, the Soviet leaders are naturally aware of the imperfections of their own system; why else would it be necessary to build walls to contain a captive population? They are, however, prisoners of the iron ideology that raised them to power, and to admit that better systems of government exist would be to confess that Communism is fallible, a heresy so profound as to be intolerable.

It was one of the tenets of the early Bolsheviks that their revolution should be exported from Russia to every country in the world, and successive Russian governments have maintained and fostered that ideal. No time scale has been laid down, and the use of force is by no means considered mandatory. If the desired results can be achieved by indirect means, such as economic disruption, subversion and the support of self-styled national liberation movements, so much the better. Actual war is to be avoided at all costs, unless the prospect of victory is immediate and beyond any conceivable doubt, since even if defeat is a virtual impossibility, a stalemate or a severe check could initiate dangerous tremors among a population that for the past thirty years has been taught as an article of faith that the Red Army is invincible.

The tragedy of the Great Patriotic War of 1941-45, with its 20 million dead, its ruin and utter desolation, is burned into the Russian consciousness to a degree unimagined in the west. The whole of Soviet thinking on defence, therefore, hinges around two focal points; never again must such a war be fought on Russian soil, and never again must the Red Army be subjected to such protracted slaughter. Instead, it is planned that any fighting will take place on the potential aggressor's territory, and that the Red Army's strength and state of preparedness will ensure a quick kill before the aggressor can initiate his move.

In the Russian view NATO is a potentially aggressive and not a defensive alliance. It matters little that NATO forces are stretched so thin as to be barely able to fulfil their defensive role; the terrible casualties inflicted by the grossly outnumbered Wehrmacht are still clearly remembered. Whatever the truth, the West is seen through Russian eyes as being untrustworthy, devoted solely to the furtherance of its own interests, and as having left the Russian people to bear almost alone the burden of two world wars.

Leaving aside for the moment the possibility of an exchange of mutually destructive intercontinental ballistic missiles and all their frighteningly detached jargon of payloads, throw-weights and survivability, let us imagine a situation that has developed beyond political containment, in which the techniques of crisis management have failed, and in which Russia feels so threatened that she launches a pre-emptive strike on Western Europe. At the present time, the prospects of such a situation arising seem so remote as to be almost inconceivable, but world events move at such a pace that the possibility cannot be discounted; it is, in fact, the only situation in which the Red Army could be committed to battle in the Western hemisphere.

Informed opinion suggests that the Kremlin believes a short, sharp *Blitzkrieg* with an easily attainable objective will effectively destroy the NATO alliance without recourse to tactical or strategic nuclear missiles. The grounds for this belief are that the Warsaw Pact's conventional forces are already strong enough to complete the task without nuclear assistance; that it would be politically undesirable to use nuclear weapons first; and that the will of western politicians *may* no longer be sufficiently strong to sanction the use of their own deterrent in a non-nuclear situation. The same arguments apply in varying degrees to chemical and biological warfare.

The objective of such a *Blitzkrieg* is the Rhine, a great natural barrier beyond which it is not necessary to proceed. With Germany occupied as far as the east bank, the linchpin of European defence will have been knocked out and the remainder of the NATO alliance rendered incapable of mounting a coherent counter-offensive. At this point, Soviet leaders may wisely announce that they have no intention of advancing further, having secured the peace of the world against aggression; indeed, a further advance is hardly in Russian interest, since it would simply harden western resolve and risk a severe check at the hands of NATO reinforcements arriving from across the Atlantic. Few would care to ignore a proffered olive branch when the alternative might be nuclear Armageddon. As to the future in a Russian-dominated Europe, the Kremlin would hope that inflationary economic pressures and continued political subversion would bring the surviving free nations of the Continent one by one into the Communist fold; the time scale is of no consequence.

Every preparation for the Warsaw Pact's *Blitzkrieg* will already have been made, ever objective detailed, every thrust line carefully chosen. For years the details have been endlessly rehearsed and every contingency allowed for and written into the master plan. Senior commanders have had drummed into them since they were junior officers that only speed will bring success, and will instinctively drive their divisions, whether tank or motor rifle, hard until their own specific goals have been attained. Assisting them will be substantial airborne forces, dropping behind NATO lines to secure the all-important bridges and communications centres so vital for a continuous advance. Numerous ground-attack aircraft equipped with a bewildering array of rockets, bombs and missiles will provide tactical support for the advancing spearheads, the boast of the pilots, like that of their NATO counterparts, being "If we can see it, we can hit it; if we hit it, we destroy it."

Heavy casualties among the first wave of assault divisions will have been anticipated; fresh divisions will be passed through them as soon as their potential has been eroded, and still further divisions will be passed through this second wave so that the hard-pressed and increasingly tired NATO defenders are faced again and again with fresh troops whose idealism has not been blunted by the realities of brutal war.

Provided they remain within the confines of the central master plan, Soviet battle group commanders are permitted more latitude than was the case during World War II, and are allowed to manoeuvre against the flanks of or possibly even by-pass areas of resistance rather than commit their troops to a series of mindless head-on attacks. As most vehicles have now been fitted with radio, even such limited tactical flexibility can be exploited to maintain the momentum required to keep a fragmented NATO defence off-balance.

Superficially there seems to be little that can stop the Warsaw Pact's run-away *Blitzkrieg*, short of nuclear involvement on the battlefield itself. On the other hand, it is important to remember that the Red Army is as fallible as any other and that it does have its problems. Its command structure remains stiff and is still rigidly hierarchical: a subaltern, for example, does not automatically inherit his company commander's powers and responsibilities if the latter is killed, and his actions when placed in this situation require the approval of his superiors, a process that can cost time on a busy radio frequency. This is in sharp contrast to the practice of western armies, in which officers are trained to think and act two steps above their actual rank, so that the subaltern can if required assume command of his company, and the company commander take over his battalion and continue the operation with the minimum of delay and the knowledge that he may use his initiative as his judgement dictates. Again, the sergeant, who has long been regarded as the backbone of western armies and who is quite capable of taking over his troop or platoon and running it efficiently, has no precise equivalent in the Red Army, whose senior NCOs enjoy considerably less power and prestige. These factors are important on two counts; first, the success of any *Blitzkrieg* depends to a large extent not only on the judgement of senior commanders but also on the initiative of junior leaders operating in the forefront of the battle, and in this latter respect the Red Army remains deficient; and secondly, while history has shown that the Russian soldier will advance unflinchingly to almost certain death in a tightly controlled battle, it also reveals that nothing depresses and demoralises him as quickly as being left without positive orders. For these reasons NATO troops have been trained to quickly identify and destroy the commander's vehicle in Warsaw Pact tank or motor rifle companies, such a target representing a queen among her pawns.

In spite of the now almost universal provision of radios, Russian commanders expect control of their formations to be subjected to constant interference from NATO's electronic warfare units. They can expect blanket jamming across the whole tactical frequency band and if this is removed it is replaced by surveillance that can monitor their command's progress and predict its next move. The slight NATO superiority in this field is acknowledged to such an extent that during exercises company commanders still employ the traditional hand and flag signals used in World War II, assuming as a matter of course that use of their radios will be denied them without warning. At one period the Red Army trained assiduously at night for what was known as the Continuous 24-Hour Battle, hoping to maintain its advance throughout the hours of darkness. In such circumstances control is notoriously difficult at the best of times and if subjected to electronic disruption a shortfall in objectives achieved will very probably result. The consequences of this could disrupt the very tight timetable that has been set, causing the second and third echelon assault divisions to pile up behind and, eventually, forcing them to fight for their own start-lines.

On the Central European sector, the Warsaw Pact outnumbers NATO by approximately three to one in tanks (20,500:7,000 or 32:10 divisions) and by two to one in motor rifle divisions (38:17). This represents the classic attack ratio, but even so may not be considered adequate by some Soviet strategists who remember that many of their offensives during the last year of World War II were made with even more favourable odds and with excellent vehicles but were still bloodily repulsed by the emaciated panzer divisions and assault gun brigades. In this equation it is not the NATO opinion of what is considered overwhelming that counts, but the Russian view, and that is influenced by historical experience.

Experience in Korea, the Indian sub-continent and the Middle East has confirmed that since the Second World War the west has overtaken and maintained its lead over the Soviet Union in the field of tank technology, particularly in the area of armament. There are now signs that the Russians are closing the gap with their T72 tank, which is equipped with a 122-mm weapon that can outrange every NATO tank except the British Chieftain. This has been achieved by reducing the crew to three and installing an automatic loading mechanism, a device considered by many experts to be a snare and a delusion, since its break-down potential is so high; others have questioned for some time the principle of direct gunfire above 2,000 metres, not only because of the difficulty in spotting a target at such distances, but also because all the pointers indicate that the tank battle will be fought at much closer ranges.

Another area in which the Red Army has its problems is that of artillery. This is surprising, since the guns have an honoured place in Russian military history and were for long regarded as the true gods of war. Notwithstanding, the fact is that much of the Warsaw Pact's field and medium artillery is still towed and therefore vulnerable in either a conventional or nuclear context. In contrast, NATO's artillery is mostly self-propelled, much of it is armoured and has an open-sights tank defeating capability as well.

Any undertaking as vast as an invasion of NATO territory must have a massive logistic backing, and here again the Warsaw Pact is vulnerable. The longer the offensive continues, the further its spearheads reach out, the greater is the cry for fuel and ammunition, while according to the rules of the game the quantity reaching the fighting troops drops proportionately. A supply column ambushed or destroyed by air attack can mean a division temporarily stranded and unable to complete its assigned task, so further damaging the workings of a master plan in which time is of the essence. Particularly significant is the concept that such interference with the enemy's logistics can be carried out without NATO's major formations being further written down to achieve the same result. It would be very strange indeed if NATO commanders have not already made suitable arrangements for the Warsaw Pact's supply lines to be disjointed well beyond what have been described as normal buggeration factors.

Perhaps the greatest imponderable of all is the degree of enthusiastic support the Kremlin can expect to receive from the armies of its client states. Superficially, East Germany seems to be the most disciplined and dedicated to the cause, but ethnically it remains a portion of an artificially divided country and in the final analysis the question must arise as to whether its soldiers are prepared to make war on members of their own families. Nor has it been forgotten that the Red Army raped its way across the country in 1945, nor that it unhesitatingly shed East German blood during the 1953 repression.

The Poles, too, are hereditary enemies rather than allies of the Russians, and are frequently at odds with their own governing Communist Party, not least on matters of religion, applied Marxism having little in common with the Christian ethic. Savage street fighting involving tanks was necessary to put down a Hungarian wave of discontent in 1956. In more recent years tanks were again used to snuff out the first glimmers of freedom in Czechoslovakia. If STAVKA has its reservations, then it has surely earned the right to them.

Unfortunately, while the Warsaw Pact does have its difficulties, those of NATO are even more complex. Western nations are only able to spend a limited portion of their budgets on defence; if they increase their defence spending it is at the expense of the living standards of their populations, and this sets up economic stresses that are fully exploited by Communist agitators and industrial saboteurs. If the free world was to expand its defences to match the force deployed beyond the Iron Curtain, these pressures would produce internal instabilities and so provide an ideal seedbed for potential *coups* by assorted elements of the Left. Obviously, such a situation is highly favourable to the interests of the Kremlin, whose tenants believe that they win either way simply by keeping huge numbers of men under arms. So far, the west has not fallen into their trap, but it has had to compromise by maintaining just sufficient conventional strength in central Europe to make a would-be aggressor consider his position carefully, as well as relying on a nuclear umbrella.

At the present time NATO employs three main battle tanks, the British Chieftain armed with a 120-mm gun, the German Leopard and the American M60, both of which mount a 105-mm gun of British design. Further tanks are under development, incorporating a variety of weapons and greatly improved armour. In general, NATO's MBTs are a better product than those of the Warsaw Pact, but are complex machines; one school of thought suggests that quantity production of a more basic design could provide a better return for the money spent without reducing combat efficiency to any great extent.

In addition to MBTs and self-propelled artillery, there are whole families of smaller armoured vehicles including light tanks, armoured cars and personnel carriers. Some of these carry guided weapons that will defeat the thickest Russian armour, and most mount a weapon that will destroy the BMP or BTR personnel carriers of the Warsaw Pact's motor rifle formations. There are also helicopters armed with anti-tank missiles, ground-based guided anti-tank weapon systems and numerous tube weapons, which have evolved from the simple bazooka and which are issued down to infantry section level. Great emphasis is placed upon tank-hunting techniques and obtaining a first-time kill.

The NATO airforces can put up between them approximately 2,000 aircraft for tactical ground support, of which 400 are also classed as interceptors. Against this the Warsaw Pact can dispose 4,000 tactical aircraft, about half of which are interceptors. To a certain extent these odds are countered by NATO's superior electronic warfare capability, which ensures deployment where it is needed most, if not actual superiority at the point of contact. Needless to say, both sides take their air defence extremely seriously, employing anti-aircraft systems that vary from the fully tracked to the handheld, from the fully mobile to the emplaced.

What, then, will be the nature of the fighting between two such armies, the one armed and trained for a *Blitzkrieg* advance, the other skilled in all the arts of defensive warfare, but much smaller? For thirty years men have asked the same question, yet the answer remains elusive; all that can be projected from the Yom Kippur War, the most recent conflict involving widespread use of modern weapons, is that the destruction of equipment (if not of personnel) is on a scale undreamed of during World War II. Successive NATO commanders will already have identified their potential enemy's major thrust lines and drawn up their response; some areas will be abandoned, others denied the enemy, while all-arms battlegroups conduct an offensive defence in accordance with the requirements of a constantly changing situation; such is the usual prediction.

And yet the opening hours of the war may well bring their surprises. A glance at a physical map of Europe suggests that the German Plain is eminently suitable for the Warsaw Pact's drive on the Rhine, there being few ranges of any consequence and only two medium-sized rivers, the Weser and the Lippe, lying in its path. What the map cannot show is a historical accident that makes the landscape of central Germany quite unlike that further west, where farms dot the landscape haphazardly. This part of the country was ravaged constantly during the Thirty Years War and for their own protection farms and farm buildings were built back-to-back, forming small hamlets that are usually equidistant from each other. Anyone who has been involved in exercises in the area will confirm that it is all but impossible to place oneself in a position where one is not within range of anti-tank weapons sited in two and probably three of these hamlets. The whole zone, in places many miles wide, is a very serious obstacle for armour if held with determination, and any Russian commander seeking to blind straight through is risking ruin.

The arithmetic is straightforward. Ten tanks destroyed is the equivalent of one company, or one third of a battalion; thirty tanks knocked out equals one third of a motor rifle division's first line tank strength.[95] A BMP in flames is not simply a personnel carrier written off, but potentially a section of roasted motor riflemen as well; three BMPs knocked out is an entire platoon, such loss constituting a company commander's tactical reserve. A further BMP destroyed reduces the company to its minimum operational efficiency; two more and serious morale factors arise. Already the pennies are beginning to take care of the pounds.

As the same topographical features exist on its own side of the Curtain, the Red Army is naturally aware of the problem and will have considered alternative solutions. It can systematically clear the zone, which will cost time when it is at its most precious and is therefore not an ideal answer; it can attempt to drive through at night, which will be a costly process because of the development of good night-sights and other night-finding aids; or, in conjunction with its mobile Frog and Scud missile carriers, which can deliver a high explosive payload, its artillery and tactical air support can attempt to erase each hamlet from the map, a formidable undertaking, which cannot guarantee success – one has only to remember the damage caused to the columnar advance of *three* British armoured divisions by the garrison of the allegedly obliterated village of Cagny during Operation *Goodwood* to realise that this method has its imperfections. Quite possibly a combination of the second and third methods offers the best chance of success, as the defenders' nerve will be shaken by constant bombardment and the efficiency of their night-sights diminished by the light from burning buildings. That the Warsaw Pact forces will succeed in forcing their way through this zone is beyond any reasonable doubt; the only unknown factors are the extent to which their schedule will have been upset and whether the losses sustained have reached unexpected proportions.

The one factor that is reasonably predictable is that their success will not be even. In the nature of things some divisions will have had a more difficult passage than others, and some of the more thrusting senior commanders will have become casualties. At this point the Warsaw Pact is vulnerable to a NATO counter-attack, which will inflict further loss and delay, but which cannot altogether contain the follow-through wave that has rolled through the wreck of the initial assault divisions.

The Soviet Commander will now seek to accelerate the momentum of his advance regardless of cost, while his NATO opposite number will try by every means possible to slow him down without committing his own jealously guarded tactical reserve. The land battle will become increasingly fluid, local engagements generally being decided in favour of the leader who has been able to preserve his command radio net. As Russian tactics have a certain predictability, divisions can be led into killing grounds and as the situation develops opportunities will arise for NATO higher formations to be employed in the Manstein tradition. Soviet tank crews will learn the painful lesson that the speed of their vehicles if far from being a complete defence against well-applied direct gunfire.

Despite and because of the huge losses that they have already incurred, the communist forces will continue to press their opponents steadily westwards. Fresh units will replace those shaken by the first shock of battle, while NATO strengths begin to drop not only because of enemy action, but also due to breakdowns that have had to be abandoned and destroyed during the retreat. Exhaustion, too, is beginning to take its toll among the western crews.

The river lines offer some temporary, if only momentary, respite for NATO commanders, who may be able to rotate some of their units. However, the Warsaw Pact has endlessly practised its river-crossing techniques and in addition to the deep wading attachments that give its tanks the ability to traverse a river bed submerged, it also has substantial numbers of amphibious light tanks and APCs, as well as large quantities of mobile bridging equipment; it will, moreover, also have selected its main and subsidiary crossing points, and these may or may not still be in possession of its airborne and air-landing troops.

The art of the river crossing lies not so much in obtaining a foothold on the far bank, but in holding the bridgehead securely and expanding it so that it can contain sufficient troops to affect a break-out when the time comes. The river crossing is the place where almost anything can go wrong – the bridging train can be partially destroyed on route to the launching site, be held up on crowded roads or even arrive prematurely while the area is still under such intense fire that it is impossible to complete the work. The permutations for trouble are endless, and a high degree of personal initiative is required from comparatively junior officers, particularly in the engineering and logistic branches, if the numerous difficulties are to be overcome; whether such initiative will be forthcoming is another matter.

If the success of the Warsaw Pact was uneven following its emergence from the frontier zone, it is reasonably predictable that it will become progressively more ragged as each river line is forced. A western commander would, as a conditioned reflex, reinforce favourable progress along certain thrust lines and abandon others less rewarding; a Soviet commander may lack the instinct or the necessary authority.

By now the NATO armies are becoming terribly tired and are beginning to suffer from equipment shortages. They, too, have suffered serious casualties and there seems as yet to be no limit to the resources of the enemy. On some sectors fresh French troops (technically not part of NATO but sharing the common aim) have moved into the line, but this has been allowed for in the Russian planning. It can, in fact, be said that the Warsaw Pact is ostensibly on the way to winning the war.

However, at STAVKA there is little cause for rejoicing. Complete air superiority has not been obtained; casualties suffered and equipment destroyed is wildly in excess of forecasts; in some cases, formations have been wiped off the board or will take months to reconstruct; the timetable is days out of phase; NATO reinforcements are crossing the Atlantic and some at least will get through; the quick kill has failed and a long war looms ahead; in a word, STAVKA is no longer controlling events.

As the foremost Russian columns probe towards the Rhine, the NATO commander asks his political masters for permission to use his tactical nuclear weapons. If their will holds, he will receive it. The most dangerous spearheads vanish in a series of blinding flashes and soaring pillars of smoke. The Warsaw Pact responds immediately in kind, and since there is no reason why a small, tired army using battlefield nuclear weapons should prevail against a stronger army employing similar devices, the question of whether or not to employ the ultimate ICBM deterrent demands an almost immediate answer. If that answer is affirmative, the few survivors of the NATO and Warsaw Pact countries would live out their lives in a landscape dominated by ruins and governed by a purely agricultural economy.

There is an alternative. After the first tit-for-tat exchanges of tactical nuclear weapons, the Kremlin can order its forces to withdraw slowly behind the Iron Curtain. Such a course of action is by no means improbable, since war *a l'outrance* in the nuclear context is completely illogical; and as the *Blitzkrieg* has failed to attain its objective there is no valid reason why it should continue. Indeed, there are substantial advantages to be gained in the political field by ordering such a withdrawal, since Russia can claim that she has taught the "capitalist-imperialist" bloc a salutary lesson, which can be repeated if necessary, and has yet saved the world from nuclear holocaust. No loss of face is involved (compare the Chinese Red Army's disengagement in Vietnam following its 1979 punitive expedition), and the NATO armies will clearly be too weak to do more than maintain some pressure on the rearguards; any attempt to follow Warsaw Pact troops into their own territory is out of the question.

This projection of possible future events is intentionally simplistic. It is also optimistic in that it assumes, for the West, the best possible solution that can be achieved even with a rein-forced NATO. The threat is always present and shows no sign of diminishing. One cannot but recall the words of a defecting Russian officer during his interrogation: "I do not understand you people. You do nothing, yet you know they're out to get you – and one day they will!"

There is, of course, the argument that if the Red Army employed western techniques and command philosophy, encour-aging initiative and permitting junior leaders to exercise their abilities to the full, its *Blitzkrieg* would succeed at comparatively low cost. That assumes permission of free thought and expression, a complete reversal of the basic communist tenet that the Party knows best, a development that constitutes a threat to the state itself and which Stalin bloodily repressed during his great purge of the officer corps. It seems, therefore, that Leninist theoreticians have something of a dilemma on their hands.

As has already been conceded, the rulers of the Kremlin are intelligent men. They are guided by historical experience and bet only on certainties. They are fully aware that the history of *Blitzkrieg* contains no example of the technique succeeding against an army that understands it and which is not flawed in some vital way, and have evidently decided that a direct attack on NATO is fraught with too many risks; as yet. Should NATO's *conventional* forces be further reduced below their present minimum safety level, they can hardly be blamed for reappraising the situation.

Select Bibliography

There is a saying to the effect that to write a book one must turn over a library, the truth of which I can most readily affirm. Therefore, rather than enumerate the very many works that I have consulted, I propose listing only those that will, in my opinion, be of greatest interest to the reader.

Good general histories of aviation and armoured warfare are contained in *The Guinness History of Air Warfare* and *The Guinness Book of Tank Facts and Feats*. The relevant areas of World War I are ably covered by Bryan Cooper in *The Ironclads of Cambrai* (Souvenir Press), by Barrie Pitt in *1918 – The Last Act* (Cassell & Co) and by Cyril Falls in *Armageddon 1918* (Weidenfeld & Nicolson), the last mentioned dealing with the Palestine campaign. The technical and theoretical developments between the wars are discussed in great detail by Charles Messenger in *The Art of Blitzkrieg*, published by Ian Allan. Alistair Horne's *To Lose a Battle – France 1940* (Macmillan) is both scholarly and immensely readable.

The view from "the other side of the hill" is provided by Guderian in *Panzer Leader* (Futura); Halder in *Hitler as a War Lord* (Putnam); von Manstein in *Lost Victories* (Methuen); von Mellenthin in *Panzer Battles* (Cassell & Co); *The Memoirs of Field Marshal Kesselring* (Wm. Kimber); and by David Downing in *The Devil's Virtuosos: German Generals at War 1940-45* (New English Library).

The defeat of the Italian Army in North Africa forms the subject of Kenneth Macksey's excellent *Beda Fomm – The Classic Victory* (Pan/Ballantine). Three important books covering the major events on the Eastern Front are *Barbarossa* by John Keegan, and *Stalingrad* and *Kursk*, both by Geoffrey Jukes, all published by Macdonald. Comparatively few Russian accounts are available in the West, but of these Marshal Zhukov's *Greatest Battles* (Macdonald) is probably the most relevant.

For the campaigns in Normandy and North-West Europe *The Struggle for Europe* (Collins) by Chester Wilmot is hard to equal; David Mason's *Breakout – Drive to the Seine* (Macdonald) is also highly recommended. *Battle* (Frederick Muller) by John Toland is, perhaps, the most lucid tactical account of the Battle of the Bulge, and contains numerous personal experiences and eye-witness accounts.

To the best of my knowledge and belief the only published history of armoured operations in Burma is my own *Tank Tracks to Rangoon*, which was also published by Robert Hale. Shabtai Teveth's *The Tanks of Tammuz* (Sphere) gives a vivid account of the Six-Day War, although the author changes the names of personalities and the identities of units slightly, perhaps for security reasons. A general account of the Yom Kippur War, with contribution from participants, is given in Arnold Sherman's *When God Judged and Men Died* (Bantam). Much excellent source material can also be found on the Arab/Israeli wars in the magazine *Born in Battle* (Eshel-Dramit Ltd, Israel), the Editor being a founder member of the Israeli Armoured Corps.

As to what one profoundly hopes will remain the future, *The Third World War – A Future History* by General Sir John Hackett and others (Sidgwick & Jackson), *World War 3*, edited by Brigadier Shelford Bidwell (Hamlyn), and *The Soviet War Machine* by Air Vice-Marshal S.W.B. Menaul and others (Salamander), all provide a wealth of expert opinion; the picture that emerges is extremely frightening, but not necessarily hopeless.

Notes

1. B.H. Liddell Hart: *Strategy: The indirect approach*. Faber and Faber. Last and enlarged edition. 1967.

2. Obersts Rommel: Infanterie Greift an. Ludwig Voggenreiter Verlag, Potsdam. 1937.

3. Ibid, page 210.

4. Gerster, Der Schwaben an der Ancre (Heilbron-Salzer).

5. The tanks belonged to D Company, Heavy Branch Machine Gun Corps, lineal ancestors of the present 4th Royal Tank Regiment. The first tank into action was Dl, commanded by Lieutenant H.W. Mortimore, which carried out a sole sweep along the edge of the nearby Delville Wood earlier the same day.

6. The name tank was simply a cover. While the first vehicles were being built the curious were told that they were water cisterns, or tanks, for the Eastern Front. A photograph shows one in the manufacturer's yard, suitably inscribed in Russian characters, "With Care to Petrograd". The French called their tanks chars d'assaut.

7. Captain G. Dugdale, *Langemark and Cambrai*.

8. Two junior officers who served on opposite sides in this campaign were the future Field Marshal Erwin Rommel and the future General Sir Richard O'Connor. Rommel drove his men to their limit but took 9,000 prisoners; O'Connor was awarded the Italian Silver Medal for Valour. Both were light infantrymen.

9. The French employed a similar system, but withdrew their Battle Zone out of artillery range.

10. As communication between tanks was impossible, this was often the only way in which officers could exercise effective control over their commands. Four Victoria Crosses were awarded to members of the Tank Corps during the Great War, all for dismounted action; the recipients were Captain Clement Robertson

(1st Bn), Captain R.W.L. Wain (1st Bn), Lieutenant C.H. Sewell (3rd Bn), and Lieutenant-Colonel R.A. West (6th Bn). Captain Robertson deliberately sacrificed his life leading his tanks on foot right onto the objective during an attack near Ypres on 4th October 1917. Later some tanks carried a primitive set of semaphore arms, but the arrangement was of doubtful value.

11. The Whippet, otherwise known as the Medium A, was a three-man tank with a speed of 8 m.p.h., armed with three machine-guns. It was designed to assist the cavalry fulfil their exploitation role, but in practice it was soon found that the two arms were quite incompatible.

12. The actual title of Fuller's paper was The Tactics of the Attack as affected by the Speed and Circuit of the Medium D Tank.

13. Only 1st Tank Brigade was absent, being in process of converting to Mark Vs.

14. The Gun Carrier was a variation on the tank theme designed to overcome the difficulties of getting artillery across No Man's Land following a successful attack. It carried either a 60-pounder gun or 6-inch howitzer, which would be dropped in the new gun line. During the Third Battle of Ypres the 6-inch howitzer was fired from the carrier itself during several night actions in which the vehicle's mobility was used to prevent effective German counter-battery fire. In general, however, the Gun Carrier's potential was wasted in the role of supply carrier, which effectively reduced the world's first self-propelled gun to the status of a pack animal.

15. Major-General J.F.C. Fuller, The Decisive Battles of the Western World.

16. Medium tank layout had by now been standardised with the main armament housed in a fully rotating turret; tankettes were lightly armoured fully tracked machine-gun carriers.

17. Formed by the amalgamation of mechanised cavalry regiments and Royal Tank Corps battalions into one body in 1939. To avoid confusion the RTC changed its title to Royal Tank Regiment while the cavalry retained their own designations.

18. Fuller for one did not return the compliment. He loathed all aspects of Bolshevism and made Tukhachevsky his particular target. Tukhachevsky was a former Tsarist officer with marked sadistic tendencies.

19. Panzer Leader.

20. The episode known as Grierson's Raid is a case in point. In April 1863, Colonel Benjamin H. Grierson's brigade of Union Cavalry was despatched from La Grange, Tennessee, on a long-range raid to destroy Confederate rail links with the fortress of Vicksburg. Having completed his mission, Grierson declined to turn back (a course that would have involved contact with the Southern forces

pursuing him) but continued to ride south to the Federal base at Baton Rouge, thus crossing the entire Confederacy from north to south.

21. Panzer leaders were also adept at forming *ad hoc* battlegroups for specific missions from the various elements of their divisions. Such battlegroups could be formed at very short notice, since the German Army relied on spoken as opposed to written orders to a greater degree than others.

22. A number of future marshals of the Soviet Union fought in Spain, including Koniev, Rotmistrov, Rokossovsky and Malinovsky.

23. Alistair Horne, *To Lose a Battle*, Cox & Wyman Ltd, London.

24. Stuka is an abbreviation of Sturzkampfflugzeug, literally Diving Combat Aircraft. In spite of his major contribution to German war potential, Professor Hugo Junkers was an outspoken critic of the Nazis, for this, Milch ruined him.

25. Me 109 pilots found a certain snob-value in being shot down by a Spitfire; some became quite indignant when told they had been downed by a Hurricane.

26. The Light Divisions were similarly organised to the Motorised Divisions, but contained a battalion of tanks.

27. A. Armengaud, Batailles Politiques et Militaires sur l'Europe, Paris 1948.

28. The "PzKw V" was actually a multi-turreted tank built in 1933 under the cover name of Neubaufahrzeuge (NbFz) or New Construction Vehicle.

29. The effect of these few Trojan Horse parties, known as *Brandenburgers* in the German Army, was out of all proportion to the numbers involved. Parachutist scares multiplied all over the Allied rear areas, reaching panic proportions; the oft-sighted nuns in hobnailed boots are but one variant of this over-excited theme.

30. In some German records the engagement is referred to as the *Panzerkampf bei Hannut;* in others as the *Panzerschlacht bei Namur.*

31. Georges and Gamelin were barely on speaking terms and Doumenc was an intermediate link in the chain of command deliberately interposed by Gamelin. Georges was not a well man, never having completely recovered from wounds received during the assassination of King Alexander of Yugoslavia in 1934.

32. 3rd DCR re-assembled the following day and was thrown against the *Grossdeutschland* Regiment, holding the southern shoulder of the penetration at Stonne. The *Grossdeutschland* was severely mauled in several days of mutually destructive combat and had to be relieved, but 3rd DCR could have been found more useful employment elsewhere.

33. As quoted by Alistair Horne in *To Lose a Battle*, Macmillan & Co.

34. Hobart was serving as an NCO in the Home Guard when Churchill, appreciating his true potential, recalled him to active duty. He raised and trained the 11th Armoured Division and later commanded the famous 79th Armoured Division, being personally responsible for many of the tactical techniques practised by its specialised armoured vehicles.

35. The regiments were 3rd Hussars, with light tanks; 2 RTR with cruisers; and 7 RTR with Matilda II infantry tanks.

36. By November 1940 the Division was at full strength and consisted of: 4th Armoured Brigade (7th Hussars, 2nd and 6th RTR), 7th Armoured Brigade (3rd and 8th Hussars and 1st RTR), the Support Group (4th RHA, 1st KRRC and 2nd Rifle Brigade), plus the divisional armoured car, anti-tank and anti-aircraft regiments, and service units.

37. Apart from Gruppo Maletti and 1st Libyan Division, 2nd Libyan and 4th Blackshirt Divisions were also removed from the board during the operations of 9th/10th December. In general, the Libyan divisions put up a tougher resistance than the purely metropolitan formations.

38. O'Moore Creagh insisted that each of his regiments should contain one squadron of cruisers at least. 3rd Hussars and 2 RTR achieved this by exchanging their respective B Squadrons.

39. After Sidi Barrani, 7 RTR's operational strength seldom rose above that of a strong squadron, largely because of heavy wear on the Matildas' delicate steering clutches. Of the Seventh's performance at Bardia, Mackay commented that each Matilda was worth a battalion of infantry to him.

40. In addition to specific bombardments carried out by heavy units of the Mediterranean Fleet, the Italians had been harried throughout the campaign by Force W, composed of China river gunboats and monitors, whose long range but extremely accurate gunnery more than compensated the British for their lack of purpose-built ground-attack aircraft.

41. The Division's famous jerboa symbol began appearing on its vehicles about this time; the earlier divisional symbol had been a simple white disc on a red square.

42. The 13 Corps' anti-tank guns were the 37-mm Bofors and the 2-pounder, both small weapons that sustained damage when towed across the desert's varied going. An answer was found by mounting the gun on the back of a cut-down lorry known as a *portee*, the intention being that it should be dismounted before going into action, although in practice this was seldom done. 3rd RHA's 2-pounder *portee* batteries were usually allocated one to each armoured brigade and one to the Support Group.

43. O'Connor was himself captured while coming forward to take control of the deteriorating situation. He succeeded in escaping in 1943 and commanded VIII Corps in Normandy.

44. Elsewhere, the Finnish Army, with German support, would recommence hostilities with Russia.

45. In Russian military terminology a Front is best defined as a Command Zone.

46. Bogeymen, or things likely to frighten children.

47. After the French campaign Hitler had ordered that all PzKw IIIs should be up-gunned with a 50-mm L/60 weapon. To his subsequent fury his instructions were disobeyed and the less powerful 50-mm L/42 gun fitted instead. The position was speedily rectified following early experiences in Russia.

48. Hitler's War Directives 1939-1945, Professor H.R. Trevor-Roper.

49. 4th Panzer Army was now commanded by Colonel-General Hermann Hoth, who had moved across from 17th Army.

50. *Decisive Battles of the Western World*.

51. The precise nature of his role remains obscure, but was evidently exaggerated in later years, for on 29th June 1919 the city fell to General Wrangel's White Army, the Bolshevik defence collapsing when penetrated by a single Mark V Tank with a British crew commanded by a Captain Walsh. In those days Stalingrad was known as Tsaritsin; today it is called Volgograd. The geo-political aspect of Russian military history remains an inexact science.

52. Panzer Leader.

53. At the same conference Manstein put forward the sensible idea of appointing a Commander-in-Chief Eastern Front. Somewhat abstractedly Hitler put forward the name of Goering; Manstein did not press the point.

54. The twin-engined Hs 129 was introduced during the autumn of 1942 and had a speed of 253 m.p.h. It was well armoured and could carry a variety of armament, the most notable variations being a 75-mm cannon, slung beneath the fuselage, and a six-tube 75-mm rocket launcher. The Ju 87G carried two 37-mm cannon in under-wing pods. Both aircraft were formidable tank-busters.

55. *Panzer Battles*.

56. This vehicle took its name from its designer, Dr Ferdinand Porsche, and carried an 88-mm gun in a heavily armoured fixed superstructure. Porsche had a genius for interesting Hitler in Doomsday machines such as this and the 185-ton Maus tank, and even produced plans for a fighting vehicle whose weight would have

exceeded 1,000 tons. Guderian considered his ideas to be quite divorced from reality, and made a point of saying so.

57. For the sake of tradition, the M3 thereafter appeared in the branch colour of orange-gold on the black guidons of TDF battalions.

58. The M10 was powered by twin diesel engines, the M10A1 by a single petrol engine.

59. In the eleven months following D-Day, thirty-nine battalions of the Tank Destroyer Force knocked out 1,500 tanks and other armoured vehicles; destroyed 684 anti-tank and other guns, 614 machine-gun posts and 668 bunkers; shot down eighteen aircraft; and took more than 40,000 prisoners.

60. Development of Artillery Tactics and Equipment 1939-45.

61. Ibid.

62. Ibid.

63. Panzer Leader.

64. It was not uncommon for wounded Russians to open fire on the enemy's clearing parties after an action. This unpleasant habit had been encountered by the British during the Crimean War; with grim humour such men were termed Resurrectionists and despatched a second time. The custom, arising from fanatical dedication, was still being practised in World War II.

65. The Firefly remained the most powerful tank in British service until the arrival of the 77-mm gun Cruiser tank Comet in 1945.

66. Exceptions were the 2nd and 3rd Armored Divisions, which had two armoured regiments each of one light and two medium-tank battalions. The standard US armoured division had 186 medium and eighty-three light tanks; the British armoured division 246 medium or cruiser and forty-four light tanks. The Light tanks were American Stuarts.

67. On 25th June XXX Corps had launched a preparatory attack to secure O'Connor's right flank, but was only partially successful in achieving its objectives. On 30th June eight panzer divisions, five of them SS, had been identified on the British sector, and one on the American sector, a measure of *Epsom's* strategic success.

68. Author's italics.

69. Many infantry divisions included a substantial number of Poles and Russians who had chosen to fight for Germany rather than remain in prison camp. They

deserted in some numbers, many of the Poles joining their compatriots fighting with the Allies.

70. Third Army consisted of the US VIIIth, XIIth, XVth and XXth Corps.

71. The M7 105-mm self-propelled howitzer was known in British and Canadian service as the Priest. "Un-frocking" meant removal of the howitzer and closing the aperture with armour plate.

72. Nor is the fact that the Allied bombing offensive of Germany, which involved both the RAF's Bomber Command and the USAAF in cruel losses, tied down a considerable percentage of the deadly dual purpose 88-mm anti-aircraft/anti-tank guns, which would otherwise have been put to efficient use on the Eastern Front.

73. On some maps the location is spelled Zvenigorodka.

74. A.N. Shimansky, p2,136, Purnell's *History of the Second World War.*

75. Panzer Leader.

76. The month-long Ardennes campaign cost each side about 800 tanks. The Germans suffered 100,000 personnel casualties, the Americans 81,000 and the British, 1,400.

77. *History of the Second World War,* Purnell, Vol 2, p.799.

78. Yamashita's brilliance as a field commander was marred by a streak of paranoia. He saw insults where none were intended and, because of some half-forgotten political activity in his younger days, imagined that his superiors were constantly plotting to ruin him. He was commanding the Philippines when the Americans landed in 1944, and was executed as a war criminal two years later, more because of his achievements than for any specific acts.

79. Alexander was almost captured at the outset. The commander of the Japanese 33rd Division had decided to take Rangoon by a flank march to the west of the city, i.e. by using the Indirect Approach. To guard the passage of his troops across the main road leading north from Rangoon, he established a temporary roadblock at Taukkyon, unwittingly trapping the Army Commander and a large body of troops to the south. Once 33rd Division had crossed the road, the block was abandoned and traffic began to flow north again towards Mandalay.

80. Chennault's unit is, perhaps, better known by its unofficial title – The Flying Tigers.

81. The British armour proved such an obstacle to Japanese plans that at one stage they issued a frangible glass grenade, filled with an incapacitant gas for use against

the tanks. The device was not very successful, but was an interesting experiment in the use of chemical agents against fighting vehicles.

82. The failure of a tank attack caused certain officers at GHQ in Delhi to conclude that armour could not be used effectively in Burma. Fortunately, they were overruled.

83. At Imphal 254 Tank Brigade consisted of 3rd Carabiniers with Lees, 7th Light Cavalry with Stuarts, and one squadron of 150 Regiment RAC, also with Lees.

84. 255 Tank Brigade was an all-Sherman formation, commanded by Brigadier Claude Pert. Its three regiments were Probyn's Horse, the Royal Deccan Horse and 116 Regiment RAC (Gordon Highlanders).

85. Throughout the war in Burma the Japanese infantry had never fought shy of Allied tanks and had availed themselves of every opportunity to scramble aboard and kill the crews with any means at their disposal. To counter this, the tanks were given their own specially trained infantry escort, usually drawn from Bombay Grenadier battalions, for operations in close country or during street fighting.

86. 116 Regiment RAC, which had remained with 7th Division during the Meiktila operations, had now rejoined 255 Tank Brigade.

87. One of Yamada's Army Commanders was Lieutenant-General Iida, victor of the 1942 Burma Campaign.

88. *The Vietnam War*, Salamander.

89. Ibid.

90. Shabtai Teveth, The Tanks of Tammuz.

91. Sagger is the NATO codename for this wire-guided missile which has a range of 2,500 metres and the ability to penetrate fifteen-and-a-half inches of armour. It is known in the Red Army as Milotka.

92. On this occasion Saggers were deployed fifty per kilometre of front, or approximately 100 to the mile.

93. The old M3 half-track had now been supplemented by M113 APCs; self-propelled artillery included the modern M107 175-mm gun and the M109 155-mm howitzer.

94. By this stage of the war the effect of the SAM had been much reduced as a result of electronic counter-measures provided by the United States, including the Shrike radiation-seeking air-to-ground missile.

95. The motor rifle division's tank regiment has, in addition to its ninety-five battle tanks, an immediate reserve of a further fifty-one vehicles with which to replace breakdowns and battle casualties. This provides some idea of the anticipated wastage from all causes in a total war situation, but as each division does not expect to spend more than a few days at the spearhead the percentage of reserve strength to the whole seems unreasonably high to NATO eyes. Obviously, the Red Army feels differently, and some Russian officers probably feel that it is not high enough.